Television,
Sex and Society

Television, Sex and Society

Analyzing Contemporary Representations

EDITED BY

BASIL GLYNN, JAMES ASTON

AND BETH JOHNSON

continuum

Continuum International Publishing Group
A Bloomsbury Company
80 Maiden Lane, New York, NY 10038
50 Bedford Square, London, WC1B 3DP

www.continuumbooks.com

Library of Congress Cataloging-in-Publication Data
Television, sex and society : analysing contemporary representations / edited by
Basil Glynn, James Aston, and Beth Johnson.
p. cm.
Includes bibliographical references and index.
ISBN 978-1-4411-7945-6 (hardcover : alk. paper) – ISBN 1-4411-7945-3 (hardcover : alk.
paper) – ISBN 978-0-8264-3498-2 (pbk. : alk. paper) – ISBN 0-8264-3498-3 (pbk. : alk. paper)
1. Sex on television. I. Glynn, Basil. II. Aston, James, 1973- III. Johnson, Beth, 1980-
PN1992.8.S44T45 2012
791.45'6538–dc23
2012002887

ISBN: HB: 978-1-4411-7945-6
PB: 978-0-8264-3498-2

Typeset by Fakenham Prepress Solutions, Fakenham, Norfolk NR21 8NN
Printed and bound in the United States of America

Contents

Foreword

Television is a political medium. But the citizenry is often unmoved by this politics swirling around their privacy; too readily allowing reception to occlude engagement. Until sex happens. Sexual representation in any medium is never innocent (in all meanings of the word), and it is naive and disingenuous (even scandalous) to pretend otherwise. Moralists seek to censure on behalf of 'common sense' or 'decency' (while denying they are 'political'); radicals seek to celebrate sexual representation as though there were no political problem with this. And it is television – the most political of media – which is the most potent arena of sexual images. TV screens are the banners and barriers wherein the images move, and the domestic space becomes the virtual agora. The representation of the supposedly most private of acts (a fiction, of course; a furtive disavowal of libidinal histories and erotic genealogies) in the private space of the home, the family, can spark a politics like no other form of representation. Dramatic, comedic, cartoonish, factual, satiric, educative – the genres of sexual representation in the televisual medium all have one thing in common: sexual representation. And it is that which drives the writers in this collection.

What does it mean to represent sex on television? This simple question is at the heart of this collection of essays. And the answers are as various, urgent, worried, celebratory, messy, ordered and exuberant as sex is; and as multi-valent, engaged, complex, sophisticated, informed and enjoyable as television.

The question, though, is both more contained, and more various than I might suggest. There is a necessary periodicity that circumscribes the televisual texts chosen. And this is what makes the collection so necessary now, and what will ensure it becomes a key historical marker as the question of representing sex in television continues to fascinate scholars in years to come. The writers of this volume are attentive to the contemporaneity of their discourses – discourses both televisual and sexual: which is to say political. This is a book of politics, a book that situates popular texts mostly consumed in domestic spaces in the full glare of the social world. And by specifying a world that is post-DVD, post-digital, and massively de-regulated in the US and UK contexts; and which benefits from a concomitant trans-nationalizing of popular discourses from previously segregated markets such as South Korea, these essays collectively offer a tentative global view.

The global reach does not, however, seek to simplify or homogenize the practises of representation. The politics of this collection is located in specificity – the specific production contexts of the shows, the specific theoretical and political traditions that inform the essay's argument. These various specificities work against the over-arching moral certainties of voices that would seek to contain both the particular instantiation of sexual activity and its representation into totalizing schemes of abjection, revolution, domination, control or whatever; but are nevertheless energetically committed to an understanding of these discourses.

The particularity, care and attention of each essay to its text, to its moment, to the specific questions posed by its particular form of representation provides a profound set of specific insights. But the totality of the collection, without forcing an agenda or determining a position, offers a more generalized politics of response. The collection as a whole understands television as politics; representation as politics; but equally it understands politics as representation – which is to say that the act of creating a televisual aesthetic to represent a sexual act, encounter, conflict or whatever is understood as political gesture. This gesture is implicated in histories of television, of commerce, of art, of sexuality, of exploitation and liberation. It cannot seek to offer answers (television is a political medium, and politics offers no answers) but the gesture, by virtue of being political engages the polis (however unaware or unwillingly) in its newly articulated space of political action, its living room, or kitchen, or bedroom agora.

And this book is further part of that politics. It offers articulations, histories, contexts and arguments that serve to provide parameters for debate, positions for dispute. Like the shows they discuss, the essays challenge, interrogate, unsettle, amuse, delight and frustrate in equal and splendid measure. Television is a political medium (aesthetic and the industrial) and sexual representation is always a political action (aesthetic and libidinal) and this book analyses, celebrates, engages with and critiques these intersections of different modalities of the political.

These modalities will shift, and when they do this book, as well as the shows it discusses, will be essential in the emerging histories of television, sexuality, politics and representation. Would that all academic books had such ambition.

Matthew Pateman
November 2011

Introduction

As the title of this edited volume indicates, *Television, Sex and Society: Analyzing Contemporary Representations* aims to provide a critical overview of representations of sex on television from the 1990s to the present day. Focusing specifically on representations of tele-sex in the United Kingdom, United States of America and East Asia, the purpose of the collection is to both intervene in and add to debates concerning the various screenings of sex, sexuality, gender, im/morality and the societal ideologies regarding sex that such programmes convey in the everyday. There is a need to do this because as Feona Attwood (2009) has recently stated, there has been a gradual 'mainstreaming of sex' in the contemporary age. And yet, although Attwood discusses a wide spectrum of cultural manifestations from commercial media production to amateur and/or DIY creations covering disparate forms such as advertising, literature, music and cinema, little is aimed at television and in particular *how* sex is represented within the medium. The need therefore to readdress television as an important cultural site in the representation of sex is essential, especially seeing as television is integral to everyday discussions and representations of sex, evidenced by the sensational and salacious headlines garnered by many contemporary productions, be it the 'films, football and fucking' (Dawn Airey cited in Moyes and Robins, 2000) of early Channel 5, the biting bloody sex in *True Blood* (HBO, 2008–), the teenage titillation in *Shameless* (Channel 4, 2004–) or the 'sexing up' of the 1990s BBC television adaptation of Jane Austen's *Pride and Prejudice*. Sex on television then is a 'sexy' and significant issue, and, more so than ever, stitched to the fabric of the everyday. It is because of the centrality of sexual representations on screen and the increasing cultural significance they hold in contemporary society – intervening in both political and popular spheres of debate about censorship, sexual ethics and the very value of sexuality itself – that this book aims to intercede. In doing so, it will situate televisual sex alongside the growing proliferation of academic discourse on contemporary representations of sex by accounting for and addressing the mass medium of television and the wide range and variety of sexual types, images and narratives that have been produced, screened and watched in the contemporary era.

Public approaches to sex on screen in the twenty-first century are vast not only in their volume, but in their opinions regarding why audiences desire, or not, to watch sex on screen, what time sexualized content is acceptable for broadcast, what types of representations are hot, or not, the legitimacy of sex as a television subject and the blurring of public and private representations of sex and sexual practice in contemporary society. That is to say, sex on television is still a contentious and highly political issue. While Mary Whitehouse may well be viewed as a comical and repressed figure from a former age, concerns about the mainstream media's proliferation of sexualized representations remain rife. Politically, culturally and sociologically then, representations of sex matter in and to contemporary society. As such, compelling questions need to be asked about such representations like: How, if at all, does sex on screen interject and shape the everyday of sex in the real? What do these representations mean on a political level? Is watching sex on screen another means of societal self-pleasuring? And, in what sense do such images trouble or adhere to dominant ideologies of sexual correctness? For example, Attwood (2009, p. xv) has underlined the importance of sex in the modern era by saying, 'As sex appears to become more and more important to contemporary cultures, permeating every aspect of our existence and providing a language for talking about all kinds of things, its meaning becomes more elusive and more ambiguous'. The latter point is picked up by Ariel Levy who, in discussing the impact of representations of sex on feminist politics, recently argued in her monograph *Female Chauvinist Pigs: Woman and the Rise of Raunch Culture* (2006, p. 198) that: 'We are still so uneasy with the vicissitudes of sex we need to surround ourselves with caricatures of female hotness to safely conjure up the concept "sexy"'. Therefore, despite the growing proliferation of sex in society and its centrality in the public sphere and the everyday, its practices either remain hidden, distorted or unclear. A need to render the sex act transparent in cultural manifestations is thus essential and *Television, Sex and Society: Analyzing Contemporary Representations* aims to address this imbalance and provide much needed analysis on the how, why and for what purposes sex is represented on television. In doing so, academic analysis surrounding the representation of sex will become more visible and insert itself within everyday discourse providing a necessary extension of academia into the everyday where the issue of sex, both its production, its practice and its reception is now, more than ever, vital to an open and public debate.

Following on from the research and analysis of recent screen and sexuality scholars such as Kim Akass and Janet McCabe (2003), Feona Attwood (2009), Ariel Levy (2006), Brian McNair (2002), Susanna Passonen (2007), Clarissa Smith (2007b) and Linda Williams (1989; 2009), the essays that make up this collection consider mainstream texts such as *True Blood*, *Shameless*, *Pushing Daisies* (ABC, 2007–9) and *The Tudors* (Showtime/Working Title/ Octagon/Peace Arch/Reveille, 2007–10). Each ask through close textual analysis if televisual sex broadcast via our everyday screens showcases more or less democratic representations of sex and as such provides a significant move away from earlier historical productions. That is, do these texts exploit, critique, or challenge the 'dominant male economy' (Williams, 1989, p. 4) of culturally produced sex? Do these television programmes reinforce gendered production, content and viewing practices that position the male as a central agent or, do they instead provide a riposte to the dominant patriarchal hierarchy involved in the televisual production of sex? As Brian McNair (2002, p. 207) argues, 'The whole point of a sexual politics worthy of the adjective "democratic" is that we gain and exercise the right to find, articulate and celebrate our own sexualities, while showing due respect for the tastes, desires and sensitivities of others'. Therefore, this collection will ascertain whether contemporary television can indeed be seen as pushing the boundaries of sex so that their representational strategies promote a more progressive, inclusive and democratic form.

With the question of the democratic potential of contemporary television in producing public and everyday representations of sex and sexual practice at the forefront, the collection will engage with the texts via broad cultural, political, national and sociological frameworks. In doing so, important questions will be asked such as how does contemporary television define the limits of sexual representation now that the surrounding discourse has become more evident within the public sphere? What are the impacts of new viewing formats on adult television spectators? Is sex still, in the twenty-first century, seen as 'dirty'? How are the texts analysed in this collection shaped by the time and context in which they are produced? The collection is not focused on governmental policies regarding the screening of sex on television or on arguments regarding censorship. Rather, *Television, Sex and Society* aims to address the shifting cultural relationship between sex and society and how television contributes to, challenges and complies with everyday notions of the sexual realm in contemporary society. That is, by looking at sexual representations from British, American and East Asian television, the triumvirate of production, representation and reception can be analysed so that the interconnectedness between consumption, lifestyle, social condi- tions and the private and public sphere can be mapped out. In doing so, an understanding of exactly what representations of sex, and the how and why can be effectively marked out so that we begin to explain and address the crucial role television plays in the public and everyday discourse over sex.

Part One: TV and the Democratization of Sex

The four essays that introduce the first part of this collection 'TV and the Democratization of Sex' consider three hugely popular cult television texts; the BAFTA winning UK television series *Shameless* created by Paul Abbott, the sassy series *Buffy the Vampire Slayer* (WB/UPN, 1997–2003) created by Joss Whedon and the seductive vampiric US text *True Blood*, created by Alan Ball. Asking if and how such texts can be understood to interject in debates regarding contemporary representations of, and dialogues about a shift from sex driven by patriarchal desires to a more democratic female agency, the essays consider the narrative structures, aesthetics, points of view, marketing techniques and creative contexts employed by these shows.

In the opening essay 'Shameless: Situating Sex Beyond the City', Beth Johnson explores how the unashamed representations of the sexual desires of four female characters in *Shameless*, namely Monica Gallagher (Annabelle Apsion), Fiona Gallagher (Anne-Marie Duff), Sheila Jackson (Maggie O'Neil) and Karen Jackson (Rebecca Atkinson), are connected to and cartographized through the fringe spaces of the 'Chatsworth Estate'. Contemplating the ways in which the UK series moves away from high-end US visions of slick surfaces, spaces and bodies, found, for example, in series such as *Sex and the City* (HBO, 1998–2004), the chapter analyses the social positions, dominant sexual desires and complex narrative functions of these women, arguing that in the series, female desire is unashamedly repositioned at the centre rather than at the peripheries of the narrative. As Johnson argues: 'The interests of the characters do not revolve around "looking good" while having sex, or having sex in good looking places. Rather, Monica, Fiona, Sheila and Karen gain pleasure from the real of their desires, be they reflected or enacted in a clapped-out camper van, on a cheap kitchen floor, in character as a dominatrix or on the backseat of a car on the edge of the council estate.'

Attesting that one of the most powerful themes of the series is thus its revelation of the absence of female sexual shame, Johnson argues that the privileging of women's space and desires in the series lays bare a new democratic concourse of pleasure achieved primarily through female rather than male agency. Actively rejecting traditional female stereotypes centred on finding the 'right man' and 'settling down', *Shameless*'s women find pleasure in excess and unrestraint. Moving away then from middle class performances of sexual 'properness', Monica, Fiona, Sheila and Karen desire sex and demand satisfaction in the diegesis of the series. As Johnson notes: 'One commonality of all these female characters is that their sex drives are repetitively shown to be much higher than those of their male counterparts.

BDSM sex, one-night stand sex, extra-marital sex, lesbian sex – it is these engagements through which the women achieve pleasure.'

In Madeleine Smith's chapter based on the cult television series *Buffy the Vampire Slayer* entitled 'Sex, Society and the Slayer', the author considers the tensions between the realms of sex and society prevalent in Joss Whedon's representation of contemporary American culture. Engaging with the work of Jeffrey Weeks (1985) in relation to the dialectic between acceptable and unacceptable sexuality as well as acknowledging and adding to debates regarding the socio-political, sexologist and feminist theories keyed out by previous readers of the series, Smith explores the contours of socially repressive and liberatory models in *Buffy the Vampire Slayer* by looking intently at textual moments or, what Jason Jacobs (2006) refers to as 'cherished fragments' of the televisual.

Providing close analyses of various sex scenes between Buffy Summers (Sarah Michelle Gellar), Angel (David Boreanaz), Parker Abrams (Adam Kaufman), Riley Finn (Marc Blucas) and Spike (James Marsters), Smith illustrates hypocritical attitudes towards gender, frames sex as a means of direct conflict regarding 'insider' and 'outsider' societal status and exposes the ambiguous position of *Buffy*'s men, struggling to find a new place in the world. Nominating Buffy's relationship with sex and society as a 'pedagogical one', Smith goes on to discuss the significance of representations of casual sex, patriarchal prejudices, desire and sexual degradation in the series. Arguing that such representations highlight and engage with contemporary political battles concerning gender, power and social place in contemporary American society, Smith notes: 'Buffy can be viewed as intrinsic to enabling discussions around American culture's most complex and contested issues regarding what is desired and/or expected of its inhabitants'.

Moving on to considering frequently violent representations of sexual encounters in *True Blood*, Melanie Waters chapter 'Fangbanging: Sexing the Vampire in Alan Ball's *True Blood*', considers the 'non-normative erotic spectrum' occupied by vampires and reads the series through this spectrum as one bound up with contemporary sexual socio-politics. Arguing then that sex on screen is rendered graphic and provocative in *True Blood*, Waters contends that the vampires are 'not only used as a means of querying prescriptive accounts of sexual identity, but also as loci for exploring vexed questions about promiscuity, consent, prostitution, and even rape'. Focusing on the gender politics of the debased body, Waters suggests that the series is able to condone some of its violent excesses through pushing front and centre representations and rituals of purification. Yet, she notes, the series shows a worrying trend in its solicitation of female, homosexual or non-white victims.

Recognizing the vulnerability of such bodies as sites less able to resist invasion, Waters goes on to analyse the shape shifting 'telepowers' of vampires that are 'obsessively concerned with questions related to bodily boundaries and their transgression'. Going on to discuss the gothic preoccupations of the show, Waters argues that vampires are cast as 'enemies within' and thus draws out parallels between the violent and frequently erotic invasions that the series depicts and the actual context of the shows production in a post 9/11 world. Recognizing the series' ability to expose democratic representations of sexual pairings that go beyond white heteronormative relations, Waters suggests that sadly, *True Blood* fails to celebrate such diversity, instead, rendering it as dark, dangerous and potentially deadly.

Emily Brick also writes on *True Blood* but her focus is distinct in that her chapter concentrates on an analysis of '*True Blood*, Sex and Online Fan Culture'. Contemplating both the original novels on which the series is based as well as Ball's televised re-creation, Brick argues that the clear framing from novel to film of male vampires as objects of desire make them particularly appealing to the fantasies and fan fictions of female television audiences. Noting the female centred point of view that dominates the show, Brick suggests that both the series itself and the numerous media platforms that supplement the show (and add to its success) demonstrate a fantasy of female democracy in both a social and sexual realm.

Looking at fan conversations concerning the distinctions between the book and television series on sites such as 'Facebook' and 'Yahoo!', Brick suggests that the sexual aggression of key male vampiric figures is, while rendered explicit on television, also 'mainstreamed'. Such a reframing allows and encourages the opening up of spaces to female fans. The numerous representations of sex screened in the show function like fantasies themselves and, in this sense, Brick concludes, the TV series can be seen to 'operate as a form of fan fiction itself, adding in fantasies and sexual encounters which are absent from the written text'. As such, *True Blood* can be seen to punctuate the closed borders of traditional textual narratives, offering a fantastic dialogue of democracy.

Part Two: TV and the Absence of Sex

The four chapters comprising the 'Absence of Sex' part of the collection offer a variety of approaches and national contexts to examine how the representation of 'no-sex' sex can challenge or comply with dominant modes of representations that oscillate between a rigid patriarchal ordering of sexual imagery toward more democratic forms of production, portrayal and reception. All four chapters discuss at length how the representation of sex can act as a barometer for social mores and attitudes as well as either forwarding a progressive or conservative approach to sex, sexual activity and its position in the everyday and public realm.

In her essay 'Beekeeper Suits, Plastic Casings, Rubber Gloves and Cling Film: examining the importance of "no-sex" sex in *Pushing Daisies*', Rebecca Feasey explores how the show offers an alternative to the majority of American prime-time series, such as *Desperate Housewives* (ABC/Cherry, 2004–) and *Dirty, Sexy, Money* (ABC/Berlanti, 2007–9) which utilize the trope of sex as a means to offer entertainment and anticipation to viewers. Utilizing the format of a fairy tale-murder mystery in which the two main characters, Ned (Lee Pace) and Charlotte/Chuck (Anna Friel), are unable to touch, or be touched by one another, *Pushing Daisies* addresses the complex, controversial and contested terrain of televisual representations of sex. However, rather than offering a conservative riposte to the growing sexualization of mainstream television through its safe-sex or no-sex content, the show instead provides a subversive template through which to engage with discourses surrounding the representation of sex. As Feasey clearly points out, 'it is not the hyper-sexualisation of society that reminds us of the importance of sex', but rather, the 'depiction of "no-sex" sex that tells of the role, function and significance of sex [...] in the contemporary period'.

In the case of *Pushing Daisies*, this 'depiction of "no-sex" sex' between Ned and Chuck in which they engage in 'alternative sexual practices' to circumvent the impossibility of contact, allows for detailed examination of the successes and limitations surrounding the representation of sex. On the one hand, the show's focus on the romantic coupling of the two leads promotes the attributes of love, emotional connection and fidelity that dominate the narrative, providing, as Feasey explores, a conservative reading relating to how the show can be seen to 'stand out against, and perhaps speak out against the pornification of society and the role of sexualisation and female exhibitionism in the contemporary social period'. On the other hand and despite the show's reliance on the 'no-sex' issue between the leading couple, there are, nonetheless, continuous references to normative sexual practice and penetrative sex. Feasey posits that the recourse to more traditional inter-pretations of sex is connected to how important sex is in people's lives and thus its pervasiveness in a wide-reaching medium such as television. As a result, the lack of touching in the relationship between Ned and Chuck was received as depressing and debilitating by audiences rather than liberating or empowering, reinforcing how pervasive patriarchal conceptions of sex are in society and the difficulty of providing countervailing representations of sex.

In 'Television X-cised: restricted hardcore and the resisting of the real', James Aston analyses how restricted hardcore representations of sex can provide a challenge to the 'dominant male economy' of pornography that may conceive of a more democratic form of representation. Aston explores the largely overlooked site of adult cable channels in terms of how the 'real' dominates discourses on the representation of sex by developing Linda Williams' work surrounding the 'frenzy of the visible'. That is, by analysing the content of the UK's largest adult subscriber channel Television X, an examination of the 'representational strategies involved in the show and what implications this has on production practices, textual representations and reception' can be forwarded, which is of special importance considering that the sex on Television X is of a restricted and censored nature.

Aston examines a number of aspects of Television X's schedule such as its representation of gender, class and geography in order to ascertain whether or not the channel's restricted hardcore can provide a progressive pornography that articulates female desire and agency. Similar to Feasey's conclusions on Pushing Daisies, so too does an examination of the content of Television X provide a contradictory response. On the one hand, the lack of hardcore representations relegates the symbols of male desire and authority, such as the erect phallus and male ejaculation, to the periphery of on-screen representations, providing a more dominant position for women as they become the instigator of the sex and more vocal in expressing their desires and pleasures. On the other hand, and especially within the class-based scenarios of Television X's programming, women are positioned as 'other' stripping them of a definable voice and demarcating them as abject. This move from the real to the representational is inextricably linked to viewer demographics and viewer practices, which are 'positioned as resolutely male' within the programming schedule of the channel. Thus, taken as a whole, Aston surmises that the content of Television X's schedule 'vacillates between conventional phallocentric pornography and a restatement of female sexual desire', but which ends 'ultimately by reinforcing pornography as produced by men for primarily male consumption with female agency limited or unrepresentable'.

Ruth Hung's chapter on the popular 2007 Chinese television drama Woju (Huayi Brothers/Taihe Film Investements, 2009) addresses the 'forms of life of a newly urbanized Chinese experience in an increasingly competitive and commercialized metropolis saturated by global capital'. In particular, Hung analyses the character of Haizao (played by Li Nian), who takes on the role of a xiaosan (a version of the mistress, though set apart from the more tradi-tional conception of the concubine as the xiaosan is financially independent and socially mobile) in the series to a mid-level government official. Hung outlines how Haizao represents a new historical figure in China at the turn of the twenty-first century as the country moved toward the materialism of Western style capitalism. That is, as the figure of the *xiaosan*, Haizao comments on the new neoliberal landscape and socio-political economy of China by using her sex and sexuality as a means with which to advance her standing, both socially and financially. In this respect, the *xiaosan* is liberated from 'traditional forms of gender oppression and hierarchies' as she belongs to a newly emerging professional class of young women, both socially mobile and financially secure, who contravene the more restricted and oppressed roles of historically comparable figures such as the concubine.

However, Hung continues by cogently deconstructing the way the *xiaosan* is portrayed in *Woju* in that, rather than providing a progressive conception of modern femininity and womanhood in contemporary China, the programme forwards the *xiaosan* as a commodity to be consumed and traded by male admirers. While the exploitation and marketization of the sexual value of the *xiaosan* might provide a critique on contemporary China's headlong rush into commodity culture and materialism, the programme does not problematicize the *xiaosan*, marking her actions and treatment as 'something retrospective and sympathetic, despite the tragic cost to [Haizao]'. Therefore, the series transforms the *xiaoson* into a desirable commodity negating any critique of contemporary China's fast paced change to neoliberal policies and Western style capitalism. It is with this latter point that Hung's article continues the 'no-sex sex' theme of this part. By eliding the controversial aspects of the *xioasan* figure whereby sex, romance and love are 'by-products of a most corrupted trade and exchange' in favour of normalizing consumer culture, the series offers a limited critique of the reality of how female sex and sexuality is being commodified and marketized in contemporary everyday China.

Finally, Jeongmee Kim's chapter on the 2005 South Korean drama serial *My Lovely Sam-soon* (Munhwa Broadcasting Corporation) focuses on how the absence of sex in the popular and pervasive *hallyu* (Korean Wave) drama is challenged by the realistic reassertion of sexual activity in the show. *My Lovely Sam-soon* authentically portrays sexual activity among young Koreans, especially from the perspective of the titular female character Sam-soon (Kim Sun-ah). In doing do, the show critiques the traditional and conservative positioning of 'pure love' in *hallyu* dramas whereby the materialism of modern living is combined with 'the values of a bygone age in which family obligation and innocent, highly romanticized and non-physical love are paramount'. For *hallyu* drama, love is about romance and not sex and as such represents strict gender categories along the contours of rigid patriarchal expectations over correct and desired male and female behaviour. In opposition to the 'old fashioned attitudes' that preside over the representation of sex and love within *hallyu* drama, *My Lovely Sam-soon* instead replaces the 'impossible ideal of "pure-love" [...] with the complexity of more everyday love'. That is, the series repositions sex and sexual activity as a central part of young people's relationships and although not explicitly represented in the series it nonetheless forms an ever present feature in the characters' needs and desires.

Therefore, Kim concludes that *My Lovely Sam-soon*'s critique of the sentimental idealization of love, absence of sexual desire and strict traditional gender categories found in *hallyu* drama enables the series to forward a more realistic treatment of the sex lives of young Korean people. However, for Kim, the oppositional stance of *My Lovely Sam-soon* engenders larger questions centring on gender identity to be asked that address how *hallyu* drama constructs 'impossible values' as straightforward, obtainable and desirable. In tackling these questions, *My Lovely Sam-soon* positions sex as the representational tool with which to dismantle notions of 'pure-love' and the 'perfect' people that it involves in favour of more marginal, excluded and everyday people and their honest and realistic relationships. Unlike the previous three chapters, Kim's chapter on *hallyu* drama analyses how the representation of sex can challenge the traditional and dominant cultural values of 'no-sex sex'. Yet, the chapter similarly confronts the complexity of televisual representations of sex (or their absence) and thus serves a succinct ending to the examination of the successes and limitations of 'no-sex sex' in contemporary television.

Part Three: TV Sex and Heritage: Sexual Representation and Re-presentation

Part 3, 'TV Sex and Heritage: Sexual Representation and Re-presentation', explores various ways in which the sexual codes and conventions from British history have been reconstructed. The sexual norms, behaviours and transgressions of the past, often incomprehensible, strange or confusing to contemporary audiences have in television period adaptations been re-presented in ways that make sense or are acceptable to mainstream modern viewers. The televisual representations of historical sexual practices have been carried out in numerous ways in television drama with fidelity to historical factuality ranging from casting light on and explaining sexual practices of the past to excusing, reconstructing or even disregarding them. The three chapters in this part all look at the varying degrees to which the past has been faithfully brought to the present and the problems and triumphs that have resulted from the attempt to engage with modern television audiences.

In the first chapter in this part, Jonathon Shears examines post-1990s Jane Austen adaptations in '"Why Should I Hide My Regard?": Erotic Austen'. In his discussion of the various television and film adaptations in the 1990s and noughties of *Pride and Prejudice, Sense and Sensibility* and *Northanger Abbey*, Shears argues that the complex codes of courtship and 'social mechanisms for erotic regulation' that were comprehensible in the Regency period have been restructured and unfaithfully re-enacted in favour of modern comprehensibility, narrative consistency and 'a contemporary need for adherence to issues such as romantic consistency, character coherence and conservatism'. In Austen's novels the reader, both through the thoughts of the characters and the voice of the narrator, is provided with access to the inner lives of characters. In the television adaptations, various 'visual and metaphoric' solutions have been utilized to represent the inner lives or interior consciousnesses of these characters in ways that will work on screen and exteriorize and make legible their interior lives. In his discussion of the solutions deployed, Shears is critical and argues that they have taken the form of 'an over-simplified on-screen vocabulary' that has 'sacrificed the rigorous balance' of courtship in Austen and coarsened 'the lines of socialised Regency behaviour'. As a result of the 'symbolic motors that drive romantic screen drama' the socially coded behaviour of the past is recodified and reframed into a visual grammar that depicts Regency sexuality in modern television terms and neglects many of the intricacies of Regency courtship.

In the second chapter in this part, Amber Regis in 'Performance Anxiety and Costume Drama: Lesbian Sex on the BBC' discusses two BBC costume dramas, *Portrait of a Marriage* (1990) and *Tipping the Velvet* (2002). As Shears does in his analysis of Austen adaptations, she also examines the strategies used to re-present the past in the present, in this case in relation to enabling the representation of historically-set lesbian characters and lesbian sex. Since the 1990s lesbian sex has enjoyed a greater presence on television in soap operas, American shows like *The L-Word* (Showtime/Viacom, 2004–9) and, perhaps surprisingly because of its association with traditional values and middle-class audiences, BBC costume drama. Yet perhaps less surprisingly given such associations, Regis argues that in costume drama the controversial subject matter is contained and mediated by the 'use of a legitimating, heterosexual framework' so that rather than undermining the dominance of normative sexuality, lesbian sex serves as constitutive of 'the conservative traditions of quality programming'. As expected for BBC costume drama, the past was sumptuously recreated for *Portrait of a Marriage* in terms of period detail and living spaces making it 'subject to two distinct legitimating discourses: quality programming and authentic representation'. The subject matter of lesbian sex detracted little from either because it was dealt with in a manner that scrutinized heterosexual sex rather than lesbian sex. As well as there being a lack of self-identified lesbians among the cast and crew, the aesthetics and storytelling also supported a heterosexual approach to the subject matter through a 'careful (re)setting of desire in terms of heterosexuality'. With its depiction of a lesbian relationship as consisting of one lover associated with masculinity and one with femininity, a butch/femme binary was offered to audiences in an 'imitation of the norm'. The series, Regis argues, buried 'lesbianism within a heterosexual framework to protect the series' appeal to middle-class respectability'.

In contrast to *Portrait of a Marriage*, which offered 'a strange denial of lesbianism in the face of its presence', *Tipping the Velvet* was promoted as 'the most sexually explicit period drama ever shown on British TV'. Yet in spite of its emphasis of lesbianism, Regis argues that it too rendered its depiction of 'deviant' female sexual desire safe through its highly stylized production which emphasized performativity and thus highlighted its own inauthenticity. At best unsettling, at worst 'adapted for, and consumed by, the heterosexual male gaze', both series, Regis concludes, never seriously challenged the heterosexism of BBC costume drama.

Like Shears and Regis, Basil Glynn in the third chapter in this part, 'The Conquests of Henry VIII: Masculinity, Sex and the National Past in *The Tudors*', explores how the past is re-presented in the present in costume drama. In this case, however, his discussion of *The Tudors* focuses on a text that does not overtly strive for or rely on notions of 'authenticity' or 'faithfulness' in its retelling of British historical events. Lacking an Ur text such as Austen's novels or *Portrait of a Marriage*, Glynn argues that *The Tudors* conforms to a broad and highly masculinized depiction of history and sexual activity that is neither nationally nor temporally specific. Rather than the demure tradition of British costume drama, *The Tudors* instead belongs to today's multinational, multi-company historically-set television co-productions (along with series such as *Camelot* (CBC/Ecosse/Octagon/Starz/Take 5, 2010) and *The Borgias* (Mid Atlantic Films/Octagon/Take 5, 2011–) where, be it in dark age times or medieval times, in Italy or in England, sex is conducted in a modern, athletic and spectacular manner. Rather than commenting on or giving access to the sexual practices of the past, series like *The Tudors* instead accommodate an international consensus image of Western heterosexual WASP ascendency. *The Tudor's* international production status, Glynn argues, is reflective of the international audience it is created for who, in a post-9/11 world, are being offered white Western historical heroes occupying positions of impressive defiance against menacing religious and foreign powers and ideas. In paving the way for the present, the uniformity of behaviour of these white virile historical heroes, irrespective of their historical place or time, serve the function of 'a masculinist rescue of white Western heritage from its threatened present' for the 'many countries [that] have been drawn into questionable military expeditions abroad and heightened security at home'.

Whilst there is no need perhaps to state explicitly the difficulties and pleasures of both representing and viewing sex on contemporary television screens, what is at stake in a collection such as this are the politics of the everyday, of democracy, of gendered expectations and representations, those that previously and perhaps even presently are ignored or dismissed from cultural communications, as well as those pushed evocatively and erotically right in front of our faces. Such representations necessitate cultural conversations – 'Did you see the shagging on *Shameless* last night?' or 'Mr Darcy: Sex-pot or what?' More than this though, representations of sex on contemporary television facilitate a sharing of experience and cultural expectation. What types of sex are represented on television, what such representations can tell us about contemporaneous social relations, about differing class expectations for example, are crucial to our understanding of each other and the world at large. Sex on television cries out for, screams and salaciously demands our attention. It's about time we talked TV sex.

PART ONE

TV and the Democratization of Sex

1

Shameless: Situating Sex Beyond the City

Beth Johnson

The multi-award winning television series *Shameless* (Channel 4, 2004–), is set on the outskirts of contemporary Manchester, England, on a housing estate named the 'Chatsworth'. Centred on the dysfunctional Gallagher family and extended community, *Shameless* arguably subverts social realist designations of dilapidation via situating and maintaining a televisual focus on and around discourses of pleasure, intimacy and sexual desire. Importantly, pleasure is integral *to* the socio-realistic environment represented in *Shameless* rather than being achieved *in spite* of it. Moreover, on the 'Chatsworth', it is female sexual desire rather than male sexual desire that is accentuated. While this accentuation can of course be understood in-line with creator/writer/producer/director Paul Abbott's background in soap-opera writing, this chapter argues that the prevailing situational and sexual dominance of the female characters in *Shameless* series 1–2, demonstrates and determines a shift away from patriarchal power in the hub of the city, instead, enabling, via the situation of a more 'real', female-centred, urban environment, a more democratic repositioning of sex. This repositioning operates hand-in-hand with what Lez Cooke (2003, p. 187) nominated recently as an emerging trend in British television drama from the 1990s to the present in which: 'female characters were at least equal to their male counterparts and often more interesting'. The hyper-mobility and diversity of female characters and female sexual desires represented in *Shameless* is crucial, I suggest, to understanding twenty-first century televized constructions of women as powerful sexual subjects.

Concentrating upon the mother/daughter characters of Monica Gallagher (Annabelle Apsion), Fiona Gallagher (Anne-Marie Duff), Sheila Jackson (Maggie O'Neill) and Karen Jackson (Rebecca Atkinson), this chapter offers a close-analysis of key scenes in which female sexual desires are cartographized and aligned with the environment from which they emerge: Monica, a 'Chatsworth' resident for 18 years before disappearing, is unashamedly promiscuous, engaging in both hetero and homosexual marital affairs with residents both within and outside of the estate and, pursuing her lovers above and beyond her husband, Frank Gallagher (David Threlfall) and children; Fiona, Monica's twenty-year-old daughter born and raised on the 'Chatsworth', utilizes sex as a symbol of enjoyment rather than as a means of escape; Sheila acts out her role as a strong sexual dominator in unexpected BDSM (Bondage and Discipline/Dominance & Submission/Sadism & Masochism) games with Frank (tying him up and penetrating him with a strap-on dildo), thus subverting the audiences' expectations of her as a maternal, weak, submissive, home cookery addict; teenage Karen engages in sexual activity as a means of personal empowerment and commercial exchange (giving blowjobs for example, in return for help with her homework) thus subverting conventional power relations.

Sex and the 'sink estate'

In *Shameless,* women's socio-sexual behaviours are given a position of proud centrality in the series narrative. While this in itself is certainly not new, *Shameless* differs significantly from other contemporary popular televisual series that have foregrounded female sexual desire such as *Sex and the City* (HBO 1998–2004) and *The L Word* (Showtime 2004–9), in that the sexual desires represented are divorced from glamorous cityscape surfaces. Whereas, according to Stella Bruzzi and Pamela Church Gibson (2004, p. 117): '*Sex and the City* exemplifies the identification of Carrie with Manhattan via intercutting images of Carrie strolling along the side-walk with low angle shots of familiar skyscrapers and the Brooklyn Bridge', the 'Chatsworth' is determinedly not Manhattan or West Hollywood, but rather a Mancunian, poverty ridden 'sink-estate'. As Stephen Baker notes of the opening sequence of *Shameless*: 'A montage of tower blocks and council housing recalls the milieu associated with "social exclusion", "welfare dependency", petty criminality and violence' (2009, pp. 455–6). No veneers of impossible perfection inhabit the 'Chatsworth'; sex does not take place on silk sheets, Brazilian waxes are not the norm and no designer Cosabella lingerie or Manolo Blahnik shoes are in sight. Neither charming tycoon, Mr Big, nor the irresistibly impulsive but beautifully seductive Shane McCutcheon exist, instead, Frank Gallagher – a drug-addled, alcoholic, work-shy and neglectful father – fills their designer shoes with his own piss-covered ones, that is before his wife, Monica, leaves him and the estate.

In order to begin this analysis and consider the representation of shameless sex brought forth in the series, it is important to ask where the women on whom this chapter will focus are situated in the opening of the series narrative. The differing 'Chatsworth' cartographies, social positions and narrative functions of these characters are integral to the ways in which their sexual desires are formed, framed and fantasized. Monica is positioned initially as the absent mother, in essence, the hole at the centre of the Gallagher household. Fiona is the eldest of the Gallagher siblings. Aged 20, we learn that for the last three years since Monica's disappearance, Fiona has taken up the key role in the family – running the household, organizing finances (or lack of them), ensuring the other siblings eat, attend school and are properly cared for. Seemingly, Fiona has taken on the role of both mother and father in the household as Frank, while still present, woefully neglects his parental duties choosing to drink, take drugs and party 24/7. Sheila Jackson is a mother of one and lives in a more affluent area of the estate due to her large government incapacity benefits. Married to Eddie (Steve Pemberton) initially (1.1), Sheila is shown to be a nymphomaniac (if only Eddie would comply), and agoraphobic. After years of unsatisfactory sex with her husband, Eddie, he leaves, nominating her and their daughter, Karen, as 'perverts'. Sheila becomes Frank's girlfriend and carer soon after. Karen Jackson is Sheila's teenage daughter. Sexually active and as sexually desiring as her mother, Karen is initially positioned as the daughter who feels 'left out' of the new relationship between Frank and Sheila, despite going out with [Phil]Lip Gallagher (Jody Latham), Frank's son. One commonality of all these female characters is that their sex drives are repetitively shown to be much higher than those of their male counterparts. BDSM sex, one-night stand sex, extra-marital sex, lesbian sex and sex as a form of exchange – it is these engagements through which the characters attain pleasure.

Making Out with Monica

In the opening sequence of series 1 of *Shameless,* Monica Gallagher is introduced as the absent mother of six Gallagher children, namely, Fiona, Lip, Ian (Gerard Kearns), Debbie (Rebecca Ryan), Carl (Luke Tittenson/Elliot Tittenson) and Liam (Joseph Furnace). Having left the family home to buy a loaf of bread and failed to return, Monica's significance is associated with and determined through her remarkable absence in the first two series of the programme. Yet, throughout this time, the audience learn much about Monica via the conversations of other family members. Frank, for example, notes in the opening sequence to each episode that Ian is 'a lot like his mum – handy for the others as she has disappeared into thin air'. If this statement is read in the context of both a similarity in personality and sexuality, a parallelism between Monica and Ian can certainly be drawn. Ian, like Monica, we infer, is sensitive, gullible and naive, yet also egotistical and self-centred. Important members of the family, both Monica and Ian are known to acknowledge and actively pursue their sexual desires above and beyond the welfare of others. In episode 1.1, Ian's homosexuality is revealed after his brother, Lip, finds gay pornographic magazines in their shared bedroom and further, realizes he is having an affair with a local married man, Kash Karib (Chris Bisson). Similarly, we learn later in the series that Monica has left her family to embark on a lesbian relationship with another woman, Norma Starkey (Dystin Johnson).

In episode 1.6, Monica returns to the family briefly with lesbian lover, Norma in tow. The return comes not through guilt for leaving her children or husband however, but is presented as an act of rage and defiance after being tricked by Frank. In an effort to attain money from her, Frank dupes Monica into thinking she has won a giant teddy bear in a competition at her local 'Cost-Chopper' supermarket. Considering Monica's previous behaviour, the teddy bear serves to inform the viewer that Monica does indeed have a 'soft side', demonstrating her child-like, selfish and naive characteristics. More interestingly however, the fact that Frank finds out that Monica shops at a 'Cost-Chopper' supermarket functions to convey the fact that while Monica may have left the poverty of the 'Chatsworth', her new surroundings are, seemingly, equally socially deprived. Yet, despite this, Monica's costume indicates a veneer of fake glamour. Emerging from a brightly coloured monster truck, Monica is first seen in the series wearing black strappy high heels, tight cerise silk stretch pedal-pushers, a pink t-shirt, a black leather jacket and large gold hoop earrings. Her hair is red though her dark roots can be seen and she wears full make-up while waving at a camcorder on which she is being filmed. All this of course takes place in a 'Cost-Chopper' car park. The fact that Monica acts like a movie-star in this scene tells the audience something important about her desires for a different, more glamorous life than the one we infer that she had with Frank. She may still shop at 'Cost-Chopper' but, in her new life, she is driven there in style by a partner who allows her to act out her fantasies in her real-life. The juxtaposition of Monica's attempted glamour amidst the drab concrete car park is ironic yet also highly fitting.

When the person holding the camcorder removes their hood, it is revealed to the audience that Monica's new partner is not a burly male trucker but a woman, Norma, with iridescent black skin and a sweet smile.

Highly aware of her sexuality, Monica's costume helps to paint her character as a woman who is both sexually aware and a woman who is willing to use her sexuality to manipulate others. Dressing provocatively in tight, age-inappropriate clothing, Monica's costume demonstrates her will to be young and carefree again. Despite this, Monica's sexual relationship with Norma is implied rather than shown in her brief return in series 1. After turning up to confront Frank, the Gallagher children invite Monica and Norma to dinner. On being asked why she just disappeared by Fiona, Monica remarks: 'I'm a lesbian Fiona. How was I meant to come back and tell you that?' (1.6). Fiona's reply belies her role as a stand in mother to the other Gallagher children: 'Gently, in stages [...] or never'. While Fiona's final assertion of 'never' may imply on the surface that Fiona believes that Monica should live a lie, this aspect of her response in fact serves as her own way of letting her mother know that she is not entirely convinced by her claims to lesbianism. Monica's seeming inability to answer the question honestly is aligned with her next lie – a lie which nearly all of the Gallagher children outrightly reject. In episode 1.7, the children collectively agree that Monica should leave the family house after she states that she has not visited them in three years because she was unaware of where they were living. Of all the children, only Ian says he believes her explanation as the others look incredulously at him. Again, the similarities in personality between Monica and Ian are revealed – like Monica, Ian is easily manipulated, desiring what he wants to believe rather than what the facts of his abandonment really indicate.

Fooling Around with Fiona

Fiona's sexuality is associated with and seen through her general exuberance to make the most of life. In episode 1.1, Fiona and her best friend, Veronica (Maxine Peake) go to a local night club to drink, dance and have a good time. As diegetic music pulsates through the club, Fiona is seen wearing a red dress, shaking her head and body in time with the music. She is not however positioned as the centre of attention nor, seemingly, does she want to be. Fiona laughs more than dances in the packed club, closing her eyes and wearing a look of absolute pleasure on her face. In terms of the cinematography of this scene, one of the most striking features is the dramatic energy captured via the combination of quick diegetic club-mix beats and quick cuts back and forth between Fiona and a male, Steve (James McAvoy), positioned on a club balcony watching her. Rapid editing ensures a dynamic narrative tempo in this scene making visible the exuberance of Fiona's character. Unbeknownst to Fiona, she is also being watched by a second man: a thief who is waiting to steal her handbag. As Fiona is lost in the pleasure of the music, the thief sees his chance and takes her bag before running toward the exit of the club. As the camera pulls back, the strobe lighting, loud music and mass of people work here to ensure an element of confusion for both Fiona and the viewer. Indeed, only Steve sees the crime clearly and races after the thief. Throwing himself at the man, Steve misses him, instead landing on a glass covered table. It is at this point that Fiona first notices him. After trying and failing to rescue Fiona's bag from the thief, Fiona, Veronica and Steve are kicked out of the club. Steve punches the bouncer who bars them after Fiona indicates that she knows that he knows the thief, and thus, by implication is 'in' on the scam. Fiona then unashamedly takes Steve back to the family home.

The *mise-en-scène* of the following scene is particularly interesting. The house, ironically named 2 Windsor Gardens, is blatantly cramped causing Steve to ask 'How many people live here?' The Gallagher children – Debbie, Carl, Lip and Ian – are sat on any available surfaces as the one sofa is too small and the decor is worn, sparsely accessorized and mismatched. Fiona however shows no concern regarding the obvious disparity between Steve's expensive cream linen suit and the dilapidation of the family home. Again, as in the club, Fiona is interested in having a good time. After the children have gone to bed, Steve moves into the kitchen closely followed by Fiona. Framed in the centre of the shot, the kitchen is established as a 'real' space in which a cluttered notice-board, rusty yet working fridge and temperamental washer-dryer are visible. The walls are painted sky blue and cheap nets partially obscure the windows. Fiona flirts with Steve before rapidly removing his clothing. In the next shot, we see Fiona and Steve in close-up, red-faced, fucking noisily on the cheap kitchen floor. Holding onto a worktop for balance, Fiona accidentally pulls open a kitchen drawer revealing plastic carrier bags and thus reminding the viewer of the ordinariness of her day to day domestic life – shopping and looking after her siblings. Framed from behind in a medium shot, Fiona is shown experiencing sexual abandon. Sitting on top of Steve, Fiona is dominating him. With her dress around her waist, her face flushed and her body moving mechanically on top of Steve's, Fiona's pleasure gains increasing prominence both through the visuals and via the dominance of her diegetic moans.

Fiona and Steve do not get to finish their coupling though as they are suddenly interrupted by sharp knocks at the door. Steve answers the door to find a police officer, Tony (Anthony Flanagan), who has arrived to return a comatosed Frank to the Gallagher homestead. Tony looks at Fiona longingly and it is revealed that Fiona has recently had a one night stand with him. Though Tony makes it clear he wants more, Fiona defiantly but gently tells him it was 'one night – no strings'. She tells Steve the same thing. When Steve returns to her house the next day she tells him that she is not interested: 'You're not that desperate. You can get laid anywhere, Steve.' However, unlike Tony, Steve's persistence and his gift of a new washer-dryer indicates to Fiona that he is not only interested in her body, but in the realism of her day-to-day life too. Fiona's exuberance, her realism, has, he tells her, seduced him long before he was able to speak to her. Telling Fiona that he first saw her a month prior to their club meeting, who she was with and what she was wearing, Fiona avers that her friend Gemma (who accompanied her at the time) was and is much better looking than herself. Asking Steve why he was not focusing on Gemma his reply is telling:

Gemma's dancing for an audience and you're dancing like there's nobody else in the room. You're life's not straightforward Fiona and a little bit of that travels with you but you don't stop it showing. You're not fake. You're not vain. You're not lost so you don't need finding. You're not trapped so you don't need springing [...] I swear to God Fiona, you make me want to enjoy my life.

Steve's clear assertion that Fiona is not 'trapped' in Chatsworth is poignant and serves to remind the audience that Fiona's desires have emerged from the real life that she lives, not a life that is based on surface products, superficial facades and the associated will to attract an audience.

This nomination of the 'real' of Fiona contrasts greatly with Steve's assertion about Gemma's glamorous and fake surface: 'This whole town belongs to the Gemmas of this world and I'm sick of the fucking sight of them'. The 'Gemmas of the world' could easily be translated in an aesthetic sense to glossy and decadent surface aesthetics found in the aforementioned series *Sex and the City*. Speaking of *Sex and the City*, Glen Creeber (2004, p. 145) notes that the series: 'deliberately sets itself up as an ostentatiously glamorous show that reproduces a world of beauty, wealth and cosmopolitan decadence. Not only does it seem obsessed with affluence and consumption, its explicitly colourful, glossy and expensive mise en scene appears to take great delight in displaying and indulging in material wealth and glamour'. Indeed, as Jonathan Bignell (2004, p. 217) argues: 'the fascination with clothes, shoes, hair and personal style is a focus on relatively trivial aspects of women's lives, in contrast to questions of gender equality and the difficult[ies] that real women face'. The stylistic fakery of 'Gemmas' denounced by Steve thus operates in-line with the *mise-en-scène* of the Gallagher household as well as Fiona's real sexual desires. Fiona's energy in sex, her pure enjoyment of it, reflects the 'real' of her surroundings and the honesty of her desires and emotions. The wanted, noisy, messy, imperfect sex that Fiona engages in with Steve can be understood as authentic; as concrete as the 'Chatsworth' itself.

Screwing Around with Sheila

Sheila Jackson is first seen on screen allowing Lip into her house to help her daughter, Karen, with her physics homework. Devoted to her husband, Eddie, Sheila flirts with him in a playful manner. After making his lunch in 1.1, Sheila playfully asks Eddie to 'guess' the filling of his sandwiches in exchange for a kiss. Smiling yet coy and looking directly at Eddie, Sheila is swiftly rejected by Eddie who refuses to engage with her and instead says he will 'find out what he has when he eats them'. In order to make it clear to the audience that this is not a specific rejection but rather a common occurrence, the camera pulls back to reveal two Gallagher boys, Ian and Lip in full earshot sat at the kitchen table. Eddie thus makes no attempt to hide his rejection of his wife's advances and the ordinariness of Sheila trying to attract him via guessing his sandwich filling demonstrates the day-to-day battle between the pair. Discussing his wife in the pub with Frank later, Eddie notes, with disgust, that her only pleasures are 'sex, TV cookery and drawing maximum benefits from the cash strapped State'. This description is revealed to be fairly accurate in the next scene when Frank, leaving the pub, goes in pursuit of Sheila who Eddie has left nominating her to be a 'pervert'.

Within minutes, Frank has manipulated his way into Sheila's home yet, while this scene may initially place Frank in a dominant position, it is soon Sheila who gains the upper-hand. After running Frank a bath in response to his sob-story about putting his own need for cleanliness behind those of his children – and thus there never being any hot water left – Sheila places clothing outside of the bathroom door for him to wear. Frank, emerging from a steamy mist drops his towel and Sheila is shown placing her stiletto shoe on it to prevent him for picking the towel up. The flow of the picture is suspended as a still shot is used to show Sheila's unexpected sudden dominance. Noting that a naked man is a sight she has 'not seen for a long time' she goes on to tell Frank that 'it always had to be pitch black for Eddie' and that Frank must be 'over the moon with a chap like this'. Close up facial shots of Frank and

Sheila staring at one another (Sheila looking down toward Frank's off-screen penis and Frank looking at Sheila's face) denote a sexually charged atmosphere concentrated most dominantly on Sheila's desire for Frank. Frank then tells Sheila to 'give it a feel if you're tempted'. Moving from the role of carer to dominatrix, Sheila then places Frank's towel over his head and roughly pulls him into her bedroom and handcuffs him to the bed. Removing her shirt to reveal sexy lilac matching underwear, Sheila reaches into a large flowery box that she has retrieved from underneath her bed and adorns her hands in long black silk gloves. As Frank complains about the tightness of the cuffs, she states: 'The more you beg, the more you're in for! Relax Frank, Relax!' Looking off screen toward what the audience now infer is Frank's waning penis, Sheila states that he should not relax 'too much'. Frank is then seen in close-up, looking down towards his genitals, appearing hot and stressed. His strained voice then notes 'It's fucking vanished!'. Sheila's retort is swift. Seemingly rubbing his penis off-screen she notes that Frank should 'give it time – we've got plenty'. Smiling, Sheila then implies that Frank's erection has returned. As Sheila moves on top of Frank the camera demonstrates her dominance by framing Frank in a high angle close-up shot. As his movement is restricted by the handcuffs, Sheila puts herself in his eye-line, ensuring that he can only see her. The camera angle then changes to a medium shot, the camera situated at the end of the bed framing Sheila sat astride Frank. She is seen from behind taking off her bra. Frank's face is then seen in a close-up staring at Sheila's naked breasts. Suddenly, however, the camera tilts downwards revealing an extremely large black dildo in Sheila's hands. Frank's face is then seen again in close-up, his eyes wide with shock and fear. The scene is then cut.

Next, we see Frank wearing a comedic knitted liquorish allsorts jumper entering Sheila's lounge. He is moving uncomfortably and slowly from which we infer that Sheila had indeed used the large dildo on Frank. A cross-cut then shows Sheila emerging from the kitchen with two large plates of hot food, smiling serenely. Telling Frank to 'sit himself down', before pouring him a beer, Sheila places a cushion on Frank's chair. While this gesture is not acknowledged by Frank or Sheila in dialogue, the inclusion of it again bolsters the audiences knowledge of what happened after the cut. While Frank has engineered entry to Sheila's house and bedroom, once inside it is clearly Sheila who takes and retains sexual control. Acting out her desires and fantasies of domination, Sheila penetrates Frank off-screen utilizing his penis as her own masturbatory tool. It is, after all, Frank who needs Sheila not vice versa. Indeed, Sheila is able to provide all of the things that Frank desires – a nice home, warm food and copious amounts of sex. In a democratic exchange, Sheila desires to dominate him in the bedroom. After years of sexless marriage to Eddie, Sheila's pleasure in controlling and commanding the space around her and the position of any new man wishing to penetrate it, reveals a purposeful shift: the house is no longer her prison but her sexual playground.

Getting Kinetic with Karen

Karen Jackson is Sheila's teenage daughter. First introduced in episode 1.1 Karen is visited by Lip in order to help her with her homework. Framed sat on one side of the kitchen table while Lip sits at the other, the table is adorned with textbooks and Lip is speaking to her about physics. Sheila can also be seen in the background following a television cookery show and cooking alongside it. As Lip continues to discuss physics, Karen responds with flirty questions regarding Lip's future intentions rather than academic ones. Tilting her head to the side and smiling at Lip, Karen is shown to be much more interested in Lip than in her homework. Discussing his latest physics mnemonic, Lip, drawing a diagram relays his knowledge: 'Everybody continues in a state of rest or uniform motion, unless acted upon by an external force'. As Lip is explaining this and looking intently at the papers in front of him, Karen is seen to slouch down in her chair and disappear under the table. Framed from behind on her hands and knees, Karen moves seductively towards Lips' crotch. As he is finishing his mnemonic '[...] unless acted upon by an external force', the diegetic sound of his voice is suddenly overtaken by another – the distinct sound of a clothing zip being undone. Lip's face is then seen in close-up before the camera pans out to reveal Lip, appearing panicked, looking at Sheila only a few feet away seemingly focused on her television cookery programme. The proximity of Sheila, Karen's mum, to this scene of implied fellatio, initially causes Lip to hiss 'Karen, Karen, don't do that.' This is quickly followed up by him noting that 'To be honest, I could do with the money'. In a high angled shot Karen rapidly emerges from under the side of the table, placing her head above the cloth that has thus far given her some privacy. 'What money?' she demands, clearly perturbed. In response, Lip, looks down at her and states: 'I charge for homework. I thought you knew.' Karen looks up at him and immediately responds: 'I'm skint'. Lip's face is then seen in close-up. His eyes look upwards, indicating brief thought. He then looks back down at Karen and says 'OK'. Karen smiles broadly, appearing happy before quickly placing the table cloth over her head. While the fellatio occurs off-screen, a long shot shows Lip smiling in seeming sexual ecstasy.

Later, discussing the occurrence with his brother, Ian, Lip notes: 'I got a blow-job today. Karen Jackson! I didn't ask. I didn't even know until she yanked it out!'. This description, like that aforementioned of Karen's mother Sheila, shows a female sexual dominance and determination to be sexually satisfied. As a favour to Lip for helping her get an 'A' in her homework, Karen also agrees to give Lip's brother, Ian, a blow job. After finding out that he is gay, Lip asks Ian to try it out and see if it turns him on. While unhappy about engaging in sexual relations with Karen as he has no desire for women, Ian eventually agrees and Karen is seen again under the kitchen table – this time on her hands and knees between Ian's crotch. Later, when asked by Lip if Ian 'was hard' she says replies nonchalantly that he was not. Karen's desire for sex and sexual activity is not however restricted to the act of fellatio which she is seen to enjoy very much (for example, shown through Karen licking her lips after fellating Ian). Just two episodes later, Karen, feeling ignored by Sheila and her new man, Frank (who has moved in and is implied to be enjoying a highly sexual relationship with Sheila), sets out to seduce Frank.

Episode 1.5 opens with a close-up shot of two sets of legs sat on steps. One pair is obviously male, adorned in jeans and placing trainers on his feet. The other set of legs appears youthful, tanned and female. As she puts on long boots the camera tilts upwards revealing that the figures are Frank and Karen. Karen is wearing a very short red and white sundress which is seen to be highly inappropriate as they stand and Frank puts up an umbrella to shield them from the rain. Walking down the drive the pair turn and wave at Sheila who is stood in the window giving them a thumbs up. Frank waves the car keys at her and when they turn around it becomes apparent that Frank is taking Karen for a driving lesson.

Once in the intimate and enclosed space of the car, the camera is placed on the back seat revealing Karen sat in the driver's seat and Frank sat in the passenger seat. With a vast amount of thigh on show, the camera switches position, moving in front of Karen and Frank to expose their faces and seated bodies. Frank asks Karen if she has 'enough room' and Karen smiles at him in a flirty manner. Frank then reaches over and places his hands between her legs adjusting her seat position. Looking directly at one another Frank avers that 'Failing to prepare is preparing to fail'. At this point, Karen grins widely at him and shows him three condoms. The charged atmosphere is suddenly however broken when Lip jumps into the back seat. Having earlier stated that Karen is a great girl and the best sex he's ever had, Lip goes on, in a voiceover, to nominate that 'the difference with this one was that I'd never been in love before'. Frank, having to switch back into a more formal mode in front of his son and Karen, Lip's girlfriend, asks Karen to remember the lesson last week. Breaking the flow of realism Karen's memory of the previous lesson takes the form of a very fast paced montage accompanied by a quick paced non-diegetic musical score. Legs are quickly seen entwined, naked, coming out of the back-seat of the car window. Having been exposed to these legs in several earlier close-ups, it is clear that the legs are those of Frank and Karen. Other shots include Karen's naked and spread legs appearing out of the car sunroof while the vehicle is visibly rocking.

The knowledge that Frank and Karen are engaging in a forbidden relationship here is made all the more poignant by the proximity of both Lip (Frank's son and Karen's boyfriend) to the pair and Sheila, still presumably looking out of the window of the house she now shares with Frank and her daughter. Indeed, the audience are given knowledge above and beyond that of Lip and Sheila. Karen and Frank are having a passionate and forbidden sexual relationship unbeknownst to Sheila and Lip. Karen and Frank's seeming lack of shame regarding this betrayal is interesting. As shown later in the episode, Karen actively encourages the relationship purposely setting out to seduce Frank. After being asked by Sheila to tape a television programme for her while she has a bath, Karen crawls on all fours towards the video player, wiggling her bottom at Frank and exposing her white lace knickers to him. Going towards him again on her hands and knees with a video cassette in her mouth she stares directly at him. Noting the name of the cassette when she reaches him – an ironically named television programme entitled *Wish You Were Here* – Karen sexually teases Frank. Purposefully taking his hand and placing it on her breast and then off screen between her legs, Karen shows determination to have Frank. After expressing concern that Sheila is upstairs, Karen's persuasion soon has the desired effect and the next shot shows Frank's naked bottom moving up and down in front of the television screen. Again then, Karen's desires are shown to function as a driving narrative cause – the sexual relationship being the planned seductive effect. Later, after refusing to go to parents evening with Karen she threatens Frank – telling him that 'He is SO coming tonight.' The double entendre however takes a more sinister turn when Karen follows it up by noting that 'We have a free pass for a couple of hours and Mum will notice I'm upset if you don't come. She has a way of always getting the truth out of me'. Effectively, Karen is blackmailing Frank, forcing him to attend her parents evening and have sex with her or she will tell her mum about the relationship – or, at least a version of the relationship. The implication is that Karen can and is prepared to ruin the relationship between Frank and Sheila – thus denying him his home comforts. Here then, Karen is shown as forceful in her desire; prepared to do whatever it takes to fulfil her sexual demands. Indeed, while Frank may be in a position of having sexual relations with both mother and daughter and thus consider himself to be 'lucky', it is, in fact, Karen who has the control over the relationship and directly over Frank's future.

While her relationship with Frank ultimately fails, Karen's ability to use her sexuality to achieve what she wants is not curtailed. In series 2, Karen moves out of the family home and into the Jockey pub after telling lesbian licence holder, Jez (Lindsey Dawson), that she is also a lesbian. Adorned in short skirts to reveal her skimpy and alluring white underwear, Karen purposefully flashes at both Jez and other customers in order to secure her new job, home, increase her tips and gain control over her environment. Like her sexual liaisons with Lip, this behaviour can be seen as a form of economic exchange however, importantly, Karen does not use her sexuality to manipulate under financial duress. Rather, Karen chooses to engage her sexual desires in this way. After leaving the family home but prior to moving into the Jockey, Karen reveals that she has a flat of her own. Seeing a financial opportunity to make more money, she quickly sublets this, lying to Jez and telling her that she is homeless. Again, as with Sheila's relationship with Frank, while a surface reading of this situation may conclude that Karen is taken advantage of by Jez, Karen, like Sheila is ultimately and decidedly revealed to be in control of her own space, desires and their fulfilment.

Conclusion

This repositioning of female sexual desire at the centre rather than at the peripheries of the narrative inevitably forces a questioning of how the desires and behaviours of these female characters link back to the title of the series, *Shameless*. Ultimately, I argue, one of the powerful themes of *Shameless* is its revelation of the absence of female sexual shame. Female sexual shame is recast and transformed in the series, given over to the judgements of voyeuristic audiences rather than to the strong female characters who demand satisfaction within the narrative. Again, while the same could be said of *Sex and the City*, a distinct difference can be seen in that *Shameless* rejects what Creeber (2004, p. 145) nominates as the 'inherently old-fashioned stereotypes that, despite their open sexuality, [the four main female characters in *Sex and the City*] still centre their lives around finding the right man to settle down with'. Unlike *Sex and the City*, the women in *Shameless* do not actively look for the 'right man', rather, they enjoy their lives, their friendships and their freedoms. While happy for a man who can fulfil their sexual desires to find them, the process of actively looking is absent from the women of *Shameless*. In place of 'Mr Big', wife status and a perfect closet, the desires of Monica, Fiona, Sheila and Karen are invested in sexual pleasure, sexual freedom and unashamed play. While the characters indeed have to make certain compromises in order to achieve fulfilment, they do so on their own terms, in their own spaces. These characters interests do not revolve around 'looking good' while having sex or having sex in good-looking places. Rather, Monica, Fiona, Sheila and Karen gain pleasure from the real of their desires, be they reflected or enacted in a clapped-out camper van, on a cheap kitchen floor, in character as a dominatrix or on the backseat of a car on the edge of the council estate.

The questions that remain, however, can be understood as follows: why the move from patriarchal power toward female agency/authority and power in *Shameless*? And, to a lesser extent, what drives the shift from 'fake' or inauthentic female desire, toward more 'real' desire as expressed in Steve's nomination of Fiona as 'genuine'? Rather than expressing equality economically, within the family, or workspace, it is sexual equality and even female dominance in sexual relations that is foregrounded in *Shameless*. As a series driven by conceptions of social class and unashamedly focused on and around underclass rather than middle-class spaces, *Shameless* is able to highlight its disassociation with middle class etiquette, etiquette that as Bev Skeggs (2004, p. 99) notes, frequently centres around: 'restraint, repression, reasonableness, modesty and denial.' In the sprawling underclass spaces of *Shameless*, the broken homes, the smashed windows and the dilapidated sofas, attaining perfection is not on the radar. The richness of *Shameless* life exists *in* its imperfection, in its excesses, its unrestraint, and its refusal to deny pleasure where it finds it.

The representations of the four women considered in this chapter demonstrate, I suggest, a visible democratization of female desire and certainly, in the first two series of *Shameless*, a move away from patriarchal dominance in sexual relations. But, what happens to these women as the series continues? Do their sexual excesses continue to empower them and why is this important? Traditionally, televisual texts featuring strong, sexual, desiring women frequently culminate and conclude in the punishment and demise of such characters. As *Shameless* continues into its ninth UK series, Monica and Karen still inhabit the screen. In series 9, we see Karen attempting to utilize her flagrant sexuality to win back her husband after having a public extra marital affair – something she successfully achieves. Monica actively kidnaps Frank (preventing him from marrying someone else despite the fact that she doesn't really want him) because she can. Interestingly, Fiona and Sheila are absent figures, but, they are not punished figures. Fiona is absent due to leaving the country with Steve while pregnant with another man's child. Sheila, similarly, gives Frank an ultimatum, demanding that he leave Chatsworth with her for foreign climes, or, she leaves him forever. Frank is, unsurprisingly, late. Sheila has sailed. Unpunished, unashamed, unrepenting, these women take control, keying out a new and exciting trend in positive female representation. Forget 'Big'. These women are giants.

2

Sex, Society and the Slayer

Madeleine Smith

This chapter will discuss the conflicts surrounding 'sex' in relation to 'society' in *Buffy the Vampire Slayer* (hereafter *Buffy*) (WB, 1997–2001, UPN, 2001–3) with regard to the presentation of the character Buffy Summers' (Sarah Michelle Gellar) sexual relationships. The chapter will argue that, rather than siding with 'sex' or 'society', *Buffy* displays sets of oppositions integral to both, enabling further discussion and debate within representations of sex and gender. The premise of the show, focusing on a teenage female vampire Slayer's life, friends and love interests within a multi-generic context, allows for a fluid and extensive engagement with the tensions between the realms of sex and society prevalent in contemporary American culture, because both are prominent features in *Buffy*. The debates surrounding the two areas are various and widespread, including socio-political, sexologist and feminist theories. Respective of this, the chapter will operate within a general awareness of the conflicts such theories present, and will attempt to situate the portrayal of sex and society in *Buffy* in relation to the on-going debates that arise from such perspectives. It must also be acknowledged that the 'society' discussed in this chapter is not the only 'society', yet is necessarily restricted to white, heterosexual middleclass American society for the purposes of responding to and informing certain values towards sex and gender present in *Buffy*. The relevance of the show to debates surrounding sex and society will be discussed shortly, but firstly, the conflicting theoretical approaches towards the opposing realms, outlined by Jeffrey Weeks (1985), need to be addressed in order to highlight how *Buffy* provides an exemplary case study with which to discuss the interaction of sex and society in popular culture.

This chapter will primarily use Weeks' 1985 essay 'A never-ceasing Duel? "Sex" in relation to "society"' (pp. 96–124) rather than other theorists' work on such areas for several reasons, primarily because Weeks directly addresses theories relevant to discussing sex and society portrayals, both of which are present in *Buffy*. Consequently, his work enables an analysis of both representations in the show. Weeks effectively outlines the evolution and development of sexology and sociology theories, including Henry Havelock Ellis (1910) and Alfred Kinsey (1948), providing instances of stasis and/or development such as a progressively libertarian attitude (Weeks, 1985, p. 282). Weeks also summarizes each theoretical approach, analysing the work of writers like Margaret Mead (1948) and E.O. Wilson (1978) to indicate commonalities such as the importance of judging each society within its own merits (Weeks, 1985, pp. 108–9). Weeks' extensive approach highlights problems with or omissions from previous works on sex and society, such as Mead's 'ability to ignore [...] counter-evidence to her conclusions' (*ibid.* p. 105). This suggests the ability of Weeks' work to effectively explore tensions and contradictions in sex and society theories. Such a comprehensive overview regarding the relationship between sexuality and the social allows this chapter to operate within a general awareness of the merits and problems of each theory.

Weeks (*ibid.*, pp. 97–9) asserts that there is 'an opposition, even antagonism' between sexologists and social theorists regarding the sexual and the social, stating that 'neither [...] is able ultimately to confront the complexities involved in the making of sexuality'. From this, Weeks (*ibid.*, p. 98) establishes two main responses that have derived from the formulation of 'sex' versus 'society' that are a central part of the approach to *Buffy* in this chapter; the 'repression model' and the 'liberatory model'. Simplified for the purposes of discussion in relation to the show, sexual repression is intrinsically conservative, promoting procreative and heterosexual union within the bounds of cultural values and social institutions. In contrast, sexual liberation foregrounds the individual's sexual desires, upholding a more relaxed attitude towards sexual choice and alternate activities, such as homosexuality, as the right of the individual over restraining societal values and is inherently democratic as a result. These opposing views find each other equally destructive, generating tensions between, respectively, the social and anti-social, humanity and animality, culture and nature, and society and the individual. Similarly related to such oppositions and fundamental in understanding the intrinsically conservative values that have shaped and continue to inform Western society, and in particular American society of which *Buffy* has been a popular contemporary expression, is the complex issue over what exactly is regarded as 'natural or unnatural, good or bad,' in relation to sexuality (*ibid*).

Weeks (*ibid.*, p. 104) addresses the dialectic between acceptable and unacceptable sexuality by outlining two key approaches to the repressive/ liberal models. Firstly, the sociological approach expansively positions culture against primitivism, promoting static social views towards family, gender and race alongside positive eugenics. Such a focus on proper social conduct and 'breeding in the best' supports the 'racist fantasises of eugenics', forwarding conservative attitudes to sex and desire. Procreative sex is foregrounded alongside instinct and natural patterns of behaviour that are also taken as given: monogamy, jealousy, heterosexual union and the primacy of genital sexuality. This strain of thought strives towards a mythic, healthy Self and society and is generally at conflict with instances and 'exceptions' such as homosexuality. Secondly, the biological approach focuses on innate human behaviour and urges in order to 'understand the animal in man' (*ibid.*, p. 110). Within this, the individual becomes a focus, raising aspects of 'selfish' desires versus altruism and outlining both biological and psychological differences between the sexes. It must be acknowledged that these two areas are controversial, complex and contested and do not exist as separate realms or as diametrically opposed to each other. For example, the focus on 'Man' in both approaches ultimately suggests a phallocentric view, forwarding male primacy and agency, and provoking much debate regarding such rigid gender positioning in sex and society amongst feminists such as Susan Griffin (1981) and Linda Williams (1989). Indeed, Weeks (1985, p. 120) argues that these theories 'cannot function without some notion of "natural man" with women as the natural other'. This suggests that sex and society conflicts naturalize the subordinate position of females within patriarchal culture despite other differences that may be evident. With this in mind, a truly liberal or democratic approach to sex and society is one that challenges rigid gender assumptions and procreative and genital primacy, highlighting the position of sex and gender as intrinsically political forces that both determine and derive from society.

It is in this respect that *Buffy* is relevant to conflicts between sex and society due to the ways in which the show represents gender, sex and sexuality along the contours of the repressive and liberatory models and the concomitant socio-biological approaches. Although much has already been written on sex in *Buffy*, highlighting the relevance of such discussions to modern culture, a link has yet to be made between sexual representations in the show and their relevance to contemporary sex and society conflicts. For instance, discussions of sex in the show by Rhonda Wilcox (2005, pp. 111–28) and Justine Larbalestier (2004, pp. 195–218) focus on themes such as love, loss and heterosexuality and do not specifically address sex and society tensions. Lorna Jowett (2005) considers the presentation of gender in *Buffy*, and although her discussions are widespread, they primarily serve as introductions to gender and sexology studies. For example, Jowett's analysis (2005, p. 106) of Buffy and Riley's (Marc Blucas) relationship centres on 'emotional' and 'physical' gender attributes that are not specifically related to sex and society conflicts. None-the-less, such discussions highlight and illuminate the challenge *Buffy* poses to patriarchal society but are necessarily limited in that they do not intend to analyse how sex, gender and sexuality are demarked in positive or negative terms in relation to wider societal debates. Thus, whilst the discussion of gender in the show has been extensive, conflicting and contradictory elements of sex and gender portrayed in *Buffy* have yet to be discussed in relation to sex and society, and it is this gap that the following chapter intends to address.

It must be noted that the representation of sex and society is widespread and varied in the show, such as in the role of Willow (Alyson Hannigan) as a gay character, and Xander's (Nicholas Brendon) rejection of patriarchal values as he leaves Anya (Emma Caulfield) at the altar in 'Hell's Bells' (6.16). Similarly, the vampire family in the series often appear to express more liberal approaches to sexuality and gender relations, such as during Drusilla's (Juliet Landau) sado-masochistic and dominating torture of Angel (David Boreanaz) in 'What's my Line? Part 2' (McCracken, 2007, pp. 124–5) and through Darla (Julie Benz) and Drusilla's promiscuous and bisexual indulgences in the *Angel* (WB, 1999–2004) episode 'The Girl In Question' (5.20), challenging constraining gender roles. Although they are seemingly more progressive and democratic as a result, the vampires ultimately represent the anti-social realm, existing apart from and in opposition to society, making any comparison of them within sex and society conflicts contestable. Because they operate outside of the social realm they do not allow for extensive discussions of sex and society debates. As such, they are not discussed in this chapter. Conversely, Buffy can be categorized as a white middle-class heterosexual American and thus a predominant representative of Western society that is in direct conflict with her outsider status. However distant from society 'regular' Buffy is due to her position as a supernatural demon Slayer, she strives for normalcy and predominantly fights for and represents society, maintaining social order by defeating destructive forces that threaten it. This makes Buffy's relationship with both sex and society a pedagogical one in which interconnected conflicts can be properly addressed. Such an approach may uphold Weeks' assertion that it is not possible to resolve tensions between sexuality and the social, yet it is essential that in-depth and insightful critiques are produced so that it is possible to explain how such representations of sex operate in relation to society and culture. As such this chapter's focus on Buffy's sexual relationships serves as an example of the conflicting and often contradictory viewpoints in *Buffy* that epitomize debates between sex and society outlined above. Such relationships outline the series as progressive and democratic, particularly those centring on the representation of sex and gender. Thus, by looking specifically at how *Buffy* navigates the realms of sex and society, a more nuanced account can be forwarded that shows how the debates surrounding the opposing realms are both complex and contested, complimenting Weeks' theory and underlining its relevance to the study of *Buffy*.

Buffy and the Beast: Sex, 'No-Sex' Sex, and Gender-Bending Bites Back

Buffy's first sexual relationship with ensouled vampire Angel presents several conflicts between sex and society, with a prevalent focus on their sexual relationship from the outset. Their first meeting in 'Welcome to the Hellmouth' (1.1) introduces tensions between sex, gender and society. For instance, Buffy challenges gender expectations when, after being followed by Angel into a dark alley, she unexpectedly attacks and throws him to the ground in a display of physical prowess, reversing active/passive assumptions. The following cut to Angel, panting heavily on his back with a satisfied smile as Buffy stands over him, parallels sexual activity. This is both heightened and undermined by his assertion that, 'I know what you're thinking, but don't worry – I don't bite'. The vampiric act has been likened to sexual activity by writers such as Rosemary Jackson (1981, p. 119). Its inclusion here connotes both impotent masculinity and sexual abstinence, heightened by the use of repressive religious icons that serve as 'protection' and promote conservative ideals, as Angel throws a crucifix necklace to Buffy. However, the traditional meaning of this imagery is undermined and subverted in 'Angel' (1.7) as Angel and Buffy kiss and the necklace burns into his skin, indicating alternative masochistic sexual activity. Such conflicting uses of the crucifix present the 'rival absolutisms' of sex and the social, highlighting both Weeks' repressive and liberatory models (1985, p. 98).

The episode 'Surprise' (2.13) depicts Buffy and Angel's readiness to progress to sexual activity, suggested through euphemisms as they acknowledge that their sexual urges are 'getting harder' to ignore. The episode also includes a discussion about sex between Willow and Buffy, the pair emphasising tensions between individual drives and societal expectations as Buffy excitedly gushes, 'To act on want can be wrong, but to not act on want [...] I think we're going to [...][have sex]'. Writers such as Wilcox

(2005, p. 112) have outlined the metaphorical significance of sex for Buffy in that 'a young woman's worst fear is realized when, after they sleep together, her partner's behaviour is monstrous'. Such discussions suggest a liberal attitude towards depictions of sex amongst youths, engaging openly with 'real' concerns. Bragg and Buckingham's (2009, p. 132) considerations of commonly encountered teen problem and advice pages support this. Buffy's comments present sex as a choice that she is able to decide and instigate on her own terms, advocating individual choice as emphasized in Weeks' liberatory model. However, the word 'sex' is never actually spoken in 'Surprise', suggesting the prevalence of repressive social codes that undermine the more liberal topical inclusion.

The approaching moment of sexual intercourse between Buffy and Angel in 'Surprise' and its aftermath in 'Innocence' (2.14) present similar conflicts. For instance, as the two passionately kiss, Angel is positioned in a passive role whilst Buffy appears active, silencing Angel's misgivings of 'Maybe we shouldn't-' with 'Don't, just kiss me'. Such reversals of traditional gender roles appear progressive, positioning Buffy as dominant and in control of her sexuality. More so, the sex engaged in is non-procreative, suggesting individual drives are foregrounded over societal progression. This demonstrates Weeks' liberatory model, rejecting the 'centrality of the reproductive urge as the yardstick of normality' (1985, p. 119). None-the-less, Buffy and Angel have sex within a loving relationship, presenting societally acceptable values. Angel's soul is released through their sexual act and he experiences a return to his 'natural' state as Angelus, whilst Buffy experiences loss; as Angelus gleefully tells her, 'Dream on schoolgirl, your boyfriend is dead'. Worse, she is blamed for the event, highlighted as Angelus taunts her, 'You made me the man I am today!'. Traditional gender traits are restored as Angelus upholds masculine promiscuity and detachment as he threatens to bite Willow and callously discards Buffy, who becomes overtly feminized and emotional, crying as Angelus throws her to the floor, returning to conservative ideals outlined in Weeks' repressive model. The placing of societal restraint over sexual urges is made painfully prominent as, returning to her bedroom in shock, Buffy catches sight of the crucifix necklace and backs away from it in horror. It is at this point in the episode that flashbacks to Buffy and Angel having sex appear, portrayed through rapid fades that show a blur of naked skin, red sheets and whispers of love. This goes some way to absolve Buffy from guilt and irresponsibility; Angel did love her, and her decision was innocent. Giles (Anthony Stewart Head), a representative of a patriarchal tradition (the Watcher's Council of men) also tells Buffy, 'If it's guilt you're looking for Buffy, I'm not your man. All you will get is my support and my respect'. This subverts conservative attitudes towards female sexuality and blame.

Angel's enforced ensoulment as 'punishment' for his primitive indulgences as Angelus by Gypsies suggests a repression of his true nature. Its violent return after sex with Buffy implies that societal restrictions over 'natural' urges can be as destructive as unrestrained drives themselves, foregrounding a more liberal attitude towards sexual activity and its repression. Such inclusions engage with sociological and biological tensions as outlined by Weeks. For instance, in 'Passion' (2.17), Angelus indulges in predatory and threatening behaviour as he stalks Buffy. His overt masculine potency and sexual threat exposes the animalism inherent in patriarchal culture's acceptance of 'violence [...] in the male role in "normal" heterosexual relations', suggested as Angelus enters Buffy, Willow and Joyce's bedrooms at night and kills Jenny Calendar (Robia LaMorte), dumping her body in Giles' bed (Williams, 1989, p. 17). This conflict is made all the more explicit in 'Amends' (3.10) following Angel's re-ensoulment, as the First Evil visits Angel and prompts him to give in to his animalistic urges to 'take' and bite Buffy. Angel is so overwhelmed by his sexual desires that he is prepared to take his own life, rejecting patriarchal norms of male dominance. He confesses to Buffy, 'I want you so badly [...] I know it'll cost me my soul, and a part of me doesn't care. It's not the demon in me that needs killing Buffy, it's the man'. As such, Angel's 'natural' and repressed drives are positioned as destructive to Buffy. This presents the animal urges in men as in conflict with yet accepted by patriarchal culture, exposing societal norms. Angel's rejection of male phallic potency ultimately presents a liberal attitude towards female subjugation and submission, undermining the 'cultural regulations, taboos and barriers' discussed within Weeks' repressive model (1985, p. 102).

As illustrated above, the release of Angel's soul following sex is configured as damaging to society, suggesting a conservative attitude towards sexual activity. This is further emphasized in 'Revelations' (3.7) as, after exposing Buffy's secret meetings with Angel, Xander angrily confronts her and declares that her actions are tantamount to '[waiting] for Angel to go psycho again the next time you give him a happy'. This attitude demonstrates Weeks' repressive model, explicitly linking sex with anti-societal behaviour and promoting conservative ideals of sexual abstinence. Buffy and Angel instead showcase 'no-sex' sex and non-genital sex, in a somewhat more progressive attitude towards sexual release. For example, in 'Revelations', Buffy and Angel do Tai Chi together; the sexual implications are obvious as their sweaty bodies move in unison, with an emphasis on the erotic and physical motions of the act as their hands lock. This imagery is supported by soft lighting, close framing and romantic music, highlighting the possibility of sexual pleasure without any obvious physical contact. However, dialogue between the two highlights sexual desire and repression through an apparent penis-metaphor as Angel suggestively says, 'It's hard [...]' to which Buffy defiantly retorts, 'It's not hard!'. This suggests that they are sacrificing pleasure for the 'good' of society. In 'Graduation Day, Part 2' (2.22), Buffy and Angel display non-genital penetrative sexual activity which forwards a more liberal approach to sex by rejecting sexual conformity, challenging 'the primacy of genital sexuality' (Weeks, 1985, p. 102). For example, to save his life, Buffy beats Angel to force his primal urges to the surface and thrusts his mouth against her neck, which Angel bites and violently drinks from. Buffy's fluid gender positioning as active/aggressive and passive/penetrable suggests the instability of rigid gender coding. The following scene is highly sexualized as, falling to the floor in dramatic slow-motion, Buffy's legs part around Angel, her hand clutching at his naked torso. Further emphasising the alternative and liberal sexual nature of the scene, the camera focuses on Buffy's enjoyment, the pleasure and pain on her face suggestive of masochism. Consequently, dominant heter-onormative portrayals of genital sex are challenged by the sexualization of the vampiric act. None-the-less, Buffy is punished for this transgressive display as Angel leaves her. Worse, he leaves to give Buffy 'a normal life', stating, 'you should be with someone who can take you into the light, someone who can make love to you'. This ultimately restates conservative ideals and positions non-normative sex as an insufficient form of sexual release, illustrating Weeks' repressive model by promoting 'sexual repression and control' as beneficial to society (*ibid.*, p. 98).

I'm Tired of You Men and Your Man-ness: The Casualties of Casual Sex

Following Angel's departure, Buffy engages in casual sex with Parker Abrams (Adam Kaufman). This appears liberal, rejecting conservative modes of procre-ative and loving union. For instance, Willow presents a progressive attitude towards Buffy's desire for casual sex with Parker in 'The Harsh Light of Day' (4.3) as she explains of Buffy's 'lusty wrong feelings' that, 'there's no wrong; you're free, you're both grown-ups.' Although this positions casual sex as guilt free and a mature step for Buffy, it quickly becomes apparent that Parker is utilizing male primacy, exploiting both dating and mating rituals and female desires for equality and agency. Whilst Weeks' liberatory model is suggested by Parker's unrestrained pursuit of sexual gratification, this conflicts with Buffy's position as subject to repressive male sexuality. The social param-eters of sexual pursuit are emphasized as he takes Buffy to a party, where he attempts to get to know her 'hobbies' and to engage emotionally with her, suggested as he says, 'It's cool to find someone else who understands.' He also makes Buffy feel like she is in control, passing over responsibility for sexual endeavours as he kisses her, emphasising an abuse of female desires for respect and agency; 'Is this okay? Because I could stop if you wanted, it's your choice'. The following sex act suggests sexual indulgence as the camera tracks Buffy's hand over Parker's body. However, the scene is intercut with Giles attempting to contact Buffy, highlighting the intrusion of sex over her societal responsibilities. After their sexual encounter, traditional gender roles of male promiscuity and female monogamy are upheld as Parker is depicted pursuing his next conquest and rejects Buffy's desire for commitment. This is suggested as Parker laughs, 'I'm starting to feel like you thought that meant some kind of commitment?'. As such, Buffy is punished for engaging in casual sex *and* for wanting more, upholding Weeks' (1985, p. 114) discussions of traditional gender profiling. Parker's manipulation of Buffy not only indicates the 'dangers' of casual sex, it also exposes the hypocrisy of sexual norms for men and women within phallocentric society. Respective of this, Buffy and Parker's encounter upholds yet exposes the 'symbolic representations of patriarchal power in heterosexual pleasure,' highlighting woman's position as Other and subject to codes of sexual and social conduct (Williams, 1989, p. 29). This is further exemplified in 'Beer Bad' (4.5), as Parker pursues yet another woman whilst Buffy labels herself a 'slut'. As such, this acknowledgement embodies yet exposes restraining conservative values towards female sexual activity.

'Good' Sex, 'Bad' Sex, and the Patriarchal Prejudices of a Corn-Fed Iowa Boy

Buffy's subsequent relationship with Riley Finn foregrounds tensions between conservative and liberal attitudes towards eugenics, gender and sexuality. In opposition to the presentation of Angel as 'bad' for Buffy, she and Riley are configured as a healthy and societally favourable union with implications of 'good' racial matching; they are blonde haired, blue eyed, middle-class and educated all-Americans who both fight demons to protect society, promoting positive eugenics. This demonstrates the promotion of 'breeding in the best' as outlined in Weeks' repressive model (1985, p. 104). However, Buffy describes Riley's conservative traits as restraining, telling Willow in 'Something Blue' (4.9) that, 'Riley seems so solid, he wouldn't cause me heartache [...] can a nice safe relationship be that intense?'. This suggests that Buffy is denying her instincts for the person society deems she *should* be with. More so, Riley's conservative attitudes towards gender and sex create tensions with Buffy's liberal views. For example, in 'A New Man' (4.12), Riley appears threatened by Buffy's dominant positioning within their relationship as, during their sparring session, Buffy allows herself to be restrained by Riley before displaying her physical prowess and throwing him to the floor. Riley's sudden aggression and determination to physically best Buffy, stating, 'I'm not even sure I could take you', links the threat of gender reversal with a fear of impotent male sexuality. Riley also displays conservative attitudes to alternative sexual relationships in 'New Moon Rising' (4.19), as he rejects Willow's human/demon relationship with werewolf Oz (Seth Green) as inherently wrong, presenting a conflict with Buffy's more liberal outlook.

Buffy and Riley's first sexual encounter in 'The I in Team' (4.13) appears progressive, as their love-making session is intercut with scenes of them fighting demons in unison. This suggests unrestrained primitive sexuality and gender equality as the two tear at each other's clothes, the implied moment of penetration foregrounding Buffy's sexual enjoyment. Conflicting with this progressive representation, Buffy and Riley are fighting to protect society from outsider threats. That her 'healthy' eugenic-friendly sexual exploits are configured as permissible when her previous sexual encounters were not forwards conservative attitudes and opposes representations of alternative sexual coupling. As such, this highlights the 'racial and racist fantasies of eugenics' prevalent in Weeks' repressive model (1985, p. 104). Conflicts between the realms of sex and society are explicitly acknowledged in 'Where the Wild Things Are' (4.18), as Buffy and Riley's copious sexual activity both releases and feeds paranormal activity, a product of repressed sexuality. In the first instance, their sexual acts are configured as damaging to society as Buffy and Riley's sexual activity manifests dangerous occurrences at a party. For example, shots of their lovemaking upstairs are intercut with scenes of sexual misbehaviour and punishment at the party downstairs as the house roars into life; displays of promiscuous behaviour during a game of spin-the-bottle are punished as the bottle explodes, injuring the players, and overt female sexuality is punished through possessed hair-hacking. However, this conservative view conflicts with more liberal imagery. For instance, Buffy and Riley are shown to be practicing safe sex, contrary to Barrie Gunter's (2002, p. 109) assertion that, in the media, 'safe sex practices are rarely allowed to surface', suggesting a progressive attitude to non-procreative sex. In the most explicit depiction of heteronormative sex in *Buffy*, Buffy and Riley's bodies are shown writhing together on the bed, barely covered by a sheet as the camera moves close to capture their raptured faces. The positioning of sexual repression as damaging is similarly liberal. For instance, Giles and Buffy's friends discover that the house used to be a children's home, where the patron punished sexual desires and activity with physical and emotional torture. That the patron, rewarded with 'thirty years of community service', performed 'baptisms on the most unclean' implies that sexuality forcibly repressed through repressive tools of religion and ideals such as 'duty' can return with devastating effects. Consequently, sexual liberation is configured as less damaging than sexual repression, although the two are depicted as feeding off each other through the paranormal activities in the house. As such, tensions between Weeks' liberatory and repressive models are exemplified. Buffy and Riley's enjoyment of the whole experience, indicated through furtive glances, supports the more democratic stance, albeit within the confines of a socially accepted relationship.

The disintegration of Buffy and Riley's relationship is presented as a result of her gender ambiguity and his struggle to accept challenges to patriarchal tradition. Riley's belief in male primacy and agency is constantly questioned by Buffy's dominant positioning as physically and emotionally more capable and active, undermining the rigid gender profiling inherent in Weeks' repressive model (1985, p. 114). For instance, in 'Shadow' (5.8), Buffy appears in control and independent, rejecting Riley's traditional role of emotional support when her mother Joyce (Kristine Sutherland) becomes sick. Riley's desire for emotional dependence and physical dominance, and his increasing instability, suggests his inability to cope with departures from fixed gender roles and traditional masculinity. Gender displacement also prompts Riley's fears of sexual inadequacy, emphasized in 'Into the Woods' (5.10) as the two make love; Buffy's sexual enjoyment is foregrounded, her face revealing pleasure whilst Riley's is not shown at all, equating her satisfaction with dominant positioning, suggesting a reversal of sexual gender roles. He is then shown leaving their bed to seek sexual fulfilment elsewhere in the form of 'suck-jobs' from vampire 'whores', restating masculine promiscuity. More so, after allowing a female vampire to feed on him in 'Shadow' (5.8), Riley violently penetrates her with a stake, rejecting his passive feminization at the hands of Buffy by reasserting potent masculine dominance. He also blames his sexual transgression on Buffy's gender ambiguity, stating that, '[the vampires] needed me [...] they had such hunger for me'. This aligns with David Gauntlett's (2008, p. 10) assertion that 'men have been "betrayed" by a society which had seemed to promise them that the traditional masculine role would deliver some ultimate happiness'. Buffy exposes Riley's conservative attitudes as she asserts, 'you can't handle the fact that I'm stronger than you'. That Riley is unpunished for his promiscuous behaviour and rigidly patriarchal outlook and leaves Buffy, whilst she again faces loss at his departure in response to her gender ambiguity, aligns with Weeks' repressive model by upholding conservative attitudes towards sex and gender roles.

Welcome to Thunderdome: Desire, Degradation and the Battle of the Sexes

Buffy's turbulent relationship with vampire Spike (James Marsters) is tinged with sexual tension throughout much of *Buffy* and most explicitly outlines conflicts between primitive and cultured behaviour, animalism and humanity, and gendered battles as outlined through Weeks' repressive and liberatory models. Many writers (Larbalestier, 2004, p. 215; Wilcox, 2005, p. 113) have outlined Buffy's doubling with Spike's on-off vampire lover Drusilla and aligned his desire to kill Buffy with a desire to have sex with her. Despite these hints and suggestions, it is their personal journeys that make possible an exploration of their true natures and sexual desires, juxtaposed with their position in society. Ambiguous and fluid gender roles play an important part in this progression, as they both fear and seek penetration and are simultaneously positioned as feminine and masculine. Spike intends to bite Buffy and avoid being staked, whilst she attempts to stake and evade being bitten, emphasising the active/passive roles of both as the notion of penetration is again sexualized. Thus the fighting and tension between them presents sexual desire and rejection; as Buffy aptly muses in 'Something Blue' (4.9), 'I think maybe we fought because we couldn't admit how we really felt about each other'. As such, Buffy and Spike suggest the potential to display liberal attitudes towards sex, through transgression of the boundaries of social acceptability (soulless vampire and human) and the possibility of sex based on primal urges.

Spike's enforced neutering by the top secret government organization 'The Initiative', via the implantation of a chip in his brain that quells his instincts to bite and hurt, suggests that Spike's humanity is a forced acquisition over his primal nature. This illustrates Weeks' (1985) discussions of sociological and biological tensions, displaying innate behaviour, urges and desires in opposition with instinct and the acquisition of culture. For instance, as revealed in 'The Initiative' (4.7), Spike can no longer feed, bite or hurt people. The sexual implications of this are made obvious as, after being unable to bite Willow, she says, 'Maybe you're trying too hard [...] why don't we wait a half an hour and try again?'. This aligns his neutered state with diminished phallic potency. Despite his involuntary propulsion towards society, Spike ends up developing feelings for Buffy that he frequently describes as 'love' ('Out of My Mind' (5.4), 'Crush' (5.14)), a notion that Buffy vehemently rejects, suggesting a reversal of expected gender roles. Similarly, after Buffy is resurrected from the dead she finds solace in kissing Spike ('Once More, With Feeling' (6.7), 'Tabula Rasa' (6.8)), yet is repulsed by the idea that it could mean more, denying his assertions that she has feelings for him in 'Smashed' (6.9) with, 'You seem awfully fixated on a couple of kisses…I'm sorry if you thought it meant more'. As such, traditional male/female gender attributes are challenged, as is the depiction of women as 'more emotional and less rational than men', suggesting a progressive subversion of patriarchal gender profiling (Gunter, 2002, p. 111).

The affirmation and reversal of gender conventions and a violent release of sexual repression further challenge society's conservative ideals in 'Smashed'. For example, Spike discovers he can hurt Buffy, equating his ability to bite and penetrate with a return to sexual potency as he declares, 'Looks like I'm not as toothless as you thought Sweetheart!'. That this is possible because Buffy 'came back wrong' emphasizes her position as Other and places them both outside the bounds of society. They violently fight, literally suggesting a release from archaic codes towards societal restraint and sexual repression as a derelict old house comes crashing down around them. Buffy becomes dominant and assertive as she throws Spike around, and is positioned as sexually aggressive as she unzips his trousers, mounts and fucks him. As Buffy triumphantly rides Spike, her sexual release is prominent as the camera focuses on her face, reversing associations of women as subservient to male pleasure. The scene positions Buffy as active and her sexual needs as paramount, illustrating Weeks' liberatory model by presenting a progressive representation of sex over societal constraints.

This seemingly progressive depiction of sex in 'Smashed' still conflicts with society, however, upholding Williams (1989, p. 153) assertion that 'in the war between the sexes, the female loses the game of power if she wins that of pleasure'. For example, in 'Wrecked' (6.10), Buffy is subsequently unable to resist Spike's sexual advances, their ambiguous gender roles now in conflict with each other. This is illustrated as Spike physically attempts to stimulate Buffy, an act which Buffy fights before giving in to. This conservative representation of women evokes the 'rape myth [...] wherein the woman initially resists [...] but eventually enjoys it', suggesting a restating of male primacy and submissive women (Gunter, 2002, p. 116). This is emphasized further as Buffy appears unable to resist Spike's sexual advances in 'Doublemeat Palace' (6.12) and 'As You Were' (6.15). However, when inflicted with accidental invisibility in 'Gone' (6.11), Buffy experiences true liberation from the confines of society, acting on her sexual impulses without repudiation. For instance, she visits Spike in his crypt and becomes physically aggressive as she pins and sexually accosts him, aligning her invisibility with sexual and gender dominance. This is further emphasized by her unseen naked state as the camera instead follows and sexualizes Spike's naked body. As Buffy explains, 'For the first time [...] I'm free; free from rules [...]'. This suggests that Buffy feels unable to act out her sexual urges within the confines of society, making the inclusion of Invisi-Buffy a temporary solution to social repression.

Buffy and Spike also showcase alternative sexual practices in 'Dead Things' (6.13). For example, Spike reveals Buffy makes sex 'hurt in all the wrong places', suggesting masochistic indulgences. Similarly, submission and domination sex games are indicated through images of Buffy riding a hand-cuffed Spike. This illustrates Weeks' liberatory model, presenting a relaxed attitude towards creative sexual energy and sex for pleasure within a casual relationship that is clearly on Buffy's terms, emphasized as she rejects the emotional attachments that Spike feels. None-the-less, their sex acts also uphold degrading images of women unable to resist male advances, suggested in 'Dead Things' as Spike forces Buffy to watch her friends dance below them as he fucks her from behind. This not only emphasizes the conflict of 'selfish' sex with society, but it also foregrounds Spike's dominance over Buffy, suggested by shots of his smug and jubilant grin as he penetrates her. This demonstrates Weeks' repressive model by positioning sex as destructive and antisocial. Buffy's ultimate rejection of sex with Spike in 'As You Were' signals a return to social confines and conservatism, as Riley's brief return restates a sense of social decorum over sexual gratification in Buffy after he witnesses her having sex with Spike. Patriarchal expectations upon women are similarly reaffirmed as Buffy rejects her urges and her selfish treatment of Spike, explaining to him that, 'I do want you [...] but I'm using you [...] I'm just being weak and selfish, I have to be strong about this'. As such, although Buffy rejects pleasure to regain power, she also rejects her degrading treatment at the hands of Spike.

The denunciation of female submission suggests a very liberal image of women in *Buffy*, and is most explicitly enforced during Spike's attempted rape of Buffy in 'Seeing Red' (6.19). At the beginning of the rape scene in Buffy's bathroom, rigid gender roles are imposed as Buffy is feminized in a soft bathrobe, suggesting vulnerability and passivity. Spike appears rigid and overtly masculine in black, a phallic and threatening figure against the softness of the bathroom. As the scene progresses, gender roles are reversed and restated several times. For example, Spike desperately pleads to Buffy, 'Love me [...] let yourself feel it', and she tells him to 'Get out [...] please stop this'. Spike's penetrative threat is asserted as he grabs at Buffy and throws her to the floor, the scene suddenly escalating with panic and tension as Spike pins her arms and pulls at her clothes, trying to forcibly penetrate her. Buffy's vulnerability is emphasized by her exposed thighs and kicking slippered feet as she screams and cries in fear. In a final reversal of conservative gender roles, Buffy kicks Spike away and screams, 'No!' admonishing both the rape myth and derogatory representations of women in patriarchal culture, transcending the prevalence of male primacy inherent to Weeks' repressive and liberatory models. Similarly rejecting gender profiling, Spike's rape is motivated by desperate declarations of love and desire (albeit rather warped ones), contrary to Gill's (2007, p. 141) assertion that 'rapists are not motivated by desire but by anger or by the need to humiliate and dominate women'. By refusing his rape attack, Buffy's rejection of Spike and of the conservative role of passive women marks a truly liberal representation of sex and society, positioning gender ambiguous women with progressive potential.

It's Not Over

The examples discussed in this chapter surrounding the representation of sex and society in *Buffy* primarily uphold Weeks' assertion that the conflicting realms of sexology and sociology cannot properly address the complex relationship between sexuality and the social. That the show portrays both acceptable and unacceptable forms of sex allows for extensive engagement with discourses of sex and society. As has been demonstrated, oppositions between the repressive and liberatory models outlined by Weeks (1985) are prevalent themes in *Buffy*. For example, Buffy's first sexual engagement with Angel and eventual sexual relationship with Spike presents animalism/ humanity and nature/culture tensions as both vampires are dubiously suspended between both realms with the loss or gaining of a soul, or the implementation of a restraining chip. Sociological and biological oppositions as posited by Weeks (1985) are also upheld. This is most effectively illustrated through the characters of Angel and Spike as 'bad' and as anti-social beings that threaten society and Buffy. This is further emphasized by Riley, who is positioned as healthy and socially progressive. Sex with him is configured as permissible for Buffy because of Riley's presentation as a 'good' racial match. Related to this concept, gender differences necessary for the vindication of Weeks' (1985) models, such as the prevalence of gender stereotyping in sexual responses, are similarly sustained. Again, this is accentuated in all of Buffy's sexual relationships as she experiences loss in each and rigid gender relations are foregrounded. For example, both Parker and Riley expose patri- archal social norms of sex and gender expectations permissible for men but not women.

However, the portrayal of sex and society in *Buffy* often challenges Weeks' (1985) assertions. For example, repressive and liberatory oppositions are often blurred between natural/unnatural and good/bad, accentuated by

Buffy's tenable position as human and Slayer, defender and killer. At times, this presents tensions between sex and society as in tandem with each other, suggesting that the assimilation of sex and society is made possible through the characterization of Buffy. Sociological and biological oppositions upholding procreative and genital primacy are also challenged. This is most effectively displayed in Buffy's alternative sexual relationship with Angel, as the vampiric bite is explicitly sexualized and sensualized. Similarly, albeit configured as damaging, Buffy's sexual encounters with Spike offer space for creative sexual energy to be released through bondage and masochistic sex games, without any obvious threats to society. Deriving from such concepts, the portrayal of gender in Buffy's relationships with Riley and Spike admonishes Weeks' (1985, p. 120) assertion that the theories require a 'notion of natural Man with woman as natural Other' by challenging rigid gender assumptions. For instance, Buffy and Riley exemplify the unstable nature of gender identity as roles are reversed. This challenges and undermines the phallocentric positioning of men under Weeks' models by ultimately rejecting male primacy and agency and replacing it with Buffy's gender fluid and progressive stance, most explicitly illustrated through her rejection of female subjugation with Spike. It is these instances of transcendence from social codes and limitations that present *Buffy* as a democratic and progressive representation of sex and society in contemporary popular culture. However, rather than positioning Weeks' (1985) work as redundant, such subversions of his models suggest the adaptive potential of Weeks' (1985) ideas to offer an expansive and nuanced approach to sex and society debates. This suggests that shows like *Buffy* have the ability to challenge existing modes of thought on the opposing realms and their respective theories, and to transcend the boundaries imposed by them. With no clear resolution surrounding sex and society debates, and the possibility of further discussions surrounding sexuality and the social apparent through and beyond representations in *Buffy*, one thing is certain; it's not over.

3

Fangbanging: Sexing the Vampire in Alan Ball's *True Blood*

Melanie Waters

From Samuel Taylor Coleridge's *Christabel* (1816) to Stephenie Meyer's *Twilight* (2005), the vampire has been a potent erotic symbol since its earliest incarnations in ancient mythology. When *True Blood* first aired on HBO in September 2008, it became rapidly apparent that Alan Ball's latest show, based on Charlaine Harris's *Southern Vampire Mysteries* cycle, would be no exception to the rule. Featuring graphic depictions of masturbation, cunnilingus, bondage, and other pornographic activities in the first episode, it is perhaps unsurprising that Olivia Lichtenstein (2009), writing for the *Daily Mail*, branded the series 'a shocking tale of depravity, explicit sexuality [. . .] and vile language' following its UK premiere on Channel 4 in October 2009. At a time when there is more sex on television than ever, *True Blood*'s ability to provoke such a virulent reaction would seem to reside less in its explicit portrayal of sexuality *per se*, than in its candid representation of sexuality as a species of violence. This stubborn entanglement of sex and violence is, of course, an abiding hallmark of vampire fictions. As Victoria Brownworth (1996, p. x) notes, vampirism is prevailingly invoked as a 'euphemism for sex'; sex, moreover, that is 'forbidden by social mores [and] not of a normative nature'. While this 'non-normativity' has traditionally manifested itself in the vampire's bisexuality, the serial nature of *True Blood* means that the erotic resonances of vampirism are always multiplying and diversifying. As a result, the vampires in *True Blood* are not only used as a means of querying prescriptive accounts of sexual identity, but also as loci for exploring vexed questions about promiscuity, consent, prostitution, and even rape. Within the 'non-normative' erotic spectrum across which they operate, however, the sexual activities of the vampire are enduringly sadomasochistic in nature, being marked – in one way or another – by acts of violence and the struggle for control. In this chapter, I analyse the dynamic relationship between sex and violence in *True Blood* through the lens of post-9/11 American culture and related debates about gender and power. More specifically, I argue that *True Blood* belongs to a cluster of twenty-first century television shows that instrumentalize gothic tropes as a means of exploring the parallel vulnerabilities of the physical body and the body politic.

True Blood is based on the premise that Japanese scientists have engineered a synthetic blood-substitute that has enabled vampires to 'come out of the coffin' and admit their existence to humans. The action is set in the fictional small town of Bon Temps, Louisiana, and centres on the character of Sookie Stackhouse (Anna Paquin), a telepathic waitress who falls in love with the vampire Bill Compton (Stephen Moyer). *True Blood* is, of course, just one of a number of vampire-themed television shows that have emerged in the wake of Joss Whedon's *Buffy the Vampire Slayer* (1997–2003, WB, 1997–2001, UPN, 2001–3). It would, then, seem to invite consideration alongside network series like *Angel* (WB, 1999–2004), *Moonlight* (CBS, 2007–8), *Blood Ties* (Citytv and Lifetime Television, 2007–8), and *The Vampire Diaries* (CW, 2009–). As network shows, however, such franchises are wholly reliant on corporate sponsorship and have thus tended to eschew images of sexual or visceral excess in their endeavour 'to alienate as few people as possible' (James Poniewozik cited in Grace Bradberry (2002)). Made by HBO, a premium subscription channel with no advertisers to placate, *True Blood* is bound by no such restrictions. Like HBO's most popular shows, *Sex and the City* (1998–2004), *The Sopranos* (1999–2007), *Six Feet Under* (2001–5), and *The Wire* (2002–8), *True Blood* adheres closely to the 'profanity, violence, and sex' (Leverette, 2008, p. 140) formula for which the channel's original programming is most renowned. Where its network counterparts are obliged to regulate their depiction of bloodshed and nudity, *True Blood* revels in the persistent inscription of gory violence and erotic spectacle. Indeed, the more salacious aspects of the show are aggressively foregrounded in its mainstream publicity. Released to coincide with the finale of Season 3, the September 2010 issue of *Rolling Stone* featured three of *True Blood*'s most popular stars – Anna Paquin, her real-life husband Stephen Moyer, and co-star Alexander Skarsgård (who plays the Viking vampire Eric Northman) – naked and bloodied on its cover. This cover, which has been reproduced endlessly in online forums and television blogs, actively asserted the show's liberal take on the vampire myth and helped to galvanize its status as the antithesis of the popular *Twilight* saga, its abstinent cinematic cousin. *True Blood*, then, understands itself as offering a narrative space in which the sexual urges and violent impulses that are typically relegated to a subtextual status within network television shows and teen film fictions can be wantonly unleashed.

As Stacey Abbott (2010) has argued, *True Blood* adheres to Fred Botting's (1995, p. 1) seminal definition of the Gothic as a genre that is rooted in 'excess'. Concerned, in Alan Ball's words, with 'nature, emotions, and intimacy',[1] *True Blood* moves away from the repressive themes of his previous HBO show, *Six Feet Under*, in order to explore what happens when the mechanisms of repression are removed, when secrets are exposed and everything 'that should have remained hidden [...] has come into the open' (Schelling cited in Freud, 1919, p. 148). For Abbott, *True Blood*'s tendency towards 'excess' is writ large in the show's treatment of vampire death: where the vampires of Buffy's Sunnydale are neatly dispatched in a puff of computer-generated dust, those in *True Blood* suffer a more lurid fate, gushing into an oozing heap of lumpy, viscous effluvia. Certainly, the show's gory explosions of tissue and matter would seem to materialize the logic of the gothic in ways that other vampire fictions cannot, marking the point at which what is hidden and contained (in this case, quite literally, the internal tissues of the vampire body) is revealed, brought to light in a spectacle of compelling sanguinary splendour. *True Blood*'s treatment of sex is similarly candid, requiring frequent nudity from its male and female stars and dispensing with the discreet, soft-focus, fade-out shots that have characterized love scenes in other recent vampire fictions.

Like all gothic texts, *True Blood* is obsessively concerned with questions relating to bodily boundaries and their transgression. While a number of recent vampire fictions – including those to which I have already referred – incline towards the strict policing and/or maintenance of the body and its borders (particularly those of the young woman), *True Blood* is more manifestly interested in telegraphing the vulnerability of these borders. Although this vulnerability is mapped insistently through images of penetrated bodies, it is also reinforced through other kinds of border-crossings.

In the first place, *True Blood* is forever querying the putative sanctity of the domestic realm. It imagines a world in which the architectural borders of Sookie's home are subject to perpetual breach; vampires, werewolves, shapeshifters, maenads, and a serial killer all find their way past the Stackhouse threshold, shattering the illusion that the home is – or can ever be – immune to the threats of the outside world.[2]

Though threats to the home are hardcoded into the Gothic, they have perhaps accrued a special currency in the wake of 9/11 and growing anxieties about terrorist attacks on US soil. Such anxieties are evoked in recent examples of the suburban gothic like *Desperate Housewives* (2004–), a show which – as I have argued elsewhere (Gillis and Waters, 2006) – seems to recast threats to homeland security as threats to the security of the home. As the houses in *Desperate Housewives'* Wisteria Lane are rendered vulnerable to various forms of surveillance, trespass, burglary, and destruction, so the safety of the Stackhouse homestead in *True Blood* is similarly compromised.

The breached status of the home is likewise articulated through the symbol of television itself. According to Jacques Derrida (Derrida and Stiegler, 2002, p. 33) television represents a distinct, if ambiguous, assault upon domestic space. Along with its growing array of audio-visual prostheses, television engages in a kind of 'breaking and entering' that 'violently' undermines the 'historical distinction [...] between public and private'. Recording and viewing technologies, after all, generate a traffic in images that cuts across the boundary which (notionally) distinguishes what is 'inside' the home from what is 'outside'. 'Telepowers', as Derrida refers to them, introduce images from the outside world into domestic space, while also making 'private' experience available to surveillance, recording, and dissemination. As an object, the television forces us into a dangerous pact as soon as we invite it into our homes; while we are beguiled and entertained by it, it carries with it the potential to undermine the fantasized 'safety' of the domestic sphere by exposing us to images of threats which would otherwise remain 'outside'. When formulated in these terms, television itself acquires a vampiric cast – seducing, deceiving, and imperilling us at the same time. Offering frequent depictions of audio-visual equipment, *True Blood* is forever commenting on its own status as television, and thus on its own 'dangerous' potential to deceive or mislead the viewer. The unreliability of audio-visual media is made abundantly evident in the opening episode when Jason Stackhouse (Ryan Kwanten), Sookie's older brother, is implicated in the murder of a local woman, Maudette Pickens (Danielle Sapia). Prior to her death, Maudette had secretly filmed herself and Jason having rough, sadomasochistic sex. After her murder the police find the tape and call Jason in for questioning. Although the tape appears to show Jason asphyxiating Maudette at the moment of climax, it soon transpires that this 'asphyxiation' was only feigned; once Jason has fled the scene, understandably horrified, the apparently deceased Maudette recovers herself, scoffs at his gullibility, and turns off the video camera with which she was secretly filming their sexual escapades (1.1). This blurring of reality and representation speaks to television's capacity to deceive and draws attention to *True Blood*'s own need to mislead its viewers by exposing them to horrors that *look* convincing, without being real.

While the infringement of architectural boundaries is a key motif in *True Blood*, the show is equally interested in the penetrability of psychic space.

Sookie's telepathy implies that psychic borders are just as permeable as the walls of the home. Again, this is consistent with a number of recent examples of gothic television: *Medium* (2005–11, NBC, 2005–9, CBS, 2009–11), *Ghost Whisperer* (CBS, 2005–10), and *Tru Calling* (Fox, 2003–5) all feature female protagonists who are perpetually assailed, at a psychic level, by the voices of the dead.[3]

These boundary transgressions perform a key role in establishing *True Blood*'s gothic preoccupations, but I draw particular attention to them here because they provide a vital context for analysing the show's treatment of sex. In its representations of trespassing, television, and telepathy, after all, the show foregrounds the issues of violation and consent that inform its approach to sexual intimacy. As is clear from the opening episode, sex in *True Blood* is always nudging at the boundaries of what the individuals involved find permissible: Maudette, for example, confides in Jason that she likes 'rough sex', but confesses that the 'consensual' sex she had with a vampire she met at a bar was '*too* rough' (my emphasis) (1.1). In a later episode, Jason attempts to enact revenge on local waitress Dawn (Lynn Collins), another of his casual girlfriends, after she leaves him tied to the posts of her bed. Once disentangled, Jason disguises himself in Dawn's clothes and waits for her to arrive home; then, maintaining the pretence that he is a home intruder, he attempts to have sex with her. Just as Dawn's struggles grow more urgent and the viewer starts to doubt that the 'rapist' is really Jason, he pulls off his mask, at which point Dawn's protests give way first to submission and then to energetic participation (1.3). If such moments register anxieties about the proximity of desire and aggression, then these anxieties are crystallized further in the frequent intersections of sex and bloodshed in the show. Indeed, penetrative sex in *True Blood* is routinely accompanied by other, simultaneous, forms of physical violation. In one especially disturbing episode, Sookie, believing Bill to be dead, takes flowers to his grave. Without warning, a soil-encrusted hand bursts through the dirt and grabs Sookie by the ankle, dragging her to the ground. As Sookie screams and claws in resistance, the naked man to whom the hand belongs emerges from the earth, revealing himself to be Bill. Stunned and relieved, Sookie kisses Bill desperately and within seconds the two are having sex. In the midst of Bill's urgent thrusting, he draws his fangs and moves in to bite Sookie. Despite the fact that Sookie refuses this advance, telling him 'Not tonight', the scene closes on the image of a frenzied Bill sinking his teeth into her breast (1.8). While this scene has been amongst the most controversial in the show's history to date, its synchronic representation of sexual and violent penetration is by no means unique. In a subsequent episode, an impassioned fight between Bill and the woman who 'made' him a vampire, Lorena (Mariana

Klaveno), evolves speedily into aggressive, hostile intercourse. As Bill enters Lorena, he bites, scratches, twists, and tears at her bleeding flesh to a disconcerting soundtrack of his own hateful screams and Lorena's seemingly incongruous proclamations of love (3.3). Although suggestive on a number of levels, such instances – in which bodies are subject to multiple forms of penetration at once – not only serve to consolidate the connection between sex and violence, but also foreground the 'double' vulnerability of the body to erotic and violent forms of intrusion alike. Pregnant with symbolic significance, the motif of the invaded body might thus function as a springboard for analysing the sexual and cultural politics of *True Blood*: What does it imply about the relationship between gender and sexuality? What insights can it offer into the show's understanding of power? What, if anything, can it reveal about the kinds of anxieties that have informed US culture in the first decade of the twenty-first century?

Although the first book in Harris's *Southern Vampire Mysteries* cycle was published in 2001, slightly predating 9/11, Ball's series actively trades on its post-9/11 context. Certainly, it is difficult to extricate *True Blood*'s sustained engagement with images of the invaded body from the anxieties about invasion that have grown up in the wake of the terrorist attacks on the World Trade Center and the Pentagon. In many ways, the vampires in *True Blood* would seem to invite consideration alongside the extremists who perpetrated the attacks. For a start, they are part of a stigmatized and persecuted minority. They can, however, 'mainstream', aligning their appearance and behaviour to the norms and values of the society in which they live. In this way, they move amongst the population stealthily and anonymously, all the while disguising an appetite for apocalyptic violence that is only discernible when it is too late. Just as 9/11 exposed the reality of the United States' vulnerability to attack – leading to the resuscitation of once-virulent strains of Cold War xenophobia and protectionism (as exhibited in the revitalization of discourses about invasion, subversion and contamination) – so *True Blood* symbolically recasts the vampire as a potential 'enemy within', the invisible threat that insinuates itself into the body politic and undermines the physical safety of its citizens.[4]

In her two most influential works, *Purity and Danger* (1966) and *Natural Symbols* (1970;1982) Mary Douglas draws a potent connection between the biological body and the social body, arguing that attempts to impose order on the human body and its flows of matter are necessarily coextensive with anxieties about the orderliness of the social body. 'The human body', she argues, 'is always treated as an image of society and [...] there can be no natural way of considering the body that does not involve at the same time the social dimension':

Interest in [the body's] apertures depends on the social preoccupations with social exits and entrances, escape routes, and invasions. If there is no concern to preserve social boundaries, I would not expect to find concern with bodily boundaries. [...] [B]odily control is an expression of social control – abandonment of bodily control in ritual responds to the requirement of a social experience which is being expressed (1982, pp. 70–1).

According to Douglas, the regulation of the body corresponds to a collective desire for the safeguarding of social order – a desire that is tethered to a particular context and a particular moment. The spectacle of disorderly, violated, out-of-control bodies in *True Blood* might, therefore, speak to concerns about the leakiness of the American social body in the wake of 9/11. While Douglas's work focuses on how and why the body is managed, the cultural anthropologist René Girard (1972) reflects explicitly on the social function of the violence that is enacted upon individual bodies and the relationship of this violence to sex. Extrapolating the logic of Douglas's hypothesis that the human body is a symbolic synonym for the social body, Girard provides a suggestive framework for conceptualizing the staging of sex and violence in *True Blood*, arguing that the visibility of bloodshed in any given society is inversely proportional to the perceived stability of that society:

When men are enjoying peace and security, blood is a rare sight. When violence is unloosed, however, blood appears to be everywhere – on the ground, underfoot, forming great pools. Its very fluidity gives form to the contagious nature of violence. Its presence proclaims murder and announces new upheavals to come. Blood stains everything it touches the color of violence and death. Its very appearance seems, as the saying goes, to 'cry out for vengeance' (1972, p. 34).

For Girard, times of conflict generate a need for *more* bloodshed, not only as retribution, but also as a means of codifying or reasserting the conventions of violence. Ritualized forms of bloodletting, then, can be a way of restoring order to an otherwise chaotic and barbarous regime. Beginning with 9/11, the first decade of the twenty-first century has been one of the most bloody in modern US history.[5] For the vast majority of Americans, however, this bloodshed has been experienced remotely, through television and other digital media. In such a world, where the realities of violence are filmed, structured, and disseminated by various media, a show like *True Blood* might be understood as offering a ritualized (if fictional) response to the ubiquitous spectacle of bloodshed. If adapting Girard's notion of ritual helps to account for the potential social function of violent spectacle, then it does so while also foregrounding the extent to which sex is inextricable from this spectacle. Indeed, in Girard's (1972, p. 35) thinking sex and violence are so closely inter-twined – in abduction, rape, defloration, menstruation, and childbirth – that the one cannot warrant consideration without an acknowledgement of the other. If *True Blood* is a show that is committed to establishing the violent, sadomasochistic contours of sexuality, then it does so as a way of empha-sising the symbolic resonances of the sex act, situating it as one of the key means by which one body – driven by desire or necessity or greed – asserts its power over another. Stressing the complex negotiations of desire, power and exploitation that take place within the sexual encounter – and within the vampiric activity by which it is so often accompanied – *True Blood* seems to augment the more overt gestures that it makes to the troubled context from which it has emerged, and to the War on Terror in particular.

At an abstract level, the War on Terror involves a powerful nation penetrating the borders of another (weaker) nation and siphoning off its valuable liquid resources (namely oil). Indeed, the violent, vampiric nature of advanced capitalism is playfully signified in *True Blood* through a cartoonish depiction of George Bush as a vampire that sits behind the bar at the Fangtasia nightclub. This vampiric dynamic is re-inscribed in *True Blood* through the spectacle of vulnerable, penetrated, and bled bodies. These bodies are often, after all, plundered for their blood. To vampires, human blood is a valuable liquid resource that is tantamount to fuel: this relationship is cast in very literal terms when Lorena tells Sookie that she's 'no more than a bloodbank' (2.8). As a more multifunctional commodity, vampire blood – or 'V' – has currency as a hallucinogen, a curative, and an aphrodisiac. Whether vampire or human, *True Blood* recognizes the exchange value of *all* blood, ascribing a clear monetary value to it in ways that are redolent of the equation of blood and oil in the popular antiwar slogan, 'No more blood for oil'.

One of the things that the War on Terror dramatically materializes is the relentlessly exploitative dimensions of late industrial capitalism, and anxieties about this are writ large in *True Blood*. In the very first episode, Tara (Rutina Wesley) is shown reading Naomi Klein's *The Shock Doctrine* (2007), a book in which Klein argues that advanced capitalist societies have exploited crises in developing (and developed) nations in order to install economic regimes that facilitate the global operations of advanced capitalism. Klein invokes electroconvulsive therapy as a way of illustrating the plight of nations in crisis, positioning the paralysed body-in-shock as a symbol for the nation-without-defences, the nation that is (albeit temporarily) rendered vulnerable to the will of more powerful, external forces. For Alan Ball, Klein's book is a convenient way of signposting *True Blood*'s engagement with the 'dark political times' in which we live, but it seems to have a special resonance in a vampire fiction like *True Blood*, where the image of the paralysed and plundered body that Klein uses as the touchstone for her discussion of late capitalism finds a strong visual correlative in the paralysed and plundered bodies that litter the gothic swamplands of Bon Temps.[6] In short, *True Blood* traces the intimate connections between vampirism and capitalism in ways that replicate the symbolic dynamics of the War on Terror.

The links between vampirism and capitalism are both compelling and longstanding. Marx (1867; 2004, p. 342) himself imagines the insatiable, parasitic demands of capital as a species of morbid bloodlust: 'Capital', he opines, 'is dead labour, which, vampire-like, lives only by sucking living labour, and lives the more, the more labour it sucks'. If Marx posits a connection between the flow of capital and the flow of blood, then Freud is equally attentive to the ways in which the fluidity of capital might help to shed light on the dynamic exchange of other liquid assets. For Marx and Freud alike, the fact that capital moves between different parties and passes – quite literally – through many different hands, taints it irrevocably. It is always and already unclean. This connection is consolidated by Freud in 'Character and Anal Eroticism' (1908; 1953–74, pp. 173–4), where he identifies the stubborn equivalence of money and filth in the myths, fairy tales, superstitions, and dreams that comprise the cultural imaginary. Elsewhere, however, he proceeds to equate money to semen – both of which are regarded as 'dirty', but also valuable. The symbolic connections drawn by Freud and Marx – between flows of money, filth, semen and blood – are explored across *True Blood*'s various seasons, finding expression in the energized intersections of business, sex and violence.

In light of its exchange value, it is perhaps unsurprising that blood is frequently associated with theft.[7] The connection between blood and theft is rendered explicit in one of vampire Bill's flashbacks to the 1920s. In this flashback, he and Lorena seduce and feed on a rich couple they meet in Chicago. Tellingly, the 'theft' of the couples' blood is stressed by another act of misappropriation when Bill rips a necklace from his female victim and presents it to Lorena. The pair then proceed to have sex on the bed, while their female victim bleeds to death alongside them (2.6). In this instance, the violent theft of blood is connected to the act of sex, which involves another exchange of bodily fluids, recalling, again, the conjunction of blood, sperm and money proposed by Freud. Blood, then, is often stolen, but it is also insistently implicated in an eroticized economics of exchange. At one point, Sookie acknowledges that her own blood is 'like vampire crack'; as a result of its potent properties, it is traded between male vampires – namely Bill, Eric and 'Vampire King' Russell Edgington (Denis O'Hare) – without her knowledge or consent (3.11).

Still, the character who best exemplifies the intersections of blood, sex and economics is probably Lafayette, a black, homosexual transvestite who works with Sookie at Merlotte's Bar and Grill. Alongside his other business interests, Lafayette has a lucrative sideline in dealing 'V', the slang term for vampire blood. Although he has a longstanding arrangement with a vampire named Eddie (Stephen Root), from whom he takes blood in exchange for sex, Lafayette maintains that he is not a prostitute. When pushed on the matter, he defines himself as a 'survivor' first, then a 'capitalist', and a 'prostitute last' (2.2). For Lafayette, his 'prostitution' exists firmly within the register of entrepreneurial enterprise: as his survival relies on his ability to exchange, he elects to use his sexuality as a means of getting ahead.

The discourse of prostitution is forever circulating in *True Blood* and is central to conceptualizing the awkward relationship between sex and violence in the show. It is, however, equally crucial to understanding the problematic role that is accorded to consent. Fundamentally, the characters who are implicated in prostitution are – overwhelmingly – female or non-white or non-heterosexual. In the first episode, Maudette reveals that she took money to let a vampire bite and have sex with her. She and Jason then engage in rough bondage sex, while he calls her a 'whore' (1.1). Another of Jason's conquests, Dawn, is also known to have slept around, being branded 'another idiot slut who puts out for vampires' (1.3). Despite her status as a virgin at the start of the show, Sookie herself is variously referred to as an 'evil whore of Satan', a 'vampire whore', and a 'fangbanger' (1.7; 2.8). Even her clothing is regarded as a sign of her sexual availability; as Bill tells her on one of their first meetings, she dresses like 'vampire bait' (1.4). In addition to Sookie, Maudette, Dawn, and Lafayette, there are a host of more minor characters who are associated with prostitution: Janella (Roberta Orlandi) is a vampire junkie who provides sex on demand in exchange for 'V'; Jerry (Nicholas Gonzalez) offers himself around between hungry vampires in an attempt to avenge the death of his lover; Daphne (Ashley Jones), a shape-shifter who works as a waitress at Merlotte's, is labelled a 'whore' by her boss, Sam, after she sleeps with him; 'Destiny' (Jade Tailor), a stripper Bill pays for a dance, agrees to leave with him – presumably, once he has offered her more money for sex; and Tony (Michael Steger), a non-white rent boy, is given money to have sex with Russell (1.3; 2.7; 3.4; 3.10). Why does this matter? Well, of all the bodies that are coded as 'prostitutes' very few survive: Maudette and Dawn are murdered by a vampire-hating serial killer; Janella and Jerry are killed brutally by the vampires to whom they have prostituted themselves; Daphne is stabbed in the stomach; 'Destiny' is drained to death by Bill, Russell and Lorena; and Tony the prostitute is staked by Russell (1.1; 1.3; 2.7; 3.4; 3.11). The only significant exception to this rule is Jason. Despite his promiscuity, and the fact he agrees to let Lafayette film him dancing in his underwear in exchange for some 'V', he manages to eschew any violent sanctions for his behaviour. Indeed, his sexual acrobatics are situated solidly as studly play. Although Sookie and Lafayette are explicitly and repeatedly designated as whores, neither is killed. Their bodies are, however, subject to insistent, sustained and debasing forms of violent inscription: Lafayette is kidnapped, tortured, shot and bitten by Eric and Pam (Kristin Bauer van Straten), while Sookie is brutally beaten in the first episode, mauled and poisoned by a rampaging maenad, almost raped by a religious fanatic, and hospitalized after Bill drinks too much of her blood. This is all in addition to the eroticized biting to which she routinely consents as Bill's girlfriend. In short, the hailing of particular characters as 'prostitutes' or 'whores' is always and already a prequel to their violent debasement.

By using these labels to insinuate the individual's sexual visibility and availability *True Blood* seems to find a way of condoning some of it violent excesses. As Girard (1972, p. 36) has noted, after all, 'The function of ritual [violence] is to "purify" violence; that is to "trick" violence into spending itself on victims whose death will provoke no reprisals'. In other words, in order to function effectively, ritual violence must discharge itself upon 'suitable' victims. In this light, it seems telling that *True Blood*'s victims are, so often, female or homosexual or non-white. Already vulnerable, these bodies are shown to solicit invasion; they are, after all, promiscuous, consenting to forms of sex and violence in ways that might be construed as licensing the other (unsolicited) attacks to which they are subsequently exposed. The treatment of gendered violence and vulnerable bodies in *True Blood* presents an obvious question: why? Or, more specifically, why *now*? Why would female or non-white or homosexual bodies become the loci for the most extreme brutalities in these texts at this particular historical moment?

I do wonder whether some of these phenomena might be framed in relation to the argument that Susan Faludi advances in her book *The Terror Dream* (2007). Here, she observes that one of the most unusual aspects of the American response to 9/11 has been its conservative, retreatist movement back towards what we might think of as pre-second wave models of masculinity and femininity. As Faludi (2007, pp. 20–1) explains,

Of all the peculiar responses our culture manifested to 9/11, perhaps none was more incongruous than the desire to rein in a liberated female population. In some murky fashion, women's independence had become implicated in our nation's failure to protect itself.

For Faludi, the aggressive demands of the War on Terror have bolstered the anti-liberal agenda by adding fuel to fantasies about a return to old-fashioned justice and values. Faludi continues,

Mona Charen anticipated the end of the old reign of feminism: "Perhaps the new climate of danger—danger from evil men—will quiet the anti-male agitation we've endured for so long." New York Times columnist John Tierney held out the same hope. "Since Sept. 11, the 'culture of the warrior' doesn't seem quite so bad to Americans worried about the culture of terrorism," he wrote, impugning the supposed feminist "determination to put boys in touch with their inner feelings." "American males' fascination with guns doesn't seem so misplaced now that they're attacking Al Qaeda's fortress," he sniffed (p. 21).

The 'culture of the warrior' (and his stay-at-home wife) is tethered to a moment that predates the rise of minority politics and women's liberation. The current yearning for an apparently simpler world, in which men were men and women were women, seems to inform the nostaligicized stylings of post-9/11 shows like *Desperate Housewives* and *Mad Men* (AMC, 2007–). Certainly, the characters of Bree Van Der Kamp (Marcia Cross) in *Desperate Housewives*, Betty Draper (January Jones) in *Mad Men* and even Sookie in *True Blood*, seem to recall and celebrate pre-liberation fashions and 'old-fashioned' values in ways that may hold a certain kitsch appeal for the contemporary viewer. I would argue, however, that these nostalgic evocations of femininity are not purely superficial. Rather, they seem to be hardwired into the gender politics of these texts.

The sexually liberated body, with the threat it poses to the stability of the family, represents what Douglas would understand as weakness in the social fabric – a weakness that must be plugged or eradicated if the integrity and security of the US body politic is to remain intact. In this way, texts like *True Blood* and *Twilight* might be regarded as enacting a fantasy of retribution on unruly sexual bodies. This violence is acceptable because it is somehow sanctioned through the 'consent' of its 'liberated' victims. The kind of reading I am proposing – which involves considering the recent resurgence of creative and critical interest in vampires alongside the traumatic aftermath of 9/11 and related anxieties about sexuality and gender – works to reinforce the importance of the vampire as a figure in whom the fears and desires of particular societies can be meaningfully and compelling expressed.

Endnotes

1 Alan Ball quoted in audio commentary for 'Strange Love' (1.1).

2 These breaches of privacy and safety are not exclusive to *True Blood*, but are frequent features of the post-9/11 suburban gothic and are particularly pronounced in something like *Desperate Housewives* – a show in which characters' homes are eminently vulnerable to trespass.

3 See Melanie Waters (2011), 'The horrors of home: feminism and femininity in the suburban gothic', in Melanie Waters (ed), *Women on Screen: Feminism and Femininity in Visual Culture*. Basingstoke: Palgrave, 2011. 58–74

4 This context – which is vexed by anxieties about infiltration, political contamination, and the threat of total annihilation – may well account for the fact that vampire fictions are enjoying such a renaissance at present.

5 By June 2011, over six thousand US military personnel had died in combat as a result of the campaigns in Iraq and Afghanistan. See *iCasualties: Iraq Coalition Casualty Count*.[online] Available at: <http://icasualties.org/>.

6 Alan Ball quoted in audio commentary for 'Strange Love' (1.1).

7 Vampires are not immune to this category of stealing: Bill's blood is established as a potential source of income in the first episode, when he is drained by a criminal couple, the Ratrays, who intend to sell it for profit. Later in the same season, Jason and his girlfriend, Amy, steal the kindly, middle-aged vampire Eddie as a permanent source of blood to fuel their 'V' addiction.

4

True Blood, Sex and Online Fan Culture[1]

Emily Brick

With its emphasis on explicit sex and violence rather than abstinence and repression, *True Blood* (2008–, HBO) is a television show regarded by many of its fans as '*Twilight* for grown-ups'. In an interview in *Rolling Stone* (2010), *True Blood* creator Alan Ball states that 'to me, vampires are sex. I don't get a vampire story about abstinence. I'm 53. I don't care about high school students. I find them irritating and uninformed'. Therefore, this chapter will explore Ball's representations of sex on screen in *True Blood* considering both the sexually explicit content of the show, the desires of its characters, and the viewer/text interfaces (including processes of imitation and identification) that actively occur within its fan fiction. Asking questions about the queer and present sexualization of Ball's vampires, the chapter seeks to address the themes of sexuality, subversion, textual identification and on-line fan cultures.

While the series is explicitly aimed at adults and notably created by a man, Ball, *True Blood* (HBO, 2008–) is in fact based on a series of novels written by Charlaine Harris entitled *The Southern Vampire Mysteries* (2001–). Adding to a tradition of female authored vampire texts, such as Anne Rice's *The Vampire Chronicles*, L.J. Smith's *The Vampire Diaries* and Stephanie Meyer's *Twilight*, Harris's novels are not only penned by a female author but also feature a female lead; barmaid, vampire lover, telepath and heroine, Sookie Stackhouse. Akin to Meyer's *Twilight* saga (a series of novels that also feature a female lead – all-be-it a teenage girl –) Harris's focus upon Sookie allows for and encourages identification with female readers. As Anne Klaus and Stefanie Krüger (2011) argue, the focus upon a young and active heroine works to 'entice a primarily female readership'. Yet while both Meyer's and Harris's works engage with themes of romantic love and lust, *The Southern Vampire Mysteries,* arguably, unlike the *Twilight* saga, seeks to reframe or subvert what Caitlin Brown (2009) notes to be a dominant vampiric paradigm 'the crux of sexism – the male vamp/female human relationship'.

Within such a paradigm, the male vampire is traditionally active, making the human female his 'victim' – ostensibly, the object of his desire. In contrast to this patriarchal coda, *The Southern Vampire Mysteries* position and acknowledge male vampires as objects of desire and figures of sexual fantasy, challenging the gender bias so seemingly inherent in vampire fiction. In addition, it is worth noting that male vampires are not only framed as fantasy figures for human females in both Harris's novels and Ball's television creation, *True Blood*, but are also framed as objects of desire for human males. In short, the male vampire is positioned as the ultimate, supernatural, and infinitely potent sex object.

The fact that vampires have frequently been depicted on screen as sexually desirable figures is a coda that is reaffirmed in *True Blood*. Indeed, the dominance of the sexy subject matter is clearly stated through the opening title montage as the show's key themes of sex, violence and religion are made visible and jostle for position. The multiple themes here also function to highlight a key difference in perspective between Harris's novels and Ball's television show. Where Harris focuses on Sookie's singular point of view, Ball offers up multiple points of view. Though Sookie's (Anna Paquin's) privileged perspective is retained (for example, in episode 1 a tracking shot follows her as she waitresses around the bar where she works and in episode 2 we are introduced to flashbacks from her childhood), Ball also offers up the points of view of others via Sookie's telepathy as well as the perspective of her lover, Bill (Stephen Moyer), a 170-year-old male vampire.

In addition, differing points of view are also achieved via Ball's introduction of new or significantly adapted characters. For example, Tara (Rutina Wesley), Sookie's best friend, is a fairly minor character in the novels, but her role is expanded on Ball's screen. She becomes Lafayette's (Nelsan Ellis) cousin and changes race from white to black. Indeed, according to Buchanan (2010, p. 127), Tara becomes 'feistier, angrier, more profane and much more sexual' on-screen than she is in Harris's novels. In the television series, Tara's increased sexuality can be identified through her actions, for example, she has a sexual relationship with Sam (Sam Trammell), Sookie's shapeshifting boss, a relationship absent in Harris's work. There are a few other major character shifts from novels to screen. For example, Lafayette dies at the end of the first novel but is a major character in the TV show, the only non-vampire gay character, increasing the diversity of the cast. Such examples of the increased sexualization and sexual diversity of the characters on-screen ensures a more dominant and explicit representation of the sex act itself – a key trope and ideological act in Ball's creation. In addition, the dominance of sex, sexuality and sexual desire on-screen opens the door for the series to meaningfully explore sexual, social and civil politics.

Vampire Ideology

Within *True Blood*, vampires are a politicized group. Having recently emerged from the shadows, they form an organized movement, demanding civil rights. They also function as political metaphors in multiple ways. *True Blood*'s location in the Deep South of America is framed by a specific racial history (slavery) and a deeply religious context. Vampires are referred to frequently in terms of race and accordingly, the animosity towards vampire/human relationships in the series has been read as animosity towards mixed race relationships, particularly sexual relationships. Paula Rogers (2010, p. 51) argues that 'as a minority group, vamps provide a safe way to explore past racial tensions that still exist in the South'. Ginjer Buchanan (2010, p. 217), editor of Harris' *The Southern Vampire Mysteries*, explains that Alan Ball 'wanted to have the black men and women of Bon Temps feature more prominently in the series' (although there is a spectrum of different racial types within the vampires, the majority of patrons in Merlotte's are white). Bon Temps is a religious Deep South town and Sookie's sexual relationship with Bill is read as a form of miscegenation by the conservative community. Indeed, on a larger scale, the narrative mystery of season one revolves around a killer who is targeting women who 'pollute' themselves by having sex with vampires.

   In addition to the theme of miscegenation, the unique plot of *True Blood* which differentiates it from other vampire texts concerns the 'coming out' of vampires into public life, very obviously drawing a parallel with coming out of the closet. The 'God hates Fangs' slogan used by the anti-vampire movement echoes the 'God hates Fags' politics of the anti-gay movement. Lafayette, as the only openly gay human in the series, is subjected to homophobic abuse by bar patrons who also attack vampires, especially in the context of their sexual relationship with humans. The religious Deep South setting provides a context for the parallel unacceptability of alter- native sexualities, consolidated in the Fellowship of the Sun, an anti-vampire church. Vampires themselves demonstrate a range of sexualities within the text, from exclusively straight (Bill) to bisexual (Eric) to exclusively gay (Pam

(Kristin Bauer), Eddie (Stephen Root), Russell (Denis O'Hare) and Talbot (Theo Alexander)).

There is also a spectrum of social class positions within vampire society ranging from royalty to bartenders. Eric, for example, has a degree of power as a Sheriff and Nick Mamatas (2010, p. 67) describes Bill as 'a member of the vampire middle class' due to his geekish demeanour. The sheer volume of vampires within *True Blood* allows for a range of representations in terms of class, race, sexuality, kindness and cruelty. The vampires have a political structure and strict hierarchy based primarily on age – the older the vampire, the more respect and power they command. Eric's sexual appeal is linked to his age; he has had thousands of years of sexual experience. In this respect, *True Blood* fits Janice Radway's model of romance narratives in *Reading the Romance* (an ethnographic study of female romance readers) in that the key romantic heroes (Eric and Bill) are aristocratic due to both their age and financial power (Radway, 1984, p. 134). Eric in particular uses his social standing and financial power to try and seduce Sookie.

Sex, Society and Fangbanging

In popular and academic discourse surrounding vampires, sex is frequently foregrounded. Barbara Creed (2005, p. 70) argues that 'while the cinematic vampire may have begun life in an earlier century as a demon or figure of great evil, it has become [...] a figure of perverse sexuality and a changing symbol for the sexual problems of the age'. Vampires have a polymorphous sexuality and exist in a liminal state between life and death, and as such are open to multiple readings, or as Judith Halberstam (1995, p. 29) argues, the 'chameleonic nature of this monster makes it a symbol of multiplicity and indeed invites multiple interpretations'. The nature of the vampire and the close links between biting and sex along with themes of necrophilia, sado-masochism, oral sadism, the phallic nature of fangs and the link between sex and death have generated many psychoanalytic readings of vampire texts. Ernest Jones (1991, p. 398), for example, provides a Freudian reading which places vampires as indicators of 'most kinds of sexual perversions'. In addition, one of the other common readings is that of the vampire as an evolving monster who takes on many forms. Tim Kane (2006), for example, splits his study of vampires into the malignant cycle 1931–48, the erotic cycle 1957–85, and the sympathetic cycle from 1987 onwards. *True Blood* utilizes all of these tropes within its representation – vampire as abject monster, vampire as object of desire, and as sympathetic hero as well as also providing a strong psychoanalytic undercurrent.

Beyond the sexual nature of vampires and the inclusion of sex within the relationships of the characters, *True Blood* also employs a series of narrative devices to inject more sex into the storylines. *True Blood* solidifies the idea of vampire as object of desire with the presence of the 'fangbanger', people who have sex with vampires and allow themselves to be bitten and fed on. When Sookie visits Fangtasia, she says that all anyone is thinking about is sex. There is clearly an element of danger and sado-masochistic pleasure in sex with vampires – sex is accompanied by biting, although in *True Blood*, biting is concurrent rather than forming a substitute for sex as is common in classic vampire texts. One bar patron in Merlotte's describes fangbangers as 'just like those women who write to serial killers in prison' (1.4). The vampire as object of desire is clearly physically powerful and dangerous. Violence (biting) is an intrinsic part of the sexual act, placing the human in a passive and vulnerable position. Sookie describes fangbangers as 'pathetic' and her telepathy gives her a rational excuse for being attracted to vampires. Far from being the average fangbanger, the appeal of vampires as objects of desire for Sookie lies in the fact that she cannot read their thoughts, so for the first time is able to have a 'normal' relationship. That Bill understands this is made clear when he says to her: 'You can never find a man who you can be yourself with' (1.3). She is also resistant to being 'glamoured' by vampires; her love and desire for Bill are real rather than imposed.

The vampire Eddie (Stephen Root) provides an opposing example because in contrast to Sookie, he engages vampires as objects of identification rather than just desirable objects. Indeed, Eddie is the only character who actively wanted to become a vampire – by his own admission, as an overweight, middle aged man who came out as gay very late in life, he was rejected by the men he found attractive. After going to a vampire bar and seeing the sexual appeal of vampires, he begged to be turned, to become the object of desire rather than just to desire vampires.

Vampire sexuality takes on a further sexual context beyond the body of the vampire in the form of vampire blood. In the novels, when Sookie is (frequently) injured, the vampires (primarily Bill and Eric) heal her by offering her their blood. Drinking the blood of a vampire also creates a psychical connection between vampire and human allowing vampires to track humans who have had their blood. On screen, however, vampire blood takes on a more sexual quality as an aphrodisiac drug, known as 'V'. This eroticization of blood is more pronounced in *True Blood* than *The Southern Vampire Mysteries* in which vampire blood enhances strength and physical wellbeing when consumed by humans. In the TV series, Lafayette is a V dealer. He has an arrangement with Eddie who donates blood in exchange for sexual favours. The blood is then sold to enhance the sexual pleasure of others, creating a linked cycle of pleasure, sex and blood.

Desire for the blood of vampires is a repeated plot element in season one and although their blood is the source of the vampire's strength, it also makes both the addicts and the vampires themselves vulnerable. The body of the vampire therefore becomes a commodity with a monetary value as well as an object of sexual desire. In episode 1.1, Bill is attacked by 'drainers' for his blood which they intend to sell on the black market. Jason (Ryan Kwanten) overdoses the first time he tries blood (1.4). Suffering from 'gout of the dick', he ends up in hospital to have his penis 'drained' (gout being linked with overindulgence, in this case in relation to sex and drugs[2]). This does not put him off however, and he rapidly becomes addicted. When he meets Amy, another user, they capture Eddie and feed off his blood as a sexual enhancer until Amy kills him. In these examples, the commodification of the vampire through the exchange value of their blood highlights tensions within the show about the interaction of humans and vampires, between life and death and most importantly the thrill and danger of sexual contact.

The economic capital associated with blood in the series is also recognized by fans and producers of the show. *TruBlood*, the artificial blood which allows vampires to come out and removes the need to feed from real human blood is on sale as a soft drink on the HBO website, allowing the fans to copy the action they see on screen, replicating the practices of vampires. That is, similar to the utilization of the term fangbanger, the consumption of TruBlood allows fans to participate with the text, both as a form of initiation and authenticity. As will be discussed later, this type of merchandising is an important part of allowing fans to create a performative identification with the show.

Sex, Romance and Violence in *True Blood*

The narrative arc of both *True Blood* and *The Southern Vampire Mysteries* deals with Sookie's sexual awakening. She has always avoided sexual contact since she is unable to avoid reading the mind of anyone she is romantically or sexually involved with. Far from being an average fangbanger, the appeal of vampires as objects of desire for Sookie, as aforementioned, lies in the fact that she cannot read their thoughts, so for the first time with Bill she is able to have a 'normal' relationship. The romantic trajectory of the first three seasons concerns Sookie's relationship with him. They first meet in scene six of episode 1. Bill walks into the bar, shot from Sookie's point of view in slow motion and accompanied by romantic piano music. Their eyes meet and Sookie tells Sam and Tara how excited she is to have a vampire in Bon Temps. Later that night, Bill is captured by two drainers, and it is Sookie who saves him, taking them on alone, overpowering the male drainer by attacking him with a chain and threatening the female drainer with his knife. From this first encounter, Sookie is established as a brave and fearless active heroine. Later that night, Sookie dreams that Bill comes to her house to seduce her, but wakes before anything happens. By episode 3, however, she is fantasising about seducing him (an active fantasy rather than the passive one of being seduced).

When Bill next comes into the bar, the scene is again shot from Sookie's perspective. According to Tara, Sookie walks towards Bill 'like she's walking down the aisle on her goddamn wedding day' and they make a date. Sookie finally has sex with Bill at the end of episode 1.6 ('Cold Ground'). The framing of their sexual encounter is amorous as they kiss in front of an open fire accompanied by romantic music. The couple undress each other slowly, and the scene ends when Bill bites her on the neck ending the episode. Episode 1.7 opens with a continuation of the scene and cuts to the title sequence, which is followed by Bill and Sookie in the bath together. Again, the setting is romantic, this time candlelit, but disruption occurs when the scene cuts to a flashback of Sookie being abused by her uncle (which later gives Bill an excuse to kill him and defend her honour). Even in this romantic setting, biting and flashbacks to abuse mean that violence is presented as an intrinsic part of sexual relations within this universe.

The link between sex and violence is foregrounded in other scenes in season one. Of the eighteen explicit sex scenes in this season, ten feature Sookie's brother, Jason. He has sex with Maudette, Dawn and Amy and a random woman he meets at Merlotte's after Dawn dumps him. The sex scenes with Maudette involve violent role play. Unfortunately for Jason, all of these women are murdered by Rene/Drew (Michael Raymond-James) for being fangbangers, thus placing Jason under suspicion, especially when the police find tapes of his violent sex sessions with Maudette (Danielle Sapia). The very first time we meet Jason, he is having sex (with Maudette), and this sexual scene between the pair is intercut throughout episode one, establishing how sexual performance is an integral function of Jason's character, especially during season one. Within the diegesis Jason notes that he has 'read in *Hustler* that everybody should have sex with a vampire before they die'. While Jason does not fulfil the Hustler fantasy of vampire sex, his use of V and his various relationships with fangbangers denote his increasing approximation to vampiric eroticism, signifying a blurring of borders between human and animal sexuality.[3]

After season one, explicit sex is established as a key motif of *True Blood*. One particularly violent sex scene which prompted a huge amount of online discussion[4] focused on Bill and Lorena (Mariana Klaveno) (3.3), one of the few scenes involving sex *between* vampires. Winner of the 'Holy Shit! Scene of the Year' at the 2010 *Scream* awards[5] and referred to by Alan Ball as 'vampire hate sex', Lorena (Mariana Klaveno) makes Bill have sex with her (as her maker, he is powerless to resist her demands, placing Bill as a passive victim) and in the process he forces her head to twist round 180 degrees. While Bill's actions may suggest a restatement of male dominance it is left ambiguous due to the obvious pleasure Lorena takes in their sado-masochistic love-making. Considering fan responses to the sequence, Popeater.com took a poll of 11,784 people on whether the scene went 'too far' in terms of its 'unnatural' violence. 64% of respondents voted no. In the accompanying discussion topic on Facebook (88 participants, 77 female, 11 male), only a few responses found the scene offensive or shocking.

One participant in the Facebook discussion, 'Nicolette', argues that:

> This might cross the line for me and I haven't felt this way since the rape scene in 'The Hills Have Eyes' remake a few years back I am sorry, but rape is not entertainment and should not be showed in such a light manner. I think I may be dropping 'True Blood' from my viewing.
> (http://www.facebook.com/PopEater?v=wall&story_fbid=137720872905648&ref=mf)

Most fans, however, found the scene funny, camp or just stupid. 'Jennifer' writes 'I was so hoping he was going to rip her head off', 'Elizabeth' argues that 'I didn't think that it went too far. He didn't rape her. Vampires by methos are not romantic, they're sexual and deviant. This is not Mormon written *Twilight* shit' (*ibid.*).

This is however not the only 'rape' scene in the *True Blood* franchise. For example, in the novel *Club Dead* (Harris, 2003) there is a scene which changes markedly from the television series. After rescuing Bill, Sookie ends up locked in a car boot with him. Bill has been violently tortured, sleep deprived and starved of blood. In the TV adaptation, Bill attacks Sookie, savaging her neck and draining her blood so severely that she is hospitalized. In the novel however, he also rapes her. The rape is written thus:

> After a lot of fumbling and rearranging and contorting, he entered me with no preparation at all. I screamed and he clapped a hand over my mouth. I was crying, sobbing and my nose was all stopped up […] After a few seconds, his hand fell away. And he stopped moving […] I was crying in earnest, one sob after another (Harris, 2003, p. 209).

When Bill 'comes round' and realizes what he is doing, he is horrified and asks her:

'are you all right?'

'No,' I said almost apologetically. After all. It was Bill who'd been held prisoner and tortured.

'Did I. . .' He paused, and seemed to brace himself 'have I taken more blood than I should?'

I couldn't answer. I laid my head on his arm. It seemed too much trouble to speak.

'I seem to be having sex with you in a closet,' Bill said in a subdued voice. 'Did you, ah, volunteer?'

I turned my head from side to side, then let it loll on his arm again (*ibid.* p. 210).

In this narrative sequence, it is clear that Bill is acting on instinct, unable to control himself and unaware that it is Sookie that he is attacking. Interestingly, the removal of the sexual element of the attack from *True Blood* means that Bill's status as romantic hero / sexual object is less compromised than it would be if he was presented as knowingly and explicitly raping Sookie. Sookie is ambiguous about recognizing the attack as a rape, later referring to the 'terrible incident in the trunk' as a 'mindless attack' (Harris, 2003, p. 221). In the series of novels, she explicitly nominates the incident as a 'near-rape'. Although Sookie herself is unwilling to acknowledge the attack as a rape, fans on the Yahoo! Group discussion boards (http://tv.groups.yahoo. com/group/TrueBlood) concur that it is. This particular group of fans have also read the novels and are therefore aware of his potential positioning as a rapist, something which is absent from the TV show therefore retaining Bill's position as a romantic and sympathetic vampire. Milly Williamson (2005, p. 57) has stated that 'in much of the surrounding fan culture, all of the fans shared an interest in those vampire narratives where the central vampire characters are constructed sympathetically'. As Bill is one part of the main romantic relationship in *True Blood* it is essential that his bond with Sookie not be viewed negatively by fans and thus lead to non-involvement and displeasure in their reception of the text.

The adaptation of this scene in particular means that in the TV series, Bill is framed more clearly as a romantic hero and object of desire than he is in the novels. Bill is actively 'mainstreaming' – trying to integrate and be the type of vampire that Sookie can take home to meet her grandmother. Although it is less prominent in the first three seasons than later on in the novels, the Sookie – Bill – Eric love triangle (or love square if Sam is included) dominates both the narrative and fan reactions to the text. The categories used by the writers on *fanfiction.net* indicate that they see *True Blood* as primarily a romantic rather than a horror text. In the stories on fanfiction, 406 are listed under Eric and only 89 under Bill, indicating the audience preference for the potential Eric/Sookie coupling over and above her actual relationship with Bill. Not only is this an oppositional stance or resistance to the 'mainstream' relationship of Bill/Sookie but an example of how the sympathetic vampire figure, of which Eric certainly fulfils, can engender 'the concept of "romance" that has little to do with romantic love' (Williamson, 2005, p. 57) in fan reception. The concept of romance is exacerbated between Eric and Sookie when Eric tricks Sookie into drinking his blood, thus establishing a psychic bond between them (2.9). Also, having three men who are in love with her places Sookie in an active position of desire since she gets to choose. It is reminiscent of Laura Mulvey's (Mulvey, 1981) model of active female desire in which the heroine has a choice of love objects representing different, both active and passive, fantasies.

In this case, Sam (although a shapeshifter) represents a socialized normal life offering marriage and children whereas the vampires offer Sookie a more dangerous form of love and non-socialized lifestyle (marriage between vampire and humans is illegal, and they cannot reproduce). Both the official HBO site (www.hbo.com/true-blood) and a number of fansites sell 'Team Bill' or 'Team Eric' t-shirts, mimicking the Team Edward/Team Jacob merchandizing of *Twilight*. This reflects how the narrative of *True Blood* is framed by Sookie's desire rather than placing her as a passive recipient of (male) vampire desire,

True Blood and Online Fan Cult-ure

Fan culture has developed since Henry Jenkins' seminal *Textual Poachers* in which media fans are defined as 'nomads' or 'poachers' (1992, p. 25). He argues that fan activity such as fan fiction can be read as oppositional and resistant to the authority of the producer. Mark Jancovich (2008) has argued that cult fans tend to be male, middle class, and employ similar strategies to academic film studies, such as clearly demarking boundaries between the authentic and inauthentic and the mainstream and the oppositional. Joanne Hollows (2003 p. 39) reads cult fandom as masculine, but open to women who 'opt to be culturally one of the boys'. Brigid Cherry (2010) has also conducted extensive empirical work on both female horror fans and online fan culture, in particular on vampire fans. The *True Blood* discussion on Yahoo! Groups is female dominated, and echoes Cherry's (2010, p. 71) observation that more recently 'larger proportions of active female fans are to be found on the discussion groups dedicated to vampire films (the vampire genre is a particular favourite of female horror fans)'. An earlier study by Cherry (1999) found that of all the subgenres of horror, it was vampire texts with their emphasis on romance and gothic *mise-en-scène* that were the most popular with female fans. The make-up of the online discussion groups, fansites and fan fiction relating to *True Blood* looked at in the process of researching this chapter is certainly female dominated and attests to the appeal the series provides for female viewers. Indeed, female fans have traditionally been side-lined or marginalized in relation to horror texts and the positioning of vampires as romantic and sympathetic heroes combined with the strong female protagonist is particularly important to their popularity with women.

Online engagement with *True Blood* encompasses casual and regular viewers as well as the cult viewer categorized by his or her 'continuous, intense participation and persistence' (Mathijs and Mendik, 2008, p. 4) whereby an active and committed viewer/text relationship is established. In these multivaried groups fans may engage with discussions online, share clips with friends on Facebook, join in episode discussions or even create fan blogs and fan wikis which allow for a wide range of viewer/text interaction oscillating between the fan as consumer and fan as producer or casual fan and cult fan (Booth, 2010). Most fansites share a similar format: news, links, episode guides, downloadable screensavers and a forum for discussion. Many[6] are not that far removed from the official site and they are often lovingly made and maintained. For example, there are 675 members in the *True Blood* Yahoo! discussion group. Started in November 2006, the group predates the TV series by almost two years (the first episode aired on HBO 7 September 2008). The first topics are posted by fans of the novels, speculating on who should play various characters, rumours about the TV series, and whether it will be true or 'faithful' to the novels.

Overall, the community is supportive, sharing trivia, answering each other's questions and discussing or recommending similar texts to each other (e.g. *Being Human*). Often, 'it is in this environment – where everyone can have their say and everyone can be a critic – that conflict arises in the relationship between producers and consumers' (Cherry, 2010, p. 81). However, this is not necessarily applicable in the case of *True Blood* or *The Southern Vampire Mysteries* in which the authors seem happy to interact with online fans and respond to fan discussion about the texts. Charlaine Harris's website (http://www.charlaineharris.com/) encourages fan interaction 'thanks for visiting the website and posting. She loves to hear from readers, and enjoys the feedback'. There is also a forum for fan discussion in which various moderators 'speak with my voice on this site. Respect them as you would me. You're welcome here!'. Not only do the various community boards encourage fan activity and participation but the moderators who 'speak for' Charlaine Harris increase fan intimacy and connection to the author. Connections between the fans and producers of the text also exist within the TV series. Alan Ball, himself a fan of the novels, has incorporated a form of visual slash fiction into the TV show and this inclusion demonstrates the way in which the show is aware of, responds to and interacts with its fans. Ball also creates a type of slash fiction within the narrative diegesis by frequently featuring dream sequences involving two, not necessarily romantically connected, characters, such as Sam and Bill. Both these examples in *True Blood* fulfil the types of fantasies demonstrated within fan/slash fiction within the text itself.

Unsurprisingly, given the sexually explicit nature of the programme and much of the fan generated response, a significant part of the discussion pertains to the sexual content of the show, such as fans listing their favourite scenes (e.g. http://www.nerve.com/tv/eight-true-blood-sex-scenes-you-shouldnt-try-at-home). Not all the fans, however, are keen on the inclusion of extreme sexual content within the show.

'Sue' writes on Yahoo! Groups that:

> I don't need the sex scenes, most of them are just time-fillers, only a few hold real interest to the plot due to dialog or showing dreams and stuff [. . .] I find an overdose of sex in the show. I mean, once in a while, sure [...] but they could let some of the scenes be just implicit, IMHO.
> (http://tv.groups.yahoo.com/group/TrueBlood/message/9684)

Many of the female viewers and fans express their preference for plot and character and feel that the sex scenes (and discussion of them) detract from the more interesting elements of the TV show and novels. Again, this demonstrates that many fans see the show primarily as a romance text and favour the concept of romance over the graphic representations of romantic love. In addition, the often melodramatic representations of romance, especially the triumvirate between Sookie, Bill and Eric, 'ensures it a place as firm favourite with the majority of women fans' (Williamson, 2005, p. 63) highlighting how important pathos and sympathy are in establishing the viewer/character relationship.

Stargazing and Merchandizing

Jackie Stacey's study of stars and their female fans in *Stargazing* (1994) provides a useful model in order to analyse the extra-textual practices of fans and to see how *True Blood* opens up viewer/text interface for a female audience. There are obviously clear differences between identification with a star and a character in a fictional text, though the fantasy world of *True Blood* allows a wide range of practices with a real person that is central to the viewer/star relationship that Stacey addresses. For example, Stacey (1994, p. 160–70) categorizes fan activity into four broad areas: pretending, resembling, imitating, and copying which all form instances of the viewer/text interface in *True Blood*. According to Stacey (1994, p. 159), 'these processes involve the spectators engaging in some form of transformation of the self' so that they can bridge the gap between fan and the text or between themselves and the characters they engage or identify with. In a longer account Stacey (1994, p. 161) argues:

> 'Pretending' involves an imaginary practice, but one where the spectator involved knows that it is a game [...] [it] does not simply involve the privatised imagination of individual spectators [...] but also involves the participation of other spectators in the collective fantasy games.

This can be seen in online role-play, first person fan fiction, sites such as *Bloodcopy.com* (a blog written from the point of view of a vampire) or even in the adoption of tags such as 'Bill's-babe' or 'Eric's-lover' by members of forums. All these practices involve some form of pretended role play by fans that encourage active female participation.

Bridging the gap between the star and the viewer is further developed by the act of 'resembling'. Though not an outright transformation of self, it does require a link between the 'shared physical appearance' of star/viewer that is 'based on a pre-existing part of the spectator's identity which bears a resemblance to the star' (Stacey, 1994, p. 161). One key example of resembling in relation to the show is provided by the website *Coolspotters* (www. coolspotters.com). Here, the website allows the viewer to search through the characters in *True Blood*, such as Eric, Tara and Sookie, and find out what type of clothes, shoes, jewellery and make-up each wear in the series. For example, Sookie has 64 such 'coolspots' next to her character that include her Jonquil Short Ruffle Lingerie Robe, Durango Crush 7" Shorty Cross Boots and the Fangtasia Life Begins at Night T-Shirt that were all worn at various times in the show. Thus, the website allows access for the viewer to buy the exact same item of clothing or jewellery, usually by supplying a link to the brands website, which their favourite characters in the show wear. Here the viewers recognize aspects of themselves, such as particular fashions they may like, and can connect to their favourite character(s) through a defined look or personality, thus bridging the gap between the viewer/text interface.

Similar to 'pretending', 'resembling' provides feminine spheres of action, in this case shopping, fashion and 'dressing up' that again provide points of entry for female fans into the world of *True Blood*.

'Imitating' and 'copying' are closely linked. Imitating refers to the adoption of behaviours and characteristics whereas copying involves a replication of physical appearance. In the context of *True Blood* fans, both copying and imitation can be found in the nature of the official merchandise. For example, TruBlood, the synthetic blood which vampires use, is available to buy in the form of a soft drink ($16 for a four pack):

> Sink your fangs into a bottle of Tru Blood, a delicious blood orange carbonated drink inspired by Bill's favorite synthetic blood nourishment beverage. Tart and slightly sweet, Tru Blood pours like a regular soda but appears stormy and mysterious when poured into a glass. Bottoms up – and vampires, remember to drink responsibly.
> (http://store.hbo.com/detail.php?p=105736&v=hbo_shows_true-blood_tru-blood)

The desire to copy that can accompany more extensive forms of fan engagement with the text is accommodated by merchandising. The *Fangtasia* T-Shirts seen on sale to human patrons in Eric's bar in the text, the Bon Temps football t-shirt worn by Jason and Sookie's *Merlotte's* uniform are all on sale to fans via the HBO website. These differ from the other official t-shirts on sale (such as 'I Love Sookie / Bill / Eric etc.'), and they involve a form of identification and engagement with the fantasy world on screen rather than simply professing that the wearer is a fan. Where there are gaps in the official merchandise and publicity, fans create their own. For example, *i-love-true-blood.deviantart.com* has a gallery of images where fans can share their homemade *True Blood* themed artwork ranging from jewellery, embroidery, cakes, manicures, pottery and knitwear to dolls and figurines. Youtube has a range of make-up tutorials for all of the characters and the vampire is obviously a popular fancy dress costume, but the level of detail and specific nature of this type of extra-textual identification and performance dressing up is grounded in a fan culture beyond the usual Halloween vampire costume. The nature of this performance and craftwork suggests it is targeted towards a female fanbase.

Conclusion: Enhancement rather than Resistance

Sex dominates the narrative and occupies a prominent position in the popular discourse surrounding *True Blood*, even though its explicit depiction is not always popular with all female fans. The nature of female fandom in relation to *True Blood* can offer a divergent model to the more dominant and traditional masculine approaches of fan behaviour by authors such as Jankovich (2008) and Hollows (2003). The online interactions between *True Blood* fans offer a predominantly feminine space in which to share fantasies and exchange opinions about the text. Although *True Blood* blurs the boundaries between the mainstream and cult text, the types of audience/fan extra textual practices still work on mainstream principles of enhancement rather than resistance, mirroring the adaptation process. Yet, the opening up of female fan participation, both in the show and in the surrounding fan culture, does provide a more democratic space whereby female views on sex can be articulated. In this respect, *True Blood* offers a challenge to the more dominant patriarchal ordering of sexual imagery toward more democratic forms of representation and reception.

Endnotes

1 Please note that the chapter is dealing with the first three seasons of *True Blood*.

2 The Telegraph (2009), 'The gout on the rise as Britons overindulge', *The Telegraph*, [online] 4 March. Available at:

<http://www.telegraph.co.uk/health/healthnews/4936215/Gout-on-the-rise-as-Britons-overindulge.html>

3 This is developed in season 3 with Jason's relationship with the mysterious Crystal who turns out to be a shapeshifting werepanther.

4 See True-Blood Net (Available at: <www.truebloodnet.com>) and Fangbangers: A True Blood Fan Blog (Available at: < www.truebloodfangbangers.com>) for examples of fansites that covered viewer response to this particular episode.

5 'The event honouring the best in sci-fi, fantasy, comics and horror', (2010) *Spike*, [online] 19 October. Available at: http://www.spike.com/event/scream/

6 Examples of fansites are:

<www.True-blood.net> <www.true-blood.tv> <www.facebook.com/TrueBlood> <www.truebloodnet.com><www.fanpop.com/trueblood> <www.truebloodfangbangers.com><www.trueblood-online.com> <www.truebloodguide.com> <www.godhatesfangs.org>

<www.truebloodfanclub.com> <www. truebloodfanfiction.com> <www. trueblood-news.com> <www.twitter.com/truebloodfanweb> <www. truebloodfans.net> <http://tv.groups.yahoo.com/group/TrueBlood> <www. fangbangers.com>

<www.fang-bangers.net> <www.fangbangers.org>

<www.facebook.com/pages/Fang-Bangers> <www.truebloodfangbangers. com>

<www.twitter.com/fangbangers> <http://i-love-true-blood.deviantart.com/ gallery>

PART TWO

TV and the Absence of Sex

5

Beekeeper Suits, Plastic Casings, Rubber Gloves and Cling Film: Examining the Importance of 'No-sex' Sex in *Pushing Daisies*

Rebecca Feasey

Introduction

The age-old adage that sex-sells is nowhere more evident than in American prime-time television drama, with depictions of sex appearing as a common trope in a range of 'must see' programmes such as *Desperate Housewives* (2004–), *Dirty, Sexy, Money* (2007–9), *Private Practice* (ABC,

2007–) and *Hung* (HBO, 2009). Although these shows vary in terms of critical and commercial success, they have each managed to court media hype and thus rouse audience interest on the back of their portrayals of sex and sexuality in the contemporary cultural climate. However, either because of, or in spite of what recent post-feminist commentators refer to as the growing sexualization of prime-time, and the wider pornification of society (Levy, 2006), ABC recently presented a whimsical, funny and achingly romantic screwball drama, seemingly devoid of sexual contact or content.

Pushing Daisies (2007–9), the short-lived yet critically acclaimed fairy tale-murder mystery created by Bryan Fuller, featured childhood sweethearts reunited as adults, albeit adults who were unable to touch, or be touched by one another.[1] Moreover, the candy-coloured sets, retro *mise-en-scène*, vintage-inspired costumes, wall-to-wall music, fast-paced dialogue and fairy-tale trappings harked back to an earlier, less gratuitously sexual period in society. As such, one might suggest that *Pushing Daisies* was that rare example of 'safe-sex' or 'no-sex' prime-time programming suitable for the conservative or family viewer. However, rather than critiquing this series for taking a stance against the growing sexualization of society, it is worth noting that the couple in question are not presented as pure, innocent or chaste, but rather as desiring, sexual and somewhat imaginative in their use of no-touch titillation, intimacy and foreplay. With this in mind, this chapter will look at the programme in question and suggest that this somewhat nostalgic depiction of 'no-sex' sex tells of the role, function and significance of sex in society, albeit sex intertwined with intimacy and romance, in the contemporary period.

Patriarchy, post-feminism and the pornification of society

It is important that we examine the representations of sex, and in this case, examine the representations of 'no-sex' sex in popular media culture because such representations can be seen to reveal the sexual and behavioural norms of contemporary society whilst also teaching us about our sexual roles, rights and responsibilities as individuals (McNair, 2002, p. 111). Moreover, media texts distribute ideas about sexuality and sexual activity and, as such, it is crucial that we acknowledge potentially alternative messages to the current sexual saturation of the media. After all, there is a suggestion that Hollywood films, prime time television, advertising, fine art, women's publishing and men's magazines have all come to be dominated by sexual content and graphic imagery in recent years. Indeed, we are told that sex, pornography and eroticism have so infiltrated contemporary Western culture that there is 'scarcely an image, entertainment, fashion or advertisement [that remains] untouched by it' today (*ibid.*, p. 61). Extant literature tells us that British culture is 'increasingly transfixed by sex and sexual adventure' (Smith, 2007a, p. 167) and that society watches, talks about and thinks about sex with far 'greater frequency and attention to detail than at any previous stage in history' (McNair, 2002, pp. 6–7).

We are informed that 'sex' remains 'the most searched for word on the internet' (Slayden, 2010, p. 54) and that 'the female sex worker is becoming one of popular culture's most regular archetypes of paid labor' (Negra, 2009, p. 100). Second wave feminists may have opposed the Miss World beauty contests, but today we see underwear fashion shows centre stage on television, while erotic novels, sexualized autobiographies and graphically naked art prints dominate our bookshelves (Levy, 2006, pp. 24–5). Moreover, we are told that pornography has moved 'from a very narrow availability to, what at times, seems like a very mainstream acceptability' (Smith, 2007b, p. 32). In short, the sex industry has entered the mainstream and the current sexualization of the media shows no signs of abating.

I do not mean to suggest that every media text has become hyper-sexualized or that each audience member is, without exception, demanding more salacious media content. However, there is much evidence to suggest that the contemporary cultural climate has become increasingly sexualized and that women are being presented through an increasingly erotic and exhibitionistic gaze. Indeed, it would be difficult to challenge the fact that we are living in a cultural environment that is pervaded by sexuality and its representations. Terms such as 'raunch culture' (Levy, 2006), 'striptease culture' (McNair, 2002), the 'pornographication' of society (Smith, 2007b) and the 'mainstreaming of sex' (Attwood, 2010) have been recently coined to articulate the growing sexualization of the current social landscape. Indeed, the existence of the 'Onscenity' network speaks for the growth and signifi-cance of 'sex in commerce, culture and everyday life' (Onscenity Network, 2011). Although theorists are at times at odds in their attitudes towards the growth of public sexual culture, with disagreement as to whether the current mediation of sex, pornography and eroticism is powerful, positive, problematic or patriarchal, there appears a consensus in their acknowledgement of the sexual saturation of the contemporary landscape.

Conservative critics and the religious right-wing tend to view the growing sexualization of society as a problem for both individuals and the wider collective. Whether the argument is concerning the sanctity of sex or the evils of commercialization, the conclusion remains the same (Levy, 2006,

p. 8). Moreover, post-feminist media theorists are currently debating the ways in which women present themselves as bodies for voyeuristic display, be it as patriarchal visual objects or as desiring sexual subjects (Gill, 2007, pp. 73–112). Arial Levy is concerned with the rise of what she terms 'raunch culture' whereby women objectify other women and offer themselves up to an exhibitionist gaze. Her concern is not with the expression of female sexuality or female sexual pleasure, but with the ways in which private pleasures have morphed into consumer driven fantasies (Levy, 2006). However, while post-feminist critics such as Levy are bemoaning the inherent misogyny of sexual objectification that drives post-feminist consumerism, other feminist voices are applauding the changing sexual and social landscape.

Indeed, there exists a number of recent feminist and media commentators who are suggesting that the sexualization of contemporary culture is a powerful and positive development in society. Brian McNair's work on what he terms 'striptease culture' argues that we are currently witnessing a collective interest in, and ease with, the 'public exploration of sexual culture' and that such sexualization speaks less about patriarchal power or moral decline and more about post-war liberalism, the advance of feminism, the growth of gay rights and the decline in hegemonic male dominance (McNair, 2002, pp. 86). Likewise, Clarissa Smith's recent work on sex retailing in Britain makes the point that sex toys are now not only widely available in the mainstream but also fashionable with a female public. Smith concludes that such interest in sexual freedom and fulfillment can be explained as another instance of a society at ease with sex, sexualization and sexual gratification (Smith 2007a, p. 167). And yet, even though Smith is pointing to a form of female sexual pleasure and thus potential sexual power removed from more traditional and patriarchal modes of motherhood, reproduction and marriage, these sexual practices continue to position women as sexual objects (Storr, 2003, p. 91).[2] Indeed, '[s]exual liberation has been a double-edged sword, offering opportunities to expand women's potential for pleasure [...] but at the same time liberation often seem[s] to make women's bodies more accessible to men with little benefit to women' (Smith, 2007a, p. 173). Yet, irrespective of whether one views female exhibitionism and eroticism as dehumanizing patriarchal oppression or powerful female choice, sexualized images continue to saturate the contemporary social and media agenda, and it is in this sexualized media environment that *Pushing Daisies* first aired.

Pushing Daisies

Nine-year-old Ned (Field Cate) discovers that he has the power to bring dead people back to life when he unwittingly revives his mother after she suffers from a fatal brain haemorrhage. The trade off, however, is that by keeping someone alive for more than sixty seconds, another random person in the near vicinity must die in their place in order to maintain a cosmic balance. Moreover, once our young hero has used his power to bring the dead back to life, he cannot again touch that person because if he does then that person will again die and this time actually stay dead. Ned's powers do not come with a manual, however, and he only discovers these strict rulings as he watches his neighbour fall down dead while watering his lawn, acting as the trade off for keeping his mother alive. Later that same evening, he watches his mother die again, this time permanently, as she kisses him goodnight.

As if unwittingly killing your mother and neighbour in the same day was not sufficiently traumatizing for the young boy, the unlucky neighbour in question happened to be the father of his childhood sweetheart, Charlotte Charles (Anna Friel), otherwise known as Chuck. The combination of these traumatic deaths, culminating in his father abandoning him at the Longborough School for Boys, meant that young Ned grew up shirking all social contact and intimate attachments for fear of hurting anyone else that he might grow to care for. His only real pleasure at the outset of the series is seen to be baking fruit pies, like those that his mother used to make before her untimely death. Unsurprisingly, when we meet the adult Ned (Lee Pace), we are introduced to a kind-hearted and mild-mannered twenty-eight-year-old pie-maker and owner of the quaint eatery, The Pie Hole, who continues to shy away from social events, genuine friendships and sexual acquaintances. Ned's only social contact is with the wily private detective Emerson Cod (Chi McBride), and this is classed as a business venture rather than a more meaningful relationship at the outset of the first series. When Emerson was chasing a fleeing criminal along precarious rooftops, the man slipped and fell to his death, only to be inadvertently touched on the way down by our heroic pie-maker putting his rubbish in the dumpster behind his diner. Emerson witnessed Ned resurrect and then re-dead the man in question, at which point he made a business proposition to our pie-maker. Emerson and Ned entered into a mutually beneficial arrangement whereby the detective investigates unsolved murders offering rewards for information, and then Ned brings the relevant victims back to life for long enough to learn the circumstances of their death, solve the crime and collect the reward.

Although Ned appears reasonably content with his closeted world and his emotionally and in other ways frigid existence, his deliberately detached life is sent into turmoil when he hears of the murder of his one and only true love, the ever perky Charlotte Charles. When Emerson and Ned go to visit the beautiful but deceased body of twenty-eight-year-old Chuck (Emerson to solve the murder and Ned to pay his respects), the pie-maker asks to be alone with his childhood sweetheart for the allotted sixty seconds that his gift allows, before having to re-dead the woman in question. Due to a combination of love, lust, hormonal activity or what Emerson refers to as sheer stupidity (1.1), Ned resurrects Charlotte and keeps her awake long enough for the criminal minded funeral director to die in order to maintain the cosmic balance. Ned and the now un-dead Chuck embark on a seemingly chaste romance, living together but not touching and sharing verbal rather than physical intimacies to avoid making Chuck dead again.

Pushing Daisies stands out as a prime time drama that features no physical contact between romantic partners. Indeed, the very premise is that the charming and good-hearted couple at the heart of the show will fall in love and yet never be able to so much as kiss or hold hands. One might suggest that the pairing of Ned and Chuck as a beautiful young couple who cannot be together physically is merely a creative way of maintaining the sexual tension and thus holding audience interest in the romantic interludes of the pair and in the programme itself. Such a technique has been used to varying degrees in shows such as *Cheers* (NBC, 1982–93), *Moonlighting* (ABC, 1985–9), *Lois and Clark* (ABC, 1993–7) and more recently in *Buffy: The Vampire Slayer* (1997–2003), which have all borrowed the 'no-sex' ruling and the 'mis-matched coupling' of the screwball comedy that dominated an earlier generation of Hollywood filmmaking.[3] However, even with such precedents in mind, *Pushing Daisies* presents a somewhat elaborate barrier to ensure that Ned and Chuck remain physically separated and the series does nothing to change, cheat or challenge this life-or-death barrier throughout the show's short history.

Charming, Chaste and Conservative

The focus on love, romance and the general sense of feel-good nostalgia (or Capra-eque sentimentalism) that dominates the show might be said to stand out against, and perhaps even speak out against the pornification of society and the role of sexualization and female exhibitionism in the contemporary social period. If so, the seemingly quaint, old-fashioned and innocent televisual text could be expected to attract a conservative audience who are elsewhere angered and alienated by the sheer volume of sex in contemporary programming. Anna Friel makes this point in her commentary on the show when she tells audiences that the chaste doting that takes place between the central couple is reminiscent of 'the days when we watched all those wonderful black and white movies and we'd be totally satisfied with just the kiss at the very end' (Eden, 2008), concluding that 'it's the old-fashioned idea of romance' and the achingly romantic notion that 'the heart conquers all' that appeals here (*ibid.*). In one scene where Olive Snook/Kristin Chenoweth, a waitress at The Pie Hole, struggles to understand the relationship between Ned and Chuck, she asks one of the diners 'if you loved me, and we could never ever ever touch, would you eventually get over it and move on', assuming that she would find out that love is without hope if it is without physical intimacy. However, the importance of romantic love over physical pleasure is highlighted when the patron replies 'If I loved you, then I would love you in any way I could, and if we could not touch then I would draw strength from your beauty, and if I went blind then I would fill my soul with the sound of your voice and the contents of your thoughts until the last spark of my love for you lit the shabby darkness of my dying mind' (1.8).

In this way, the programme could be seen to condemn the recent sexualization of the small screen by reminding audiences of a different period, when norms of domesticity, fidelity, propriety and pleasantness were understood to be cleaner, safer and more chaste. However, although the programme can be seen to offer a 'romanticized nostalgia for the good old days' (Grainge, 2003, p. 205), we must be clear that it is not in relation to any specific historical period, social setting or political era. Therefore, the show might perhaps be less a yearning for a preferred but irretrievable past and more a 'fabricated approximation of the past' (Drake, 2003, p. 190) so that those selectively stylized clothes, cars and home furnishings 'operate as catalysts for recollection' (*ibid.*, p. 189) and mobilize a feeling of a past security, reassurance and comfort.[4] The very fact that The Pie Hole is said by the characters themselves to be 'a bells on the door, pies making mom and pop place'(1.2) rather than a ruthless, faceless, corporate franchise so popular in the contemporary period goes further to make this point.

Indeed, one might suggest that the conservative tone of the programme is less about retro aesthetics and more about the appropriateness of behaviour. As Ned and Chuck are unable to be physically intimate, the show can be seen to present alternative, and indeed rather charming, moments that demonstrate the growing bond between the pair. We see the couple sleeping in different rooms holding their hands up to the dividing wall, as if holding hands through the bricks and mortar barrier, and when they do share a room it is in small single beds on opposite sides of the space (1.1). We see what one commentator refers to as touchless hand holding (1.1) and figurines kissing when the couple themselves cannot (1.1). Moreover, there are small gestures of non-physical affection between the couple peppered throughout the show. When Ned presents Chuck with a rooftop full of bees (1.4) and lets her put her individual cup-pies on the restaurant menu (1.7), it speaks within the context of the programme as genuine love, thoughtfulness and affection. Such chasteness bespeaks of old-fashioned courtship, which when combined with the prince charming narrative that runs throughout the programme's short history, encourages us to read *Pushing Daisies* as a romantic, tender and charming (if not necessarily wholly nostalgic) text.[5]

Playful Sex and Intricate Contraptions

However, although the programme does undoubtedly and unashamedly present a number of chaste, romantic and affectionate moments between the couple, the show itself is not without sexual content. After all, it has 'a curious preponderance of male characters with names that seem to be some sort of sex pun' (Mackie, 2009)[6], pop-up books that are no longer the fare of small children but are erotic texts for mature audiences (1.7), a passing reference to key parties (2.7) and the characters that enter the colourful nursery-rhyme narrative from week to week tend to engage in a diverse range of pre-marital, marital and extra-marital sexual activities (1.2). We hear Olive tease Ned about the rolling pin hiding under his apron (1.7) and that same character tells the audience that 'we all need to be touched' (1.1). We find out that Chuck has grown up with an 'extensive collection of historic erotica' hidden in the milk cellar (1.2), we are told that Ned 'had a filthy mind as a child' (1.3) and we learn that the sense of pleasure derived from eating at The Pie Hole is akin to a 'sex addiction' for one recurring female character (1.5). Moreover, in relation to our central couple, although they cannot touch, we do see the characters in nothing but what Chuck refers to as their 'silky intimates' when they are alone (2.1). Although they can only hint at the sexual frisson between our romantic partners, the dream sequences that pop up throughout the show demon-strate a more sexually aware coupling. In one such dream Chuck falls on Ned wearing nothing but a short nightdress, and when Ned starts to tell her about the softness of her skin, she interrupts him, orders him to stop talking, kisses him intensely and then commences to take off her clothes (1.6). If audiences are more interested in the way in which the characters reveal their sexual interests beyond the fantasy realm, Chuck has been known to stand shower wet in front of the pie-maker, wearing nothing more than a red-bow in her hair and kitten heel slippers (1.7). In short, this couple may not touch, but they are not without sexual desires and physical needs.

Indeed, after the chaste romance of the aptly named 'Pie-lette' (1.1) episode, the programme shows the couple sharing kisses and intimate embraces. However, because they cannot actually touch, these moments have to include a number of sheaths, covers and coverings. For example, in one episode the couple kiss through thick body bags (1.2) and in another they share a passionate locking of lips through micro-fine cling film (1.3). The plastic being used on each occasion becomes thinner and thinner as the series progresses, trading up from industrial strength sheeting to super-fine cling-film, leaving audiences to assume that the thinner the barrier, the more satisfying the physical proximity (Keveney, 2007). Even a cursory glance at recent advances in condom manufacturing that range from ultra-fine, to, featherlite-ultra make it clear that the thinner, finer and less obtrusive the barrier the higher the potential for pleasure (Durex, 2010). Although the couple in question are not using such traditional forms of protection, the references to 'kiss-condoms' (Hinckley, 2007) and 'body condoms' (Keveney, 2007) draws the parallel. The couple also use large heavy tarps (2.9) and full-body bee-keeper suits (1.4) to hug one another, careful not to let their flesh touch, and draw on a false wooden arm to touch one another's bare skin (2.1). Ned reveals to Emerson that although he sometimes finds it hard being in a relationship where he and Chuck cannot touch one another, he has found ways to improvise and has figured out ways around the no-touch ruling (2.2). Indeed, in some of the more ingenious and imaginative images of togeth-erness, we see the couple holding hands through a rubber glove attachment rigged up in the front of Ned's car (1.2) and cuddling in bed, bodies separated by what Ned refers to as a bedtime 'contraption' (2.2).

Although *Pushing Daisies* can be read as a chaste, conservative or romantic and charming text, there is also room to read the show as frisky, sexy and potentially kinky. If one considers that 'sex sells big on prime-time TV' (Hinckley, 2007), then it is no wonder that the show contains this adult theme merely as a way to compete in the televisual marketplace. Therefore, although popular commentators were heard asking 'who first got the idea to go to a network programming chief and say: whattya think about the idea of a prime-time drama that has no sex?' (*ibid.*), it is worth noting that sexual interest and sexual activity do exist on the show in question, and one might even go as far as to suggest that such representations were necessary.

Indeed, in his work on sex, media and the democratization of desire, McNair tells us that 'sex is a central feature in our lives and needs to be portrayed as an integral part of our relationships' (McNair, 2002, p. 107). One might take this a stage further by suggesting that sex is a central feature in our lives and therefore needs to be portrayed as an integral part of those relationships that we see on the small screen. Indeed, recent statistics concerning the sexualization of popular media culture tells us that while 78 per cent of viewers think the portrayal of sex is acceptable; 64 per cent believe it is a necessary element of contemporary cultural life (*ibid.*). In short then, sex is important, it matters to each and every one of us, not merely in terms of reproduction, but in terms of physical pleasure, emotional connectedness and in defining our social period.

The very fact that prime-time television is dominated by representations of sex and sexuality can be seen to speak for a popular interest in and a public acceptance of sexual culture. The young adult audience in particular appears interested in discussing, exploring and celebrating sex, sexual activity and sexual diversity in the public sphere and it is this audience who are not only demanding access to sexual discourses, but the same audience who are watching this seemingly chaste show. Indeed, the term porno-chic has recently been employed to reflect the public interest in the pornographic area whereby popular media culture borrows from the aesthetic and narrative conventions of pornography without drawing attention to the task of arousal. While pornography proper continues to be met with moral outrage, this newer sexualized aesthete is routinely met by intrigue, interest and excitement.[7] Therefore, rather than dismiss, condemn or critique the growing commodification of sex, and the extension of sexual consumerism to a broader public body, it might be worth thinking about the ways in which the growing sexualization of the media can challenge the unconscious weight of a culture that has made sex, sexuality and sexual activity synonymous with shame, embarrassment and repression. Indeed, audience interest and investment in porno-chic might be understood as 'the byproduct of a free and easy society with an earthy acceptance of sex' (McNair, 2002, p. 199). The sexualization of prime time television might be seen to open up a dialogue about sex, breaking down traditional boundaries between previously separate areas of private practice and public discussion, encouraging a dialogue between partners, parents, friends and scholars and sending a message about both safety and pleasure in the current cultural climate.[8]

What is interesting, however, about the show in question is the ways in which the depiction of 'no-sex' sex challenges the seemingly universal attention given to patriarchal, penetrative sex. *Pushing Daisies* makes it clear that sex can be fun, playful and satisfying when you are forced to use your imagination, forced to find other ways to touch and be touched, to pleasure and be pleasured, to desire and be seen as desiring. Finding less predictable ways of expressing your sexual self appears to offer a sense of emotional safety and physical satisfaction in the short-lived show. *Pushing Daisies* offers a playful wink in the direction of alternative sexual practices, far removed from the explicit sexual conquests that dominate the contemporary television landscape. However, the fact that the series was cancelled after only 22 episodes perhaps ultimately suggests that this charming sexual content cannot compete with the more aggressive sexualization of contemporary media culture. After the 'Pie-lette' (1.1) first aired in America, a review commented that 'whether *Pushing Daisies* succeeds will depend on many factors, not ignoring the fact that explicit sex-wise, it's an intriguing island on a large ocean' an island which may or may not in the end 'be able to support human television life' (Hinckley, 2007). Intriguing indeed, *Pushing Daisies* is a programme dedicated to the playfulness rather than the explicitness of sex, a programme that focuses on the importance of chivalry and romance rather than the sexualization of society and porno-chic, a programme that is centred around the idea of destiny, soul mates and true love rather than one night stands and adultery. Perhaps we have to conclude that this overtly charming and potentially kinky text was unable to attract an audience who, although familiar with the commodification of sex, tend in the main to be familiar with the commodification of patriarchal, phallocentric, predictable and indeed penetrative sex.

The importance of penetrative, and thus, patriarchal sex is palpable when reviewers started to suggest that the lack of touching in a relationship was depressing rather than romantic (Sepinwall, 2008). Indeed, a number of characters in the programme even make reference to the heartrending nature of the relationship at the centre of the show. When Olive discovers that the couple in question cannot touch or be touched by one another, not even for a passing moment, she tells Chuck that her situation is 'the most tragic story I've ever heard, not withstanding famine' (1.6). Likewise, when Chuck's own father is resurrected, he goes on to describe their seemingly chaste courtship as a 'freak show' (2.9).

The couple themselves admits that the no-touch ruling is difficult, with a fleeting reference to the potential pleasures of polygamy and multiple partners (2.12). For example, a scene wherein Ned and Chuck refer to themselves as a couple with 'special circumstances' actually ends with Chuck telling Ned that: 'we are an us [but] maybe we just have to embrace the idea that sometimes I might have to hold someone else's hand and sometimes you might have to kiss somebody else [...] maybe there is something to this polygamy thing, maybe one person isn't enough' (1.6). Even though this scene ends with Ned announcing that 'you're the only one for me' (1.6) to his childhood sweetheart, maybe the seeds of doubt may remain in the minds of an audience more used to predictable patriarchal sexual encounters on the small screen.

That said, the problem with the relationship may be less about sex and more about intimacy, as one review puts it: 'the problem with Ned & Chuck's relationship isn't the sex part, which you can easily do without touching skin to skin, it's the intimacy part. The kissing and the hugging and the cuddling and the absolute care that would need to be taken are all but impossible' (Grunt, 2008). This echoes Chuck's earlier comments about maybe having to hold someone else's hand. The couple are not looking to have sex with other partners, but miss the tenderness of hand holding and sharing affectionate embraces, which brings us back to the charming ways in which the couple manage to overcome such obstacles by the chaste and charming 'no-touch' hand holding as introduced at the outset of the piece.

Conclusion

This chapter has tried to consider the representation of 'no-sex' sex in the short-lived *Pushing Daisies*, considering the ways in which the alternative sexual practices that are peppered throughout the show can be read as either chaste, conservative, kinky or as representing a society at ease with sexualized images in popular media culture. Although the preferred reading of the show must be as a playful, potentially post-modern take on non-contact sex in a society dominated by internet pornography, cybersex and the fear of sexually transmitted disease, there remains sufficient tenderness, romance and chivalry in the series to situate it as either a nostalgic, conservative or chaste text, and enough passing references to the importance of penetrative sex to view it as a more predictable patriarchal production. However, irrespective of whether audiences read the show as playful, post-modern or patriarchal, it is the relationship between physical and emotional intimacy that is paramount in this fairytale text.

Endnotes

1 *Pushing Daisies* proved to be both a critical and commercial success on both sides of the Atlantic. The heavily promoted pilot episode, cutely named, the 'Pie-lette' attracted over 13 million viewers in the United States when it aired on ABC in 2007. It was the most-watched new series of 2009, coming in fourteenth in the overall viewing figures for the week ending 3 October 2007. The show was equally heavily marketed in the UK, bringing in an average of 5.7 million viewers when it aired on ITV1 in 2009. Although one might suggest that 13 million and 5.7 million views do not make for ratings success, it is worth noting that the programme proved popular with the much coveted younger audience, with figures suggesting that 31 per cent of viewers were in the 16 to 34-year-old youth demographic (Topping, 2008).

2 Brain McNair (2002, pp. 1–2) makes the point that 'sex in our time is not reducible to reproduction [...] its possibilities and permutations are

constrained neither by the mechanics of male-female intercourse, nor the immediate survival needs of the gene or species. The biological imperative to transmit genes through sexual intercourse has over hundreds of millennia evolved into the psychological capacity to feel sexual desire and experience orgasm as an especially intense form of physical and emotional pleasure. Sex has become sexuality; or rather, sexualities'.

3   The screwball comedy is a popular and enduring subgenre of the Hollywood romantic comedy that dominated the American Film Industry during the 1930s and 1940s. These films tended to feature snappy banter, farcical situations, slapstick humour and a romance narrative between a seemingly mis-matched pairing. The film critic Andrew Sarris (1998) says it best when he refers to films such as *It Happened One Night* (dir. Frank Capra, 1934) or *His Girl Friday* (dir. Howard Hawkes, 1940) as sex comedies without the sex.

4   Alternatively, the programme might demonstrate its vintage furnishings and retro aesthetics simply due to the fashionability of such goods in the current marketplace. After all, retro objects are said to be 'loaded with connotative markers of taste' in the current period (Drake, 2003, p. 190).

5   On more than one occasion the omniscient voice over of the programme refers to Ned as the heroic Prince Charming and Chuck as the Sleeping Beauty of the piece (1.1; 1.3).

6   Such sex-puns have included Willie Gerkin, Shane Trickle, Bryce Von Deenis, Randy Mann and Colonel Likkin (Mackie, 2009).

7   Brian McNair (2002, p. 70) makes this point when he tells us that 'porno-chic aims to transfer the taboo, transgressive qualities of pornography to mainstream cultural production, but in the knowledge that if media audiences are in general less easily shocked than in the past, mainstream culture remains a zone where real pornography is not acceptable'.

8   The discovery of HIV in the early 1980s meant that the discussion of sexual behaviour was crucial to mainstream health education (McNair, 2002, p. 6).

6

Television X-cised: Restricted Hardcore and the Resisting of the Real

James Aston

Writing about American pornography in the 1970s and 1980s, Linda Williams, in her seminal book *Hardcore* (1989), cogently discussed the inherent irony at the heart of hardcore representations of sexual intercourse. Namely, in pornography's rush to capture the real and the authentic of physical pleasure during sex, representations are ultimately limited in that while pornography is straightforwardly able to demark male pleasure through on-screen signs such as the erection and ejaculation, it is unable to provide unambiguous representations of female sexual pleasure. Williams (1989, p. 50) describes this limitation of visual pornographic representations as the 'frenzy of the visible in a female body whose orgasmic excitement can never be objectively measured' or what Attwood (2009, p. 7) reinforces as the 'visual proof of the involuntary spasm of sexual pleasure in the female body'.

Indeed pornography has continually yet elusively engaged with the 'frenzy of the visible' in order to clearly demark reality, or the 'real' from the representation. Contemporary initiatives have centred on web-based or new media pornographies such as gonzo, amateur and realcore that forward an attempt to capture a truth about sex rather than a representational facsimile. Although the elemental limitation of making the invisible visible in terms of female sexual pleasure still continues, the aesthetic and confessional nature of much contemporary pornography does relate more to the personal, multivaried and real world nature of sexual intercourse. That these representations are still, for the main part, tied up in male desire and representative of wider societal power relations does not reduce the discursive framework they provide in which to produce, watch and talk about pornography. The internet has facilitated much of this new pornographic realism in that it has revolutionized consumer choice and consumer ease with which to view, and more importantly interact with, pornographic images. The freedom of choice, ease of consumption and the rescinding of legal, social and geographical hurdles has facilitated the mainstreaming of hardcore pornography which has bled into such diverse cultural forms as music, fashion, cinema and literature. In turn, and not without concern, this democratization of pornography engendered via the internet is indicative of a general blurring of the boundaries between the public and private spheres of sexualization and its representation in contemporary society.

Television is one such medium where this 'mainstreaming of sex' (Attwood, 2009) has emerged and is representative of larger societal discourse over the concerns, whether real or imagined, of the cultural shifts toward more public representations of sex and sexual practice. Indeed, British television broadcaster Channel 5 initially differentiated itself from other more established and popular television stations during the first few years after its launch in 1997 by providing viewers with a variety of late-night adult programming. Programmes ranged from the home-grown adult game show *Naked Jungle* (Channel 5, 2000), imported erotic dramas such as *Compromising Situations* (Showtime, 1994), *Hotline* (Magic Hour Pictures, 1994) and the sex lifestyle shows *Sex and Shopping* (Channel 5, 1998) and *UK Raw* (Channel 5, 1999). A consistent theme running through these shows is how sex and sexual practices are strongly interlinked with definitions of the self and issues relating to lifestyle, especially those that challenge and confront orthodox society. Although Channel 5 rebranded in 2003 dropping all of its adult content in a move to resituate the station as a more credible and progressive television provider, adult televisual programming that features explicit discussions and representations of sex still continue in Channel 4's *Embarrassing Bodies* (2008) and *The Joy of Teen Sex* (2010–). The mainstreaming of sex in the context of television is justified and legitimized by recourse to scientific or educational discourse. For example, *The Joy of Teen Sex* addresses serious issues facing teenagers such as pregnancy, sexuality, body image and sexually transmitted diseases. At regular stages questions posed by teenagers on the show are addressed by doctors or trained professionals in the area. While arousing and stimulating representations of sex are largely absent from British terrestrial television stations, the issue of the 'real' is nonetheless still very much a central issue underlining that the previously private domain of sexual lifestyles, sexual performance and practical advice is now very much part of an established and visible public discourse.

However, sex for pleasure in terms of both the representation and the reception of respective images is still absent from the more legitimate medium of terrestrial television. This would suggest that mainstreaming of sex is not a unidirectional and unstoppable phenomenon but one that is instead 'a case of customising sexual discourse to particular social groups in the audience in order to maximise their pleasure while minimising the offence to others' (Arthurs, 2004, p. 8). In the case of a programme like *The Joy of Teen Sex* the audience is both specific and inquisitive and thus the programme caters for a certain taste and value system while coterminously packaging the show in a scientific, medical and practical framework so as to reduce both erotic and arousing content that may be found offensive by viewers not within the target demographic. With this in mind, '*Television X*-cised' sets out to look at the sites and spaces where erotic representations of sex proliferate within the medium of television. That is, by focusing on pay-per-view and cable channels, this chapter will not only address a largely ignored area of the representation of sex on television that has obviated a thorough account of the practices of televisual pornography (production, distribution, representation and reception) but will also develop the theme of the 'real' that has dominated discourse on the representations of sex. Therefore, the UK's largest adult subscription channel *Television X* will be used as a case study to delineate in particular the representational strategies involved in its shows and what implications this has on production practices, textual representations and reception considering that the programmes featured on *Television X* are of a restricted and censored nature. Not only will this re-situate debates about the 'frenzy of the visible' contained in Williams' work, but it will also forward a critical framework with which to develop an understanding of the importance of content and taste in consuming representations of sex that will unpack the viewing habits of, primarily male, viewers of sex on television.

Television X: Restricted Hardcore as Progressive Text?

Television X started broadcasting under its original name, *Fantasy Channel*, in 1995. The station is owned by Portland TV which is a subsidiary of Northern and Shell owned by media mogul Richard Desmond who also publishes the *Daily Star, OK!* and who, in 2010, bought Channel 5. *Television X* constitutes one of the more popular British adult pay-per-view channels and has won numerous industry awards at the UK Adult Film and TV Awards, the SHAFTA's and UKAP (UK Adult Producers) during its operational history. To date, *Television X* operates three main channels which are the flagship *TVX* channel as well as *TVX Amateurs* and *TVX Brits*. The company also owns *Red Hot TV* which broadcasts eight channels including *Red Hot Fetish* and *Red Hot Dirty Talk*. Although viewing figures for adult channels are currently not supplied to the Broadcasters' Audience Research Board (BARB), due to the longevity and central position held by *Television X* in terms of providing British adult programming for a pay-per-view audience, the station provides an indicative case study of the production, content and reception of British produced pornography shown on satellite and cable networks. Therefore, the remainder of this chapter will be divided into two main areas. Firstly, an analysis of the content and themes evident in the programmes broadcast on the flagship *TVX* channel will be analysed enabling an examination of how sex is represented and its implications for viewer reception. In the second section, the reasons why viewers watch restricted and censored pornography will be explored by situating the role that television plays in structuring reception. The chapter will conclude by addressing how the restricted representational strategies of pornography contained on *Television X*'s schedule deals with notions of the real and the consequences these have for potential viewing positions and viewer demographics.

   The *TVX* channel broadcasts from 10pm till 5:30am and consists of around 18 to 20 programmes with each roughly lasting 30 minutes. The more popular titles include *John Cherry: Soccer Stud, Council Estate Skanks, Charlie Britton Exposed, Diamond Geezers* and *Lara's Anal Adventures. Television X* also has a hardcore and uncensored internet site and it is important to note that all of the programmes featured on the *TVX* station are also part of the hardcore internet line-up. That is, the actors and the locations are identical in both versions; it is the detail of representation that is markedly different. For example, in the television version the camera set-up, editing techniques and performers actions and language is modified so that explicit representations of sexual intercourse are elided. This latter aspect is significant in that it is not how normative viewing practices of pornography are structured. Thus, *TVX* purposefully conceals the visible and hence limits the potential to capture or represent the real or authentic of sexual intercourse and sexual relationships. However, in destabilizing normative pornographic practices in terms of production, content and reception interesting questions arise. Does the resulting material challenge 'the viewer [...] as a voyeur' whereby '[t] he human subjects depicted in pornographic texts are objectified as purely sexual animals, their beings stripped down to the sexual essence for the voyeuristic pleasure of the spectator' (McNair, 1996, p. 47)? In turn, can the moderated pornography of *TVX* impact on larger power dynamics between the male and female actors on screen so that patriarchal and phallocentric orientated sexuality is exposed and rendered strange? That is, can *TVX*'s recourse to sanitized pornography result in parity between female and male sexuality and desire within the text that promotes a more democratic representation of sex?

The majority of the programmes on *TVX* are heterosexual in nature although some do focus on lesbianism (*All Girl Initiation*) and transexualism (*Ladyboy Training*). In these programmes, such as *All New Ben Dover Show* and *Old and Young*, the narratives are led by men reinforcing male agency and male-dominated desire in that the women tend to be peripheral characters despite their visibility in scenes of sexual intercourse. Here, these programmes ossify the '"maleness" of pornography' (*ibid.*) through the objectification and fetishization of women while denying them a voice with which to articulate their own desires. The female as object is taken further in the programmes *Bitch in the Boot* and *Freddie's British 18's* that involve often degrading treatment of women and exposes an unhealthy attitude toward women that sees them simply as dehumanized possessions for male sexual desire. For example, in *Bitch in the Boot 1* a male character finds a woman in the boot of a car who, it is implied, he ordered. For the duration of the scene the man is shown in total control as he leads her around a seemingly uninhabited house as if she is an animal on a lead (perhaps the bitch of the title?). He ties her up, handcuffs her and dictates throughout what he requires from her in terms of providing sexual gratification for him. Afterwards he returns her back into the boot where he found her. In these types of programmes, the representations align themselves toward the philosopher Helen Longino's (1980, p. 44) oft cited definition of pornography as 'material that explicitly represents or describes degrading or abusive sexual behaviour so as to endorse and/or recommend the behaviour as described'. However, the fact that the representations are restricted means that not only do we not see the more aggressive and violent nature of the performative male sexuality but we also do not *hear* the more explicit verbalizations of the abusive relationship between the man and the woman that exists in the unexpurgated internet version. In this respect, the television version withdraws from showing the physicality of the scene and hence renders it less oppressive in its 'degrading, humiliating, subordinating content' (McNair, 1996, p. 48). While it would be egregious to suggest such restricted pornography provides a progressive text that offers challenges to the dominant patriarchal hierarchy of pornographic representations, it does nonetheless provide the potential to open up the discourse surrounding moral and ethical representations of sex.

For example, although the examples cited do conform to more established approaches to pornography that situates it as a 'dominant male economy' (Williams, 1989, p. 4) whereby male –orientated sexuality is central in articulating desire and receiving pleasure, the way the sex is filmed does allow for a more female-centred sexual identity to emerge. Despite the different themes or settings of the programmes featured on *TVX* (ranging from providing tips on how to make an amateur porn film (*Lara's School of Porn*) to Guy Richtie-esque gangster drama (*Diamond Geezers*) to social realism (*ASBO Trash Whores*)), the format is more or less the same. The scene usually commences with a striptease or a brief segment of 'girl-on-girl' before the male character enters. Then there is an extended cycle of foreplay that involves both fellatio and cunnilingus. Fellatio is either shot from behind the woman or in extreme close-up on the woman's face so that only the top half is visible. Cunnilingus is either shown from the side or from behind so that actual contact with the vagina is obscured. Sexual intercourse is similarly shot so that no penetration scenes are visible and that the sight of the erect penis is either absent or restricted to a minimum. The concluding 'money shot' that 'can be viewed as the most representative instance of phallic power and pleasure' (Williams, 1989, p. 95) is either absent or, because the erect penis is not allowed to be shown in the context of ejaculation, commences outside of the frame onto the woman's body in an obviously staged and at times artificial manner. These images of sexual intercourse are filmed through a variety of camera movements and edits that are often disjointed as the filmmakers avoid unwittingly capturing any prohibited material.

Although hardcore sex is occurring in these scenes, it all takes place outside of the frame in a type of liminal zone which at times is only millimetres outside of what the camera picks up. The result is almost like a 'frenzy of the invisible' whereby the filmmakers frantically endeavour to keep hidden and out of shot the forbidden and illicit hardcore. In doing so, the limited pornographic representations provide a distancing effect that induces 'unpleasure' within the viewer rather than producing a straightforward erotic spectacle. That is, the footage reflexively calls attention to the simulated nature of the sex despite the various scenarios of the programmes that promise 'raw', 'uncensored' and 'realist' entertainment in pragmatic environments such as behind the scenes, a day in the life and the girl next door. It also disturbs power dynamics in that male agency is withdrawn, underlined by the lack of explicit representation of male desire (the erect phallus) and unambiguous male pleasure (penile ejaculation). While viewer response to *TVX*'s use of restricted hardcore pornography may be one of displeasure, it is not an overt

or deliberate device implemented by the broadcaster to critique social forma-
tions and the spectator's relationship towards pornographic entertainment.
TVX still caters squarely for the male viewer as 'looking is equated with the
male position' (McClintock, 1999, p. 389) in all of their output. Nonetheless, it
does open up a space in which women can become more active and central
to the narrative, especially in terms of articulating female desire and pleasure.

Lara's Anal Adventures: Moving Toward Authentic Female Pleasure?

Lara's Anal Adventures is a flagship show on *TVX* featuring Lara Latex a
popular actress within the stations schedule who appears on a number of
programmes such as, *Lara's School of Porn* and *Lara's World of Nylon*. In the
third episode of this series which is the focus here, Lara is joined by Anna
Joy (a 'self proclaimed anal expert') and 'big lad' Leo. There is an extended
introduction presented by Lara explaining the show and what is to happen
later before another extended sequence featuring Lara and Anna as they get
'ready' for Leo. The scene between Lara and Anna is interesting; not only in
its absence of the male performer but also in the intimate conversation the
two women have about their needs and desires when engaging in sexual
activity. This is followed by another lengthy sequence where the two women
dress each other in revealing and erotic negligee. They then relocate to a living
room and, already over ten minutes into the programme, engage in sexual
intercourse with Leo. The resulting narrative utilizes dialogue to convey what
the viewer cannot see and this is almost exclusively carried out by Lara and
Anna. Leo, similar to the preceding scenes is absent in that Lara and Anna
not only provide a running commentary on what is happening but also dictate
the action as well. The scene ends without withdrawal or an external male
orgasm thus continuing the peripheral nature of Leo in the scene denying him
a clear expression of male pleasure and 'phallic sexuality' (Williams, 1989,
p. 20) and thus aligning him more with the elusive nature of female sexual
pleasure 'whose orgasmic excitement can never be objectively measured'
(*ibid.*, p. 50).

The format of *Lara's Anal Adventures 3* follows the pattern and structure
previously noted and provides an often fragmented representation of the
mise-en-scène as the camera violently pans away or deploys oblique angles
to obscure or avoid any explicit imagery. The female driven narrative of the
programme is also replicated in the majority of *TVX* productions, for example
Alysha's Diaries, *Stud Hunt* and *Jasmine 24/7*, which situates the women as

more active characters who seek out sexual activity and determine the direction of sexual intercourse. The result is a more consensual and democratic sexual relationship. Such representations move away from the dominant gender roles found in internet pornography and *Television X*'s own hardcore internet versions in that they downplay male aggression and sadism and thus elevate the role of the woman from that of a submissive and dehumanized sexual object. However, it would be simplistic to declare that the restricted hardcore pornography of *Television X* provides a utopian space of democratized sex. Its restricted content is solely dictated by Ofcom regulations and not some lofty ambition to challenge the hegemonic structures of mediated sexual intercourse. In fact, whatever gains are attributable to the shifting gender roles engendered by the inability to show (and describe) hardcore machinations are offset by recourse to the male–orientated consumer and general approaches to sex that circulate in society. For example, masculine prowess is exclusively attributed to penis size and sexual performance. In *Lara's Anal Adventures 3*, both women comment on the large size of Leo's penis with Lara exclaiming at one point that 'he's fucking massive'. This is replicated in other programmes such as *Life in Bras 5* whereby the woman says 'your dick really fills up my pussy' and *Charlie Britton Exposed* where one of the female actors says to Charlie (played by *TVX* stalwart Ben Dover) 'I need a big cock to break me in'. Moreover, there are a number of programmes such as *Council Estate Skanks* and *Suburban Perversions* where married women engage in sexual intercourse because their husbands cannot satisfy them sexually, which is indicative of a greater trend across the *TVX* schedule that underlines the female need for sexual expertise in the male performers. Here, the overriding aspect is of a reversion back to 'phallic sexuality' whereby the woman surrenders her own sexual identity and desires for that of 'the power and pleasure of the phallus' (Williams, 1989, p. 112).

TVX also equates sex with deviancy and while this can produce positive outcomes in that it can 'be seen as a political challenge to a prudish establishment and the stultifying rules that restrain sexual expression' (Arthurs, 2004, p. 49) whereby marginalized sexual practices and identities can be recouped, in the majority of the *TVX* shows, deviancy is clearly situated as shameful, dirty and illicit. The locations popular in programmes such as *Bitch in the Boot*, *Glory Hole*, *The Swinging Scene* and *Motorhome Pickups* take place in abandoned warehouses, industrial buildings, toilets, alleyways, uninhabited houses and mobile homes. As such the geographical mappings of these locations do not take place in established centres of the urban environment. Instead, and as an extension of the hardcore images, they exist in a liminal zone outside of the everyday gaze. The effect is to reinforce the sex, which is without exception between strangers and devoid of love or any meaningful intimacy, as furtive, forbidden and reprehensible. This is reinforced by the recurrent articulation of dirt, filth or waste in dialogue between the performers. Constant reference is made to the woman performer as a 'dirty little slut', a 'dirty fucking whore' or a 'filthy bitch' with the noun in each of these expressions emphasizing the sordid and debased nature of the women engaging in such deviant sex.

Patriot-archal Porn: The Class-based Female Other

The partial re-centring of female agency in articulating sexual desire in the content of *Television X* programmes is further restricted by the thematic strategies inherent in the programming that prevents progress in providing alternatives to the dominant patriarchal system of pornography. *Television X* prides itself on being a supplier of British pornography and all of the programmes in *TVX* are produced and filmed in the UK. In this respect the schedule has a rather parochial outlook but does give the (British) viewer a sense of commonality far removed from the exotic and polished spectacles of American pornography or the nostalgic, camp offerings of continental Europe. For example, a large proportion of *TVX* plays upon familiarity with legitimate, terrestrial British television programmes by crudely punning the titles of popular shows. We have *Life of Bras* and *Tashes to Flashes* which are pornographic spoofs of the popular BBC1 police/time travelling shows *Life on Mars* (2006–7) and *Ashes to Ashes* (2008–) and *Ready Steady Chav* and *Asses in the Attic* that play upon the formats of the BBC light entertainment programmes *Ready Steady Cook* (1994–) and *Cash in the Attic* (2002 -). The recourse to British culture and societal configurations is further exemplified in the fecundity of programmes that deal with class distinctions. Among the more popular titles are *Recession Whores*, *Council Estate Skanks*, *Pippa the Posh Bird* and *Bellenders* (itself a spoof on the working class lifestyles found in the popular BBC soap opera *Eastenders* (1985–)). Here the class-based narratives combined with the restricted hardcore of *Television X* again facilitate an opportunity to challenge patriarchal constructions of pornography by situating the women as more central and active as well as exposing stereotypical class distinctions. For example, in *Pippa the Posh Bird* we meet Pippa riding a horse through her country estate before she coerces a male stable hand into having sex with her. Pippa's character controls the scene by dictating the course of action and describing the sequence throughout. The male character is subservient in this episode underlined by his silent demeanour and an ejaculation scene that takes place off camera. Thus, the female character is dominant throughout yet the scene also exhibits fantasies centring on inter-class relations, whereby the proper and pure upper-class female engages in sordid and illicit sex with a member of the working class that conforms to rigid class stereotypes in terms of the way they dress, act and ultimately have sex. Indeed, the majority of *TVX*'s class based programmes conform to class stereotypes rather than offering any salient commentary into British based class distinctions and the representation of the real or the authentic that class-based pornography could possibly provide. In particular there is a significant focus on the working or under-class female as the abject Other, which further compromises the potential of *Television X*'s restricted pornography to destabilize traditional gender positions in hardcore pornography.

Council Estate Skanks serves as an indicative example of how these types of offerings position the woman as Other in that they locate her as abject. In the five episodes that make up the series, the motif of dirt articulated in a number of *TVX* programmes is continued and ossified, which again demarcates the woman as unclean and immoral. That is, the figure of the sexually impure woman is categorized by her infidelity and voracious sexual appetite as well as her appearance and surroundings, which are also specifically marked as soiled, unhygienic and repellent. The series of programmes that make up *Council Estate Skanks* start with a pre-sequence title that provides a definition of the word 'skank'. The caption reads 'a lewdly and disreputable person often *female*, especially one with an air of tawdry promiscuity'. Throughout each episode the filmmakers repeatedly have male performers categorize the woman as dirty or filthy 'skanks' and 'chavs'. These nominations are combined with on-screen titles reinforcing the lower status of the women with captions such as 'chavvy jewellery from down the market!' and 'what a skanky bra!'. In the narrative developments of *Council Estate Skanks*, and to a lesser extent in all of the lower-class based programmes, abjection can be seen as the breakdown between the clean and the unclean rather than engendering fears over death and decay most associated with conceptions of the abject. That is, the woman is positioned as abject by removing her from the more stable representations of cleanliness and purity and of mother or wife. For example, the dirt and squalor in which the sex takes place removes associations with it as an act of life-giving reproduction and thus marks it as purely pleasurable, sexual and reproductively consequence free. In these situations the woman is seen as sexual promiscuous, marked by the fact that the sex takes place with a stranger and while her husband or partner is absent, and as craven and self-abasing due to the contaminated locale and sordid nature of the sex act. Here, the focus on class and the Othered woman has the potential to address mainstream reaction to the difference of women, in particular culturally constructed archetypes of the sexually promiscuous, binge-drinking, violent and criminal female that has produced headlines such as 'Surge in violent females' (*The Daily Express*, 2008), 'Rise in arrests of women drunks' (*BBC News*, 2008) and 'Legacy of the Ladette: women's binge drinking is linked to alarming rise in teenage promiscuity and abortions' (Borland, *The Daily Mail*, 2010).

However, the recognition of the complex representation of woman as Other and how this is inexorably connected to notions of the abject is ultimately unrepresentable. That is, the anxiety that is produced by representing the women's bodies, both in terms of sexual activity and appearance, as abject – as craven, degraded and self-abasing, is manifest in what Julia Kristeva terms the 'Phobic object' that condenses all fears and thus is the 'fear of no thing specific or determinate' (Taylor, 1987, p. 158). The abject, therefore, the 'unnameable pseudo-object' (*ibid.*, p. 159) becomes unreachable, indefinable and ultimately out of our grasp. Similar to the hardcore pornography that exists outside of the frame and the locations of sexual intercourse that occur outside of the urban centre so too does the abject exist at the limen, or the liminal zone, which is a 'void that is not nothing but designates [...] a defiance or challenge to symbolization' (Kristeva, 1982, p. 48). Thus, the abject always excludes, similar to the waste products we flush away so that, like the sex, it is invisible while simultaneously visible. The ramifications this has for disturbing the patriarchy of pornography and the 'power of a phallic economy of pleasure' (Williams, 1989, p. 102) is that the abject is funda-mentally 'propelled away from the body and deposited on the other side of an imaginary border which separates the self from that which threatens the self' (Creed, 1993, p. 182). Therefore, presenting the woman as an abject figure who is both absent and present, attractive and repulsive, known and unknown removes viewer identification from concepts of the real into the imaginary or representational so that 'the pure/impure opposition represents [...] the aspiration for an identity, a difference' (Kristeva, 1982, p. 82). It is this difference, or the othering of women, that these programmes reinforce by denying the woman any real presence other than that of a sacred symbol, 'both pure and impure, proper and improper, holy and filthy' (Taylor, 1987, p. 168) for male viewing (dis)pleasure.

Therefore, taken as a whole, the content of *TVX*'s schedule vacillates between conventional phallocentric pornography and a restatement of female sexual desire ending ultimately by reinforcing pornography as produced by men for primarily male consumption. The example of *Lara's Anal Adventures* does situate a more active female agency but one that is still dependent on the male economy of pornography, while *Council Estate Skanks* presents the woman as unrepresentable and as ultimately out of reach. However, even though these programmes may not be able to dislodge Williams' (1989, p.

4) claim that 'for women, one constant of the history of sexuality has been a failure to imagine their pleasures outside a dominant male economy', they can still offer resistance, however tentative. That being, in *The History of Sexuality*, Michel Foucault (1990) traces the genealogy of social, economic and political configurations that have shaped conceptions of sex and sexuality, whereby he (*ibid.*, p. 95) astutely addresses the power dynamics evident in these discourses by commenting that 'where there is power, there is resistance'. What *TVX*'s representations of restricted pornography highlight is that powerful articulations of male sexuality are only truly successful within the narrow confines of hardcore, and, removed from this sphere, the discourse over sexuality presents not just the power of male sexuality but the possibility of a reaffirmation of female sexuality and sexual desire.

The Television as a Moral Guide

Television broadcasting in Britain 'is based on the principle of public service' (Scannell, 2001, p. 45) that is a complex, contested and elusive term to define and explain. The British Broadcasting Company (BBC) acts as a salient point of entry into the long and convoluted history and classification of public service broadcasting in that much of its original manifest and remit is applicable, albeit in modified form, today. The BBC's mandate was for it to exist as a public utility that was to act in the public interest on a national scale. Lord Reith, the first director-general of the BBC was keen to produce a public service broadcaster that was not simply there to entertain but which also had a 'responsibility to bring into the greatest possible number of homes in the fullest degree all that was best in every department of human knowledge, endeavour, and achievement' (*ibid.*, p. 47). Analogous with the pursual of quality and high standards within the BBC was a focus on also providing a clear moral framework to compliment the educational and entertainment aspects so that the BBC could promote a social unity through knowledge, taste and conduct. The public sector positioning of the BBC enabled the company to promote a moral, cultural, and to a lesser extent, political and social voice which listeners and viewers could structure their lives around. Although television has undergone enormous upheaval through the advent of commercial and satellite broadcasters, the concept of public service television as 'purveyor of moral and cultural "uplift" in the well-established tradition of improvement for the masses' (*ibid.*, p. 50) continues to retain relevancy and currency in the contemporary cultural sphere.

The reason for briefly detailing the importance of television as a moral and cultural barometer is to posit an opening with which to address why viewers subscribe to watch restricted pornography on television as opposed to the uncensored, and free, hardcore that is easily available on the internet. While televisual pornography does provide better technology in terms of screen size, resolution and sound than internet video images there is also the notion of television, specifically British, as a safe and regulated medium that is strongly connected to the history of television as a public service broadcaster. That is, when watching pornography on a channel such as *TVX* there is not the danger of viewing illegal, forbidden or transgressive sexual acts and representations that exists over the internet. Viewers are aware, primarily due to the censored hardcore imagery, that the pornographic material is strictly monitored, as is the case with British adult satellite channels, by the government accepted telecommunications regulatory authority Ofcom (Office of Communications). The regulated and controlled pornographic images contained on an adult channel such as *Television X* leads to another key aspect of favouring television which is viewer choice. Television is similar to the cinema in that choice is already pre-determined and necessarily limited to reflect market and audience demand. Therefore, unlike the internet where the viewer actively has to select pornographic sites to visit and images or scenes to watch, with television these decisions are wrestled away from the viewer so that they become more of a passive consumer. The importance of a lack as well as a pre-selected or regulated choice for pornography watched on television is that the viewer can dissociate themselves with the content if it is not to their liking or represents material that is threatening to boundaries of taste. Thus, there is less danger of being positioned as responsible for what is viewed. If, as is more likely with the internet, a wrong choice is made then it is the fault of the broadcaster not the viewer and thus does not reflect upon or comment on the viewer's identity and viewing practices.

Conclusion

The notion of a lack of interactivity in watching pornography on television contradicts the aim of pornography which situates itself as a substitute for interaction with the 'real' thing. As such it returns us back to Williams' 'frenzy of the visible' and the continual, but inaccessible, quest for authenticity and the 'real' in representations of sexual intercourse. In the case of *Television X* the real is circumvented in favour of the artificial. That is, the production, content and reception of pornography on *Television X* resolutely returns the sex back to representation. Firstly, the restricted hardcore of the programmes deny viewers access to the 'real' of sexual intercourse; secondly the action takes place away from visible spaces existing instead on topographical margins such as derelict warehouses, disused industrial factories and secluded rural locations; thirdly, the example of class in *Television X*'s output, which forms a significant proportion of the schedule, delineates the woman as Other, as an ultimately unknowable figure relegated to symbol and stereotype and thus as a representational facsimile of the real; lastly, the technology of television acts as a screen rather than an interface further removing the viewer from the real in that they forgo choice and interactivity in favour of safety and regulated content decided by someone other than themselves.

The reverse directional flow of the real back to representation, which resists the advance of the 'mainstreaming of sex' on television that hardcore pornography has to an extent facilitated, can perhaps be framed as a confrontation between Luddites and Technophiles. This is not to say that advancements, such as the internet, should be considered in an anti-technological and anti-progressive manner, but that in the ever increasing quest for capturing the real and the authentic in representations of sex, boundaries between public and private, regulated and uncontrolled, safe and illicit have become porous and undefined. What Neil Postman (1993, p. 5), author of *Technopoly* astutely points out is that 'people who are very enthusiastic about technology are always telling us what it will do for us. They almost never address the question of what it will undo'. Therefore, *Television X*'s undoing of the 'frenzy of the visible' and move back toward the secure domain of representation can be seen to address Luddite fears over technological innovation and the ramifications uncensored and limitless (internet) pornography can have on issues such as taste, identity and reception. *Television X*'s antiquated and unsophisticated programming emphatically excludes a younger audience who are more likely to seek out unexpurgated hardcore pornography on the internet anyway, therefore suggesting that subscribers are older male viewers who have a longer standing connection to the television and are anxious about the seemingly infinite size of the internet, its unregulated and uncontrollable content and what consequences this may have for watching pornography. It is with this last point that ultimately situates *Television X* as a male orientated and phallocentric producer of pornography. Even though the restricted hardcore of the channel does afford some space for women to direct the action, it is for the most part cancelled out by the fact that the consumer is positioned as resolutely male. *Television X* therefore reinforces Williams' point about the 'male dominant economy' of modern pornography in that it fails to incorporate female desire and pleasure into discourses of sexual representations. Thus, the potential of both the subversive and progressive quality of *Television X*'s schedule is ultimately limited due to the channels return of the real back toward representation and of its particular production practices that enables male agency and prioritizes male consumption of pornography.

7

Imagination in the Box: *Woju's* Realism and the Representation of *Xiaosan*

Ruth Y. Y. Hung

Since China joined the World Trade Organization in the 1990s, following Deng Xiapoing's declaration that 'To get rich is glorious', economic transformation, guided by the Chinese State and the Communist Party, has profoundly altered the moral and cultural landscape of China. Akin to the US and UK, the new China organizes, controls and produces itself by means of media and spectacle as much as its economic power and political structure. While China changes, cultural spectacles, especially created by newly important TV and other electronic media, have become prominent devices in transforming and stabilizing China. Therefore, reading those devices carefully has become necessary for any understanding of contemporary China. In this chapter, I propose to study the critical success of the nationwide popular TV serial *Dwelling Narrowness*, or *Woju* (meaning a humble abode in English), taking it as a critical example of these changes and how its content and reception illuminates the emerging moral and cultural realities of the new People's Republic of China (PRC).

Woju, a 35-episode television serial and an adaptation of a 2007 novel by the cyber-literature writer Liu Liu, was first broadcast on Shanghai Dragon Television in Shanghai during prime time in 2009. It became an immediate hit and nationwide networks rebroadcast it across the country. According to *Shanghai Youth News*, *Woju* enjoyed the highest audience ratings among TV serial dramas of that year (Lin, 2009; Sina Entertainment, 2009). *Woju* is a realist drama and reflects the social changes and new urban realities within the limits allowed by the State's official ideology. Television critics have called such realist serials by the term, '*zhu-xuan-lu*' (main melody) and accordingly *Woju* owes its exceptional success to the mobilization of a 'realism effect', as Roland Barthes (1986) might call it, in audience's cynical attitude toward life in the new China. One result of this achieved 'realism effect' is that audiences confuse or identify their sense of life as it is with that of life as it is supposed to be. The TV serial produces realism effects similar to those of nineteenth and twentieth century European prose. Anton Chekov wrote, for example, 'The best among them are realistic and show life as it is, but since every line appears to be imbued with an awareness of the goal [...] you get a sense of what life is supposed to be aside from life as it is, and that is what captivates you'(Cited in Bloch, 1988, p. 278). In other words, *Woju*'s realism effect mobilizes its audiences to accept the very society it in fact criticizes. Such a realism effect even opens up the possibility of critique; as a result, we see that realism in the new China can do its work without reducing itself to sentimental melodrama that merely satisfies the sensationalist and consumerist cult of a modern metropolis. *Woju* tells a modern version of the 'fallen woman' story, with the exception that this seemingly powerless young woman – played by the protagonist Guo Haizao – is not just prey to powerful men as she also anchors the material world. Her performance and role in the story embodies the experience of contemporary Chinese modernity with a tangible image.

Woju represents the forms of life of a newly urbanized Chinese experience in an increasingly competitive and commercialized metropolis saturated by global capital. Centered on the Guo sisters, Haiping and Haizao and their struggle to buy a flat in the coastal city of Jiangzhou,[1] the TV serial develops several intertwined plot lines. It tells the story of Haiping, the elder sister, and her typical ambitions to own property and her consequent life as a mortgage-slave. It portrays the joys and sorrows that the wrenching process of buying an apartment in urban China causes. It organizes itself partly as a romance focused on love found, abused, and lost. It approximates real events in portraying the city mayor's secretary, Song Siming, and his dark art of corruption embedded within his vision of China's rise in the global economy.[2] Finally, and most important, it tells the story of Haizao, the younger sister who chose the life of a married older man's *xiaosan* (literally meaning 'the little third' in English) over regular work and secured family life. Not only the narrative, but the social and ideological realities at stake in the series centre on Haizao, on the *xiaosan* and so I will return to her repeatedly throughout this chapter.

A series of problems, bigger than they could manage, set in as soon as Haiping became a 'mortgage-slave'. Because of Haiping and her property ambition, Haizao half-willingly became Song Siming's *xiaosan*, ending a relationship with her boyfriend Xiaobei and, thanks to complications of a later miscarriage, her chance at motherhood. Nearing the end of the drama, Haizao not only lost her child with Song but, because of the miscarriage, irreparably damaged her uterus. Song, driving on his way to the hospital, died in a car crash. The drama ends most ambiguously; it points to two different futures. While the TV drama's last shot of Haizao shows her sinking into a state of deep perplexity and leaving her motherland for good, its concluding shot is a close-up of a Chinese Language School named after Haiping. The language school teaches Chinese as a foreign language to foreigners residing in China.

As my summary suggests, the success of this TV serial rests upon its extended dramatization of a new sexual politics, embodied in the figure and narrative of highly-educated women in urban China, especially the *xiaosan*. The *xiaosan* is, in this sense, the dramatic key to the series. In the narrative, she anchors the materialities of urban life in neoliberal China while figurally she provides analytic access to the nature of that socio-political economy. The *xiaosan* trades her sexuality, fertility and qualifications for not just quick cash or stability but also social standing. She represents a new historical figure that emerged in China at the turn of the twenty-first century. Liberated from traditional forms of gender oppression and hierarchies, she belongs to a professionalized category of young women, enjoying social mobility and financial independence that set them apart from seemingly comparable figures such as ancient concubines or modern mistresses. In other words, the *xiaosan* seemingly has a comparative advantage in that she, rather like a designer bag, is free for sale in the exchange market and not a figure in hiding.

In *Woju*, the *xiaosan* played by the character Guo Haizao is an educated young woman, whose body and fertility the burgeoning political economy positions as commodities. Neither a prostitute nor a courtesan nor simply a mistress, Haizao grows out of twenty-first century China's populist culture of consumerism, recognizing her own value added at the nexus of market corruption and trading on it for what seems like permanent advantage. To

distinguish Haizao's form of oppression from traditional forms, *Woju* emphasizes Haizao's education as well as assimilation with activities and people
outside her hometown. Coming from an educated family in rural China
and graduate of a national 'signature' university in the city, Haizao left her
birthplace to settle down in Jiangzhou, living with Haiping and her brother-
in-law Suchun, both graduates of a 'signature' university. Since Haizao's first
appearance in the TV series as a self-motivated student determined to get
into a university in the city, *Woju* reproduces a meme common in Chinese
life and in discussions of China in the world: the migration of rural peoples to
the cities for the alloy of education and wealth. The realism effect is explicitly
familiar and semi-official: urban life is a necessary product of Chinese
modernity, urban mobility and women's liberation – which is also essential to
the processes of modernization, in the work place and new erotic spheres.

The series insists on Haizao's education because it belongs to this narrative
meme and it matters to us because it differentiates her as *xiaosan* from older
social forms that exploit women's reproductive and sexual value. Therefore,
we see how the *xiaosan* anchors the series: as the narrative moves, it follows
Haizao's 'liberation', presenting a picture of the everyday. In this way, the
series presents the fact of a modernized China's internal transformations as
an effect of its new 'normalized' place within global capital. As a result, the
new figure of the *xiaosan*, unlike the old concubine, prostitute, mistress,
or wife/partner, instantiates the sophisticated display of erotic tension and
desire new to this society. We watch the allegorical spectacle of China's
change as Haizao manoeuvres her sex between the loving boyfriend-fiancée
and the powerful corrupt official-lover. Generalized commodification, the
illusion of free agency and control, the 'rewards' of wealth and urban life – all
these gratifications spectacularized for an audience that experiences them as
'real'.

To put it simply, we could say that 'education' allows *Woju* to manipulate
the image of Haizao from a traditional sex object to a modern consumer
subject – a figure at the centre of desire in consumerist cultures. Throughout
the drama, Haizao presents herself as an agent of her own life, as an individual
making individual choices, but the narrative will soon show that her 'agency'
is itself embedded within the world of commodities and consumption. In her
role as a university graduate, audiences witness the placement of female
subjectivity within the consumerist discourse of post-Mao-Deng China. After
her first brief appearance as a high school student, Haizao soon reappeared
in the TV serial as a wage earner and bourgeois consumer, showing off to
Xiaobei her ability to identify one international designer brand after another.
The possibility that Haizao could have been a victim trapped within the realm
of modern consumerism was side-lined by her near intellectual reflection

upon her childish material fixation and the very lifestyle she learnt to embrace. A few days of work after graduation, Haizao detected the alienation of urban-dwellers as they self-contentedly submerge themselves in what Matthew Arnold (1994, p. 3), in a comparable context of mid-nineteenth century urbanizing England, calls 'our stock notions and habits' – a habituated pattern of life that capitalist subjects follow 'staunchly' and 'mechanically'. Haizao reflected:

> Everybody [...] tolerates abuses. What is the meaning of life? Is it to endure pain on an everyday basis or to seek happiness? [...] Everyone ekes out a living in the same way. All we know, indubitably, is the good ethics of laboring round the clock. One works like an ox for twenty-two days or more a month, and ramp about like a jumpy and joyful rabbit for just a day: on the pay day.[3] (Episode 4)

In this moment of self-reflection, a voice-over presents Haizao's thoughts, creating a momentary gap between the projected internal monologue and the female body. This gap fixes the audiences' amused attention to Haizao's 'deep thoughts' on China's urban lifestyle, as well as the bureaucratic corruption of the political system that lies behind the ineluctable facts of current Chinese life. However, with the subsequent appearance of an increasingly stylish and sophisticated Haizao, and with the character herself literally and loudly announcing her determination to become a *xiaosan*, the TV drama distracts the audience attention. Since then, Haizao's intellectuality is no longer at the centre, but rather relegated to the background as one of the diverse facts of life that *Woju*'s realism presents. As the drama goes on, her education increasingly becomes a visual witness to Haizao's increasingly prominent physical appearance on the screen. Halfway into the drama, the 'educated' Haizao begins to appear in hotel rooms, bedrooms in luxurious villas, huge shopping malls, posh cars, and with intensely commodified objects that mark her own status (an eye-catching scarlet overcoat, a vanity desk set topped with branded cosmetics, expensive dinners). It remodels her nerdy straight long hair to a sophisticated perm. This change is not trivial. It not only visualizes her transformation but its luxurious tone adds to the realism effect of a common and even yet highly desirable form of satisfying consumption within the new urban forms of life. In other words, the realism effect works on the audience, allowing for a significant identification with a new woman who seems to have found a space in which she is an active autonomous subject.

The educated woman as *xiaosan* spends her days and nights as though she were the master of her life, dreams and plans. In fact, the role she has embraced places her within a sexual economy unique to the emerging China

– one defined by an extensively corrupt political system and the emerging continuous flux of consumerist culture that both holds her and that she has internalized and embraced. *Woju* displays Haizao's modern urban identity makes desirable the newly acceptable proscribed sexual role for women willing to participate in this sex trade. Ironically, desire that so often disturbs works in this context as an effect of stabilization. *Woju* draws the audiences' attention to an intelligence beamed through Haizao's modernist reflection and then distracts and blunts criticism by luring the mind and seducing the gaze with a spectacular display of a woman's body, her lavish taste, and most imaginatively for the audience's gratification, the sexual fantasy she has induced in Song. Meanwhile, online polls indicate that Song Siming is a very popular character. This result puts into question the ethics and efficacy of hard work, indicating an inability on the part of the audience to command a sustainable critical position on the *xiaosan* phenomenon.[4] It is important to remember that Song embodies the worst of the new China, but that the story blunts critique of his corruption by making him yet another instance of the lovingly attractive rogue.

Under the cover of Haizao's outfits is the complex populist sentiment about the rapid escalation of consumerism in the post-Mao-Deng era that the phrase 'capitalism with Chinese characteristics' best captures. Populism of the market is also populism of women's bodies, of women's wombs, of women's educational achievements and social aspirations. Revealingly but not surprisingly, the eroticized image attracts more popular interest than it fuels social criticism. The consumer marketplace, which depends upon ever-new forms of changing fashions and lifestyles, allows *Woju* to reflect upon and elevate the problem of corruption to the curious business of the 'educated' professionals and the art of the politically and bureaucratically successful. In this sense, there is an erotic element to Haizao's experience – her romance, her outlook, her clothing and make-up. *Woju*'s carefully embroidered Haizao provides the opportunity for critical reflections on contemporary society and subtly, but inoffensively, naturalizes the patterns and ideology of the 'free market'. This is why its realism effect blunts critique. In other words, Haizao is as much a body for consumption as she is a consuming body who congregates with other consuming bodies in fashionable shopping centres and in front of the TV box. *Woju* emphasizes the ordinariness of its characters and of their lives. Tactically, this realism works to demythologize the *xiaosan* experience by suggesting that Haizao, too, is a vulnerable individual trying to live alongside the economic climate she finds herself in. In this sense, the *xiaosan* figure is the allegorization of the audience's erotics; it works on desire through desire. Like the audience, and vice versa, Haizao the *xiaosan* is erotic, active, and welcomes her oppression.

The Economy of Sexuality and the Consumption of *Xiaosan*

At this point, we should ask two questions, or take up two angles on this subject. We can ask how the new political economy produces new intersections between the media, especially TV, and a new sexual politics in Chinese culture. We can also ask how the central presentation of this *xiaosan* in *Woju* provides us special access to the constellation of forces and powers that underlie her appearance as a new functional type within the aesthetics of this differently sexualized economy. In simple terms, the economic political transformations that *Woju* draws upon and represents – corruption, a bubble economy in housing, intense urbanization and internal migration – reposition women as objects of value. The role of the *xiaosan*'s requires that a woman believe in the mythical notion essential to consumerism that she has 'choice', that she 'empowers' herself within this new sexual economy. She must believe she voluntarily trades on just the values it assigns her body as commodified organ.

In *Woju*'s characterization and presentation of Haizao, her sexual identity and her sexual mores change within the new economy and introduce a new set of judgements parallel to the new aesthetics of state influenced media. Within these media-centreed domains of desire – in production and narrative – the woman internalizes as acceptable her own new valuation and willingly changes her subjectivity to the *xiaosan*. Haizao needs not be 'sexually' submissive; however, she must have a market value. In an attempt to persuade Mrs Song to accept Haizao's existence as an essential add-on to his 'professional' life, Song Siming explains to his wife how political corruption and the market in new China gives Haizao's sex a market and exchange value:

> In our circle of government officials, everyone has a *xiaosan*. Without one, colleagues will quickly isolate and marginalize you. You will have to follow the circle's own code of ethics as long as you are in the loop. If you don't, others will [...] guard against you and keep you in the dark. This is also why I *must* be as corrupted as the rest. (Episode 19)

TV exploits the young woman's body, the desires it provokes for the fantasy of 'love', just as the corrupt official indulges his masculine fantasy. Haizao's story not only ends pathetically but also suggests that the new economy allows no humane sexual space for women's bodies, but also for men who embrace them. For Song to meet Haizao's needs, to qualify to possess a *xiaosan*, he must be politically powerful, socially resourceful, and financially strong. This reflects the sexual economy of post-Mao-Deng China, where global capitalism has leveled ideological differences – differences, in particular, between 'socialism with Chinese characteristics' and post-9/11 American-led liberal democracy. Under these circumstances, the symbolic capital of a *xiaosan* in Chinese political culture and moral life reveals that a romantic and sensationalized form of sex trade is perhaps the best the audience could find in an eroticized realism effect that offers pleasure in and expects nothing more of Chinese politics, society and institutions.

Woju turns this horrendous sex trade of *xiaosan* – a marker of neoliberal market economics in the new PRC – into an account of exchange value turned into something retrospective and sympathetic, despite the tragic cost to the young woman involved. It is 'critical' of the *xiaosan* phenomenon in the way that Chekov's analysis of the realism effect suggests. The audience can easily take the life *Woju* depicts as their own, or at least as a part of world which is continuous with their own. I have elsewhere offered a detailed textual analyses of the TV serial, in which I concluded that *Woju*'s erotic 'realistic' effect encourages the audience's receptivity towards a naturalized reality while the illusory satisfaction of desire it provides gives the audiences a refuge from the reality it displaces with a new mediatized spectacle of erotic and moral gratification (Hung, 2011).

A good example of this occurs in the sequence of Haizao and Song's first 'sex' scene, which Song has orchestrated and to which Haizao, somewhat reluctantly, has submitted. The scene takes place in episode 12, one-third into a 35-hour-long serial. By this moment in the drama, the audience should know that Song is corrupt. Because his crimes lack the dangerous edge in those TV serials that the State Administration of Radio, Film, and Television (SARFT) labels 'anti-corruption' dramas, his romantic gallantries seduce the audience, which tolerates his shortcomings.

Significantly, this 'sex' scene took place on a Christmas evening – a festive time that modern society has turned into an occasion for a months-long shopping spree. The first sex scene takes place after Haizao 'borrows' RMB 60,000 – this is the down payment on Haiping's new apartment – from Song, knowing that she has no means to repay the loan. After a few shots established Haizao's resistance to Song's sexual advances, the sequence shifts to Haizao and Song having sex on a carpeted floor. Although the plot places the copulating couple at the centre of the drama, the TV screen does something else. As soon as the drama suggests that sex is taking place, the screen size shrinks by two-thirds and creates two extra screens. One shows Xiaobei waiting anxiously for Haizao in their apartment, another shows Mrs Song busying herself with housework while waiting for Song to come home. This arrangement of screens opens up a space of relative calm that submerges, pacifies and outweighs the 'sin' of the couple's infidelity. This is one possible interpretation, which the shot arrangement supports; the rhetoric of the drama in no way insists that we should make, from the outset, any moral judgement on this sexual exchange. In fact, moral ambiguity is what the serial encourages. Soon after the end of this sex scene, the voice-over enters into the consciousness of Song:

> Song finds himself very indecent. Under the effect of alcohol, he exposes his life-battered body in front of an innocent young lady. He likes [Haizao]. Yet, why must [he] translate his feelings for her into a bodily possession? Why must he leave darkness and uncertainty to this young woman who touches [his] heart? (Episode 12)

Any excitement or indignation that the audience might have felt ends with a clear-headed voice pulling back abruptly from passionate sex. Such evasiveness and withdrawals are characteristic of the drama's attitude toward what should clearly be a relationship of corruption. Later on, in the final moments of the drama, when Song learns that Haizao is pregnant with his child, he again looks serious as he half-kneels on the floor, persuading Haizao to give birth to their child despite their proscriptive relationship. It is a moment that the camera sets Song off at his most romantic, charismatic and seductive, and it should now be easy for the audience – and even the elder sister Haiping – to imagine how Haizao has all the reasons to fall for him. All the while, the fact that their 'romance' and 'love' are by-products of a most corrupted trade and exchange remains sidetracked.

Woju is a hybrid that combines two broad types of fantasy. Like a melodrama, it offers a fantasy of erotic desire in the form of a romance and some suggestively sexual dialogues. It also creates a fantasy of an aestheti-cized and normalized reality, keeping at bay not so much the repressiveness of the strict economic and political hierarchies but genuine curiosity about the possibilities for alternative ways of living. In this context, it is no coinci-dence that rather than paying a sustained attention on other such social and political problems as corruption and high housing price that Woju raised, the audience quickly seized upon the xiaosan as a 'juicy topic' and made it the cause of a particular kind of popular criticism. These popular criticisms, in turn, aroused and exploited the audience's voyeuristic desire that shifts critical consciousness, mistakenly, into a narrow puritanical and moralistic chauvinism often found in journalistic reviews and popular cultural criticism. Albeit unconsciously, they created an opportunity for the State to orches-trate conflicting discourses and competing critical desires that, collectively downplay, and make thin the drama's potential queries about post-socialist

China's political practices, moral guidelines, social realities and cultural landscapes. In an interview (*Nanfang Weekly*), Liu Liu, the author of *Woju*, explained the sequence of events leading to *Woju*'s sudden disappearance from *Beijing TV Youth Channel*, which rebroadcast the drama:

> On November 15, 2009, a post entitled "Torrents of Thunderbolts, the Most Obscene TV Drama Dialogues in History: *Woju*" appeared in Tianya. com [an online discussion forum]. It clips and displays all "bone-baring" conversations [between Song Siming and Haizao]. It recorded eleven hundred thousand visits in three days and some three thousand responses. The government could no longer tolerate [*Woju*] and criticized it for its "negative impact upon society," saying "it relies on cooking up sex and corruption in government offices to achieve high audience rating."

Woju not only soared in the media-market but also came through the first round of broadcast across the country intact. To do so, it needs the ability to pass through three institutions. First, it must capture the profit-oriented media and mass culture, tactically with sensationalist dialogues and scenes. Second, it must capture the attention of a responsive, internet-based popular criticism that functions and matters not so much qualitatively but quantitatively. Finally and most importantly, it must satisfy the demands of a rapidly developing party-state machine that combines strategies of neoliberal governmentality with socialist authoritarian high-handedness. In this sense, *Woju*'s popular reception reflects the problem of consumer-based culture. Not only did the serial enjoy huge popularity, it benefited from the SARFT's strategic tolerance – strategic because, according to the website Danwai, the SARFT 'slipped' the drama through its guidelines only when cultural critics were busy sensationalizing and 'sexing' up *Woju*. As soon as online discussions looked beyond sex and the city, the SARFT hastened to criticize *Woju* for exploiting the themes of sex and official corruption to increase profits. In other words, popular critics' little attention to such less sensationalized topics as official corruption and the bubble economy, in comparison to the overwhelmingly negative attitude toward the merely suggestive sexual dialogues, demonstrated the absence of both serious criticism and state-sanctioned critical practices. As long as the serial served merely the purposes of eroticizing the norm, the state tolerated it. Once that eroticization turned desire towards the problems of politics and corruption, the state moved to censor it. But the state need not have worried for the series normalized the consumerism of the Chinese Communist Party's (CCP) vision for the PRC.

The explosive popularity of *Woju*, and the audience's sympathetic attitude toward Haizao's role as a *xiaosan* suggest that there are issues more at stake than the problem of mass-marketed cultural criticism and production. Although, as some Durkheimian reflectionist theorists might suggest, popular culture is no more than an expression of broadly shared values of a mass audience, it is nonetheless, only one factor among many that guide production decisions. That is, as much as *Woju* 'reflects' the ideological vacuum and nihilism of the post-Deng generations of Chinese people, it is equally true that an engaged audience reacts to and uses the collective sentiment, the Gramscian 'hegemony', that *Woju* manufactures. The *xiaosan* figure as *Woju* portrays it, for example, comes from the debris of common sense; its re-appearance and re-cognition in *Woju* requires it to engage audience as more than what is entrenched in popular consciousness.

Indeed, the *xiaosan* is the material anchor of this story of corruption and the way the series uses her imposes upon the critic the obligation not to double that effect. Within the tale, she presents herself as an erotic satisfaction to a set of recognizable desires. The series itself, melodramatically, makes a spectacle of her body, her sex and her outlook precisely as she makes a 'spectacle' of herself inside this romance of commodified desire. The series transforms romance into erotic spectacle, doubling the eroticism of commodity fetishism in the market exchange of the *xiaosan*. Everywhere, the series doubles the satisfaction it offers in response to the desire it arouses; it does the work of capital in the new China in this doubling. The series has been enormously successful in leading internet and other commentators to duplicate and to extend this machine. Responsible critical commentary, such as we attempt here, cannot easily escape that machine if it also indulges in explication or close reading of especially those scenes and images that most concretely embody the double action of the woman satisfying her man at the same time as the video satisfies the audience with its soft-core replacement for real critical thought.

Post-Mao-Deng TV Realism and the Limits of Imagination

New media culture is the marketplace of collective sentiment, with the intermediation between culture and popular values as the one element that ultimately defines both. Any analysis of the popular reception of *Woju*'s Haizao must treat the negotiable nature of this dialectical relationship in which TV drama inscribes its logics into the everyday lives from which it already emerges to create its reality effect. In a widely circulated internet post, a netizen by the name of Wang Feng suggests an answer to the question:

[*Woju*] describes the cruelty of life most realistically. As the gap between the rich and the poor widens, [...] sexual resources are increasingly flowing towards the powerful and wealthy. Some say that we have arrived at the era in which money serves as the frame of reference for all values: the kind and number of women a man can get is directly in proportion to how much money and power one has. This is widely practiced in entertainment circles and among students of performing arts, reflected in the unwritten rules of university campuses, and testified to by the number of mistresses corrupt government officials keep. Contemporary Chinese society, having been heavily exposed to the situation since the late-1980s, has become used to it and is ignoring the way the wealthy and powerful monopolize sexual resources. This is where the cruelty of *Woju* lies; it shows a good case of how money and power together beat up an urban male [i.e. Xiaobei], who is young, honest, and hardworking but having little access to the social, political, and economic resources that the powerful monopolizes (Cited in Xin, 2009).

The ethos of the twenty-first century Wang describes helps our understanding of *Woju*'s success. For contemporary China, post-socialist and secular, the end of a century stands for a voyage of hope. *Times Weekly* (Elliott, 2007) sees the post-Olympic China as one that is 'striding onto the global stage and acting like a nation that very much intends to become the world's next great power'. Indeed, the Olympic spectacle and the country's spectacular victory in the Games are talismanic for not only China's rising global status but also its neoliberal policies and transformations that have once created national and local dilemmas. Because of the country's legendary economic growth, the Chinese people have become less preoccupied with the contradictions created by the so-called 'socialism with Chinese characteristics'. Rather, they have shown a remarkable tolerance with such post-socialist reality as dramatic disparities in wealth, sharper class divisions and state violence. The National Museum on Tiananmen Square, once the CCP's exclusive showplace of the revolution's victory over capitalist exploiters, recently reopened after a four-year renovation for an exhibition on Louis Vuitton, celebrating the brand's twentieth anniversary in China and its '157 years of creativity and craftsmanship'(*The Wall Street Journal*, 2011). No longer remembered as a place for the inauguration of the PRC and, more recently, for the Chinese state's violence against its students and people, Tiananmen Square has what the museum's director, Chen Lüsheng, calls 'a fresh new identity' (*Global Times*, 2011).

Gong Haiyan, an employee of *Jiayuan.com* (a matchmaking website), although thinking that society should not define women as a 'sexual resource', believes that the show reflects contemporary China's marriage market and the attitude toward women it contains. She says in an interview with *Times Weekly*, '25-year-old boys usually want to date girls of their age. But a mid-thirties man won't want to date women in the same age range; he chases after girls in their twenties. Most of the mature, successful men who come here looking for partners have had some experience of rejection. They want to make up for their hurt feelings now that they have successful careers' (Xin, 2009). In the same interview, Gong makes an important point about the influence popular dramas and media opinions have on the masses: 'All the male characters acting in the popular dramas and who have grown up with the post-1980s generation have the same traits: they are mature, romantic, and rich. Love is always found within the framework of such Cinderella-meets-prince, dream-like, narratives' (Xin, 2009). In clearest terms, Gong sums up the situation of China's marriage market: what makes an ideal partner is above all money and power.

No doubt, the circumstances of contemporary China and its marriage market have served as the foundation of *Woju*'s conception of the *xiaosan* figure. In this context, we can understand why the audience has a sympathetic attitude toward Haizao. It would be simplistic, however, for the discussion to stop at the analysis of text-context relations, notwithstanding the common-place consensus in popular criticism that the TV series is a realistic portrayal of contemporary Chinese urban life and that its realism has an insistently critical edge. Given that this response is a result of the 'realism effect' of the series art, the question arises, how does *Woju* simultaneously manufacture such provocative images of the *xiaosan* as a generic social type while placing her within a narrative that ruins her? The answer lies in the realism effect that Barthes teaches us to recognize as itself a product of art. To explain how this works, I want to elaborate on the sequence of *Woju*'s ending. It concludes with an open, uncontroversial lesson about how Haiping's day-to-day regular work rather than what Haiping calls a 'shortcut' is the key to social success. Nearing the end of the drama, Haiping sums up the daily life of her generation in a series of numbers:

A bunch of numbers jumps out from my head [...] each morning: 6,000 Yuan for mortgage; 2,500 Yuan for food, clothes, and daily necessities; 1,500 Yuan for Ran Ran's [Haiping's daughter] nursery school fees; 600 Yuan for gifts and social activities; 580 Yuan for transportation; 300–400 Yuan for property fees; 250 for mobile phone bills; and also 200 Yuan for gas, water, and electricity fees. In other words, counting from the first breath I gasp in each morning, I will need to make at least 400 Yuan a day. This is my cost of life in this city.

This is a grand romance of the sordid business of surviving everyday life within a new regime of intense corruption and markets. The strength of *Woju*'s ending lies in the tensions between two competing forces: traditional and modern values, especially those concerning social success and a moral sense, coexist within post-Mao-Deng China. What *Woju* portrays is a version of contemporary Chinese urban life against which the meaning of social and political success no longer depends on one's ideological aspirations and revolutionary romanticism. In the new China, life's meaning depends on the ability to orient a balanced marketized life defined by transactions, costs, and balance sheets – by the illusion that the human subject is a free rational agent producing value through informed decisions. The Haiping Chinese Language School, for example, is the tangible reward of Haiping's work ethics and a token of her 'patriotism'. She who, in the course of earning extra money for her mortgage, has found teaching Chinese to Westerners a virtuous business and her responsibility as a Chinese citizen. Yet, a question on the status of the two sisters' sexuality must arise here: What makes one sister trade her sex in one way and the other sister in another way? Although Haiping's sex seems to be of the right kind – repression to the national project, Haizao too does what the nation demands even if it is tragic, for corruption and the *xiaosan* are also part of the new China. Song is the so-called '*cong-er-dai*' (poor second generation) who is a person of nouveau riche status and so buys the girl's body and social value for himself and his needs.[5]

Woju's realism clearly is not that of 'socialist realism'– sometimes-called 'critical' or 'revolutionary' realism – that has dominated modern Chinese literary history, nor does it follow the May Fourth agenda of reformist realism. There is no way to generalize from either Haizao or Haiping to the Chinese urban-dwellers and position them against the specifics of contemporary Chinese history, in which the characters can be bearers of a radical political impetus or a social message for reform. This is because the series allegorizes Haizao, makes her a figure, and so makes her a type. But it does so by eroticizing her so she works, as does the series, to satisfy the audience's uncritical desire for the life-form the show portrays and promotes. For one thing, despite the realistic portrayal through which Haizao became a *xiaosan*, her tragic ending is at once cathartic and spectacular undermining audience alignment with the preceding realism of *Woju*. While the dramatic effect pacifies the audience's instincts for moral justice, the car crash inspires awe and a visceral fear that induces the audience into a trance-like state of disbelief. In other words, while Haizao's loss of both Song Siming and motherhood shakes off the last doubt an audience might have about whether or not to sympathize with Haizao, its extremism taps into the audience's deepest desire to live Haizao's life by undermining the likeliness that such an extreme punishment will indeed happen in reality. The melodramatic nature of the ending, which contradicts the plot and external reality, blocks the development of critical perception and tragic emotion or perception on the part of the audience.

In short, the drama's realism effect undermined its critical potential and the serial gained popularity because this effect, while describing and detailing the social problems immanent in contemporary Chinese society, creates confusion about the drama's moral values – especially at the end. *Woju*'s realism effect is productive in the sense that it creates the ideological illusion that there is a plurality of conscious possibilities available in society. *Woju*'s realism moves away from older revolutionary assumptions about established practices of 'socialist' or 'revolutionary' realism that tells grand narratives about a futuristic present. The present is futurist in the sense that it is embedded with the fantasy desired future; a procedure the commodity always does via the play of desire. *Woju*'s realism, and indeed the realism of most contemporary Chinese TV serials emphasizes a real possibility of a plurality of consciousness, a kaleidoscopic composition of subjected views that is constantly shifting, shaping, and yet never in focus. This is the work of the market in life. *Woju*'s realism effect achieves its success in its open, restless, and almost inexhaustible attempt to display different modes and models of life – the kaleidoscope of the market-subject's experience. The audience, immersed in the seeming infinite openness of the drama's views of the world, consumes these only abstract 'possibilities', and takes them so utterly for granted because they are in abundance in the TV series. This realism is 'productive' for the audience and citizens who are not merely passive consumers but consumerist subjects who emerge from the process of this consumerist illusion of freedom within the market place of 'choice' and 'life-style'.

Therefore, the *xiaosan* surfaces squarely within the already saturated and uncritical space of the commodity – and her nature is part of that space. She is in and of its field. The serial privileges the triumph of the romantic love between Song Siming and Haizao, glossing over those circumstances which threaten it, or, which hold such a relationship in place. The audience responded to the *xiaosan* phenomenon as if it was a part of life, an almost inevitable piece of business in life. In effect, the drama does not elicit from the audience either moral outrage or the imagination of a new society, of new circumstances. The audience does not see the need for a new moral or political imaginary; it does not see the need for imagination itself, choosing to live instead within the conditions the serial confirms as natural and ratifies by romance. Li Nian, the actress playing Haizao, says:

> Some of my friends are like Haizao, but they are not aware of their being a *xiaosan*. Before playing in *Woju*, I couldn't understand their choice [of

---

being a *xiaosan*]. After *Woju*, I changed my mind: life has given them no alternatives. It is difficult to go back in time (*Guangzhou Daily Post*, 2010).

Since the 1980s, the post-Mao-Deng Chinese State has made plans to develop an ever-increasingly commercialized media and entertainment industry that will cohabit and collaborate with the complex ideological state institutions of market-socialism. In his attempt to answer the question 'What is Postmodernism', Jean-François Lyotard (1984, p. 81) has emphasized the link between the prefix *post-* in the term 'postmodern' and the Greek prefix *ana-*, which means recalling the immemorial to the mind. The immemorial, in the case of the post-Mao-Deng China, would mean the political extremism and ideological purity that prioritize the collective over the individual, and that glorify self-sacrifice and puritanism. If Chinese postmodernity is, as Arif Dirlik and Zhang Xudong (1997, p. 8) have rightly pointed out, 'to be grasped not only in its relationship to modernity in general but also in the relationship to a socialist and revolutionary modernity', we must understand the new sexual political-cultural economy that the *xiaosan* figure epitomizes as one that depends ultimately on *both* the State's visible hand – a new form of political totalitarianism – and the commercialism, amorality and cultural massification that post-Mao global capitalism has created. In other words, although Mao's high-handed cultural policy did not survive Deng Xiaoping's market reforms intact, and though the process of television institutionalization since the 1980s has been characteristically market-oriented, the State's effort to control its people's minds and sentiments has never really relaxed. Given the TV industry's structural relation with the State and its entangled relationships with China's mixed commercial spheres and the mass communications media, the party-state has sought only to develop that control through an approach that, overall, is infinitely more sophisticated and subtle than that of Mao's era.

Woju – a TV serial about the problem of *xiaosan*, high housing prices and corruption – exemplifies the normalizing power of popular and consumer culture over the fragmenting force of social problems and criticism. *Woju*'s realism effect not only works without essential conflicts with state censorship, it also works for the State's politics and puts serious criticism at risk by pre-empting and co-opting it within its erotics. As the figure of *xiaosan* shows, 'state interests' and 'popular culture' are not separate, self-evident and diametrically opposed categories. Rather, in the new China, these are among the differences that disappear into a flattened social cultural and intellectual world. In the new China, the two cultural sensibilities are inextricably bound to one another. *Woju*'s 'realism' does not address the role of imagination prominent in the tradition and discourse of socialist realism with which

Chinese intellectuals and popular readers grow up, nor does it direct our attention to anything interesting about the role of the imagination in contemporary Chinese visual culture.

Endnotes

1 See Zhu, Sibei (2009), 'Who should be woken up by *Woju*?', Trans. by Ren Zhongxi, *China.org.cn*, [online] 25 November 25. Available at: <*http://www. china.org.cn/opinion/2009–11/25/content_18953464.htm*>. The article first appeared in Chinese on 20 November 2009.

2 After *Woju* became a national hit, a widely circulated internet article, entitled, 'The Media Recovers *Woju*'s Historical Reference: First Male Protagonist Alludes to Qin Yu, Personal Secretary to Chen Liangyu', identifies fictional characters from *Woju* with senior CCP officials involved in the case of Chen Liangyu in 2006. Chen, former Shanghai Party Chief, took money out of Shanghai's pension fund for personal investment. The Party charged Chen with accepting 2.39 million Yuan in bribes and his personal secretary, Qin Yu, with accepting 6.8 million Yuan in bribes. The internet article identifies Song Siming, the key corrupt official in *Woju*, the fictional version of Qin Yu. See Hainan News (2009), 'The media recovers *Woju*'s historical reference: first male protagonist alludes to Qin Yu, Personal Secretary to Chen Liangyu', *Hainan News*, 4 December, Available at: <http://www.hinews.cn/news/ system/2009/12/04/010625878.shtml>; later reposted many times on nearly all the major portal websites in the Mainland. See also People.com. cn (2009), [online] 4 December. Available at: <*http://pic.people.com.cn/ BIG5/162952/162956/10511266.html*>

3 All quotations from *Woju* are my own translations from the TV drama entitled *Woju* (*Dwelling Narrowness*), first broadcast by Shanghai Dragon TV in Shanghai between 27 July and 9 August 2009; later rebroadcast by Beijing TV nationwide on 5 November 2009. It was directed by Teng Huatao; written by Teng Huatao (screenplay), Dun Cao (screenplay) and Liu Liu. Episode numbers are cited parenthetically.

4 Half of the people who participate in online polls vote for Song, the rest of the votes are shared by Xiaobei, Haizao, Haiping, and Suchun. See Ji, Mu (2010), 'An interview with Lian Si: the present condition of youths – from *Woju* to Ant Clans', *book.douban.com*, [online] 29 January. Available at: <*http://book.douban.com/review/2962892*>

5 For the definition of the term 'poor second generation', see People's Daily (2009), '"Poor 2nd generation": hot term in China', *People's Daily Online*, [online] 3 September. Available at: <*http://english.peopledaily.com. cn/90001/90776/90882/6747456.html*>

8

My Lovely Sam-soon: Absent Sex and the Unbearable Lightness of Sweet Korean Romance

Jeongmee Kim

In the late 1990s, South Korean (Korean hereafter) television drama became a cultural phenomenon throughout the East and South East Asian region and continued to be immensely popular throughout the noughties. Quickly known as Korean Wave (or *hallyu* in Korean, *haliu* in Chinese)[1] drama because of the unprecedented success and volume of exportation to neighbouring countries (including China, Japan, Mongolia, Singapore, the Philippines, Taiwan and Vietnam), Korean drama quickly had a big impact on Asian audiences. John Burton of *The Financial Times* and Norimitsu Onishi of *The New York Times* reported in 2001 and 2005 respectively how influential the wave of Korean popular culture was as it swept across the Asian cultural scene. Burton (2001, p. 4) believed its popularity abroad signified 'an important moment for the country' and Onishi (2005, p. A3) pointed out how 'the booming South Korean presence on television [...] spurred Asians to buy up South Korean goods and to travel to South Korea, traditionally not a popular tourist desti-nation.' The popularity of *hallyu* led to the strange phenomenon of Taiwanese and Chinese youths undergoing plastic surgery to look like Korean actresses such as Song Hae-gyo of *Autumn in My Heart* (KBS, 2000) and Lee Young-ae of *Daejanggeum* (*Jewel in the Palace*, MBC, 2003) fame (Shim, 2006, p. 30). In Japan, the success of the drama series *Winter Sonata* (KBS, 2002) led to the main actor Bae Yong-joon being called 'Yon-sama' by his fans (*sama* being an honorific title reserved for Japanese royalty). So numerous were these fans that the Japanese prime minister at the time, Junichiro Koizumi, was quoted as saying that 'I will make great efforts so that I will be as popular as Yon-sama and be called Jun-sama' (Onishi, 2004, p. 13). However, in spite of the fact that *hallyu* drama has become a commonplace presence on the digital, satellite and terrestrial channels of numerous Asian countries and that half of the world appears to be enjoying *hallyu* drama, outside of some vibrant online communities for Asian diasporic fans it is a form of television that remains virtually unknown in the West.

As one might expect when talking about drama, the term *hallyu* covers a lot of genres including modern day trendy drama (*Full House* (KBS, 2004) and *Lovers in Paris* (SBS, 2004)), youth-orientated melodrama (*Autumn in My Heart* and *All In* (SBS, 2003)) and historically set melodrama (*Jumong* (MBC, 2006) and *Jewel in the Palace*). This chapter will focus on Korean 'trendy drama' which as a genre capitalized on and incorporated elements from Japanese trendy drama that had been very popular in Asia in the early 1990s.[2] Just as Japanese trendy drama had done, Korean trendy drama focuses on the lives and loves of young professionals, but with added further ingredients including the pressures of family obligations and rigid Korean cultural expecta-tions for male and female behaviour (Lee, 2004, p. 269; Hirata, 2005, p. 35). This means that in contrast to the earlier Japanese trendy drama, it has a strangely dichotomous nature.

Old fashioned attitudes preside over the young modern lifestyles depicted in the dramas. In other words, Korean trendy drama deploys a conflation of modern Korean lifestyle and traditional values. Modern Korea is projected through urban settings and the enviable and fashionable lifestyles of good-looking young professionals who all adhere to the values of a bygone age in which family obligation and innocent, highly romanticized and non-physical love are paramount (Kim, 2007, p. 49). Young people behave exactly as their parents would wish them to whilst the fashionable clothes, furnishings, cafes, music, cars and apartments keep young audiences keen. As Dong-Hwan Kwon's research (2006) has demonstrated, such conservatively old-fashioned sentiment has been a highly significant factor in such dramas selling well abroad.

Angel Ling and Avin Tong's (2008, pp. 102–5) audience research reveals that Asian female audiences were especially attracted to one old-fashioned element in particular: the theme of 'pure love' which commonly appears in *hallyu* drama.[3] In Korean Wave drama, love is not about sex but about romance. Couples sleep together in the same bed and talk all night with the idea of getting naked or having sex not even occurring to them (for example, in the drama *Autumn in My Heart* the hero and heroine talk all night in bed, fully clothed and on top of the covers). Kaori Shoji, writing for *The Japanese Times* (2004) and reporting how the hit Korean TV series *Winter Sonata* brought the Korean obsession with 'pure love' (*jun-ai* in Japanese) to the nation, explains what she thought 'pure love' was:

> So what exactly is a *jun-ai* [pure love] relationship? Well, it should be platonic or, at most, include just one sexual encounter. A *jun-ai* couple should also be faced by many obstacles contrived to keep them apart and pining for a romantic reunion. *Jun-ai* quotient also rises if it's a *hatsukoi* (first love) situation—a pair who fell in love when they were 15 and somehow managed to keep those nascent emotions intact in spite of the passage of time. [...] The Japanese ... [were] convinced that the purest love comes when one has never loved before.

As lovers have usually been sweethearts since childhood (and in *Autumn in My Heart* youthful love reaches ridiculous dimensions as the hero Jin-suh is shown as a toddler gazing at the newborn heroine Eun-suh suggesting he is recognizing the love of his life), their adult sexless love is comprehensible in terms of innocent feelings. Rather than the earth moving for them, the heavens will usually fall before a young couple get around to actually consummating their love sexually. Love is spiritual, transcendental and still childishly innocent, effacing the adult sexual reality of bodily fluid swapping and genital grinding that would be off-putting to Korean family viewing and contradictory to pre-pubescent feelings. Korean Wave trendy dramas thus offer a fantasy space in which modern life is conveyed through a conservative televisual veil of oppressed (or denied) sexuality (which is a world apart from the love motels in which Korean youths commonly conduct their sexual relationships).

In 2005 *My Lovely Sam-soon* (a.k.a. *My Name is Kim Sam-soon*,[4] MBC) appeared, a drama that in several ways challenged the depiction of sex and its exclusion in *hallyu* drama, but did it so deftly and skillfully that very few people noticed its sexual content. The critical response to the series noted how realistic the female heroine Sam-soon was and how much female viewers identified and empathized with her. A weekly magazine, *Sisa Press* (2005), for example, praised the series and its depiction of the main female character Sam-soon calling her the 'Nation's Beloved Spinster'. Academic works also focused on the depiction of the character in terms of the realism of her gender portrayal and the ways in which audiences identified with her (Chung, 2007a; Hoon-Soon Kim and Mi-Sun Kim, 2008). However, it does not seem to have been sufficiently acknowledged that one of the main ways in which this particular drama was so realistic was that it depicted young people as sexually active, which is what they are in modern Korea in spite of *hallyu* drama's attempts to tell us otherwise.

While Hoon-soon Kim and Mi-sun Kim's article (2008) pointed out that Sam-soon was unusual in showing that the heroine does have sexual desires, it neglected to discuss the fact that in *My Lovely Sam-soon* she is depicted as not only having them but actually trying to act on them and that she has already acted on them in the past. Further, and most importantly, the main narrative drive of the drama is whether Sam-soon and the male hero Jin-heon will have sex or not. The sexual content of the series was never explicitly discussed in the popular press either. In my research, the only discussion of the sexual nature of the series appeared in a newspaper article (*Hankook-ilbo*, 2005) and was devoted to the 'steamy' kissing scene in episode six. It did not discuss the far more blatant sexual elements at all. As the overall critical response reflected the *hallyu* trendy drama formula of denying the existence of sex, it perhaps suggests that reviewers can be as conservative, formulaic and rigid in reading texts as producers are in creating them. This chapter hopes to rectify this critical exclusion of sex when it comes to *My Lovely Sam-soon*, as it is its inclusion that helps make it such an important, bright and witty television series.

In Korea, *My Lovely Sam-soon* was an instant hit from the moment of its first airing in June 2005, with its average rating a very healthy 37.7%[5] (at one point reaching a startling 50%) making it the fourth highest rated drama between 2000 and 2010 (*Herald Business,* 2011). Five years after the show ended, such was its popularity that it was made into a theatrical play with the same title in January 2011. The drama series did very well overseas too, with the Philippines making their own local version, *Ako si Kim Samsoon* (GMA-7), which aired in 2008.

My Lovely Sam-soon is basically a love story and tells the tale of an overweight thirty year old *pâtissier* called Sam-soon (Kim Sun-a) who, having been dumped by her boyfriend on Christmas Eve, worries that she will never again find love. By accident she meets Jin-heon (Hyun Bin), a rich, handsome and well-educated man who owns a fancy French restaurant and who is looking for a new chef. Despite continuously falling out, they gradually fall in love with each other, but several obstacles stand in their way. One is Jin-heon's ex-girlfriend who returns from America wishing to reunite. Another is Sam-soon's ex-boyfriend, Hyun-woo, who stirs up trouble. Jin-heon's mother also stands in their way as she disapproves of Sam-soon. Perhaps the biggest obstruction to their getting together, however, is Sam-soon herself who feels undeserving of love until she loses some weight. Over the course of its sixteen hourly episodes, there are misunderstandings, arguments, break-ups and tearful reconciliations until at the end, the two of them finally become a couple.

Based on the internet novel by the writer Ji Soo-hyun, *My Lovely Sam-soon* was promoted as the Korean *Bridget Jones's Diary* (dir. Sharon Maguire, 2001). Just like Renée Zellweger who had to put on weight to play the overweight Bridget, the actress Kim Sun-a put on around 5–6 kilograms prior to filming to play the eponymous heroine. The director Kim Yun-chul said that he wanted to create a British-type romantic comedy which combined fantasy and reality, referring to films such as *Notting Hill* (dir. Roger Michell, 1999) and *Bridget Jones's Diary* as his inspiration (*Joy News 24*, 2005). Kim's drama *The Swamp* (MBC) had won 'Best Television Film' at the Monte-Carlo Télévision Festival in 2004 and following this he became known as an 'arty' director (*The Kyunghyang-shinmun*, 2005) in Korea. Certain stylistic artistic flourishes are certainly detectable in *My Lovely Sam-soon*, such as his frequent use of the steadicam, but in this particular drama the artistry is less in the challenging visuals than in the challenging narrative content of the drama both in relation to the rendition of its heroine's story and, as will be discussed later, its depiction of sex.

Another important narrative strand in *My Lovely Sam-soon* is the heroine's desire to transform herself by changing her name. Sam-soon in Korea is a very old-fashioned and unsophisticated name and throughout the series Sam-soon desires to change it to a more modern and sophisticated one. The name she wants is Hee-jin, which purely by coincidence just so happens to be the name of Jin-heon's ex-girlfriend. Sam-soon is utterly determined to rid herself of her name as she thinks that it has been responsible for her bad luck with men. She also blames it for poorly shaping her destiny because she believes people have viewed her as a country bumpkin all of her life. Although she has coveted the name of Hee-jin long before she meets an actual flesh and blood Hee-jin within the drama, it is clear from the outset that Sam-soon literally wants to become somebody else. As this somebody else is soon embodied by the appearance of the traditionally beautiful, slim, stylish and sophisticated Hee-jin, the type of heroine advertised as an ideal woman by *hallyu* drama, one can conclude that this is the kind of woman she wishes she could become. However, as Jin-heon's feelings for Sam-soon develop, he goes to incredible lengths to ensure that she does not succeed in transforming herself into a 'Hee-jin'. He even goes as far as hiring private enforcers to prevent her from going to the borough council and changing her name by deed poll.

Sam-soon's attempt to transform herself (ostensibly by changing her name but symbolically by wishing to become a Hee-jin, a *hallyu* heroine and the kind of beauty paraded in television dramas) results in a *hallyu* drama somewhat remarkably reproaching *hallyu* drama for the damaging effect it can have upon women's self-esteem. Through the hero Jin-heon's resistance to Sam-soon's transformation, the undesirability of such unachievable and manufactured femininity is put forward. When towards the end of the drama Sam-soon tears up the document that will enable her to change her name (ep.16), it signifies a minor apotheosis in that she learns to love herself, her own name, her own femininity and recognizes the futility of wanting to be somebody else. The name Sam-soon becomes as important to her as it is to Jin-heon who has chosen the 'real' girl over the supposedly 'ideal' girl. The drama emphasizes its title at this moment as in Korean the name of the series more accurately translates as *My Name is Kim Sam-soon*, a title that emphasizes the female rather than the male perspective of the international English language title of *My Lovely Sam-soon*. By embracing her name, her relationship and the ownership of her own identity, the drama emphasizes also that every woman, no matter how un-pretty or unstylish, is entitled to her own love story.

Indeed, the contrast between Sam-soon and Hee-jin could not be more pronounced. Hee-jin is the first love of Jin-heon, and is not only slim but effort-lessly beautiful (to the extent that she looks fantastic even when sweating doing yoga), stylish (always looking sophisticated in designer clothes and with a fashionable hairstyle), smart (she is a medical student) and has a tragic quality to her (she has a serious illness). She is rich, lives in a huge and beauti-fully furnished apartment in the capital and drives a fancy car. Typical for a *hallyu* drama heroine, she was the childhood love of the hero Jin-heon. When they got together as adults she was a very dedicated girlfriend who cooked for him, bought his clothes and worried about his well being. Even when they split up it was, we learn, for noble reasons, as she felt she had to leave him because she did not want him to suffer or be held back because of her illness (she also honoured the request of his mother who thought separation would be best for her son). Their relationship was one of 'pure love' as it was first love, sexless, idealized and each other's needs were anticipated and accom-modated by the other almost before they arose. According to *hallyu* drama conventions, as she displays all of the credentials, the drama should logically be about her. However, in this case it is not! When, after three years apart and having largely recovered from her illness she returns to try and start the relationship with Jin-heon anew, she slowly discovers that his heart belongs to another. This other is Sam-soon. She is unstylish (often to be found in baggy t-shirts, jeans and trainers), poor, not university-educated, not particularly pretty, an overweight overeater who is constantly threatening to go on a diet and who drinks as much as the men in the drama, smokes (occasionally), older than the man who will love her and is not averse to hitting people and swearing at them. At best the comical sidekick to the heroine, this type of female character in *My Lovely Sam-soon* finally gets centre-stage.

The focus on a different type of heroine does not mean that Hee-jin was punished for being ideal however. *My Lovely Sam-soon* does not go that far. For being such a noble character there is the ideal *hallyu* drama hero for her to have a 'perfect' relationship with based upon 'pure love'. Whilst being treated for her illness in America, her doctor, Henry (Daniel Henney), falls madly in love with her. Later, when she is temporarily reunited with Jin-heon, Henry follows her to Korea, supports her and acts as her guardian angel as well as her friend. His sexless devotion and her honourable behaviour are rewarded in the drama with their ultimate sexless union and a lifetime together based on spiritual rather than physical desire (a kiss on the forehead and a peck on her lips signifying their intimate moment and their becoming a couple). They have a '*hallyu* drama' future together unlike Sam-soon and Jin-heon whose future together is far less romanticized and, in my opinion, much more interesting as a result.

The portrayal of both of these couples helps illustrate just quite how clever *My Lovely Sam-soon* actually is by contrasting the impossible ideal of 'pure love' (represented by Hee-jin and Henry) with the complexity of more everyday love (represented by Sam-soon and Jin-heon). The former couple obey all of the *hallyu* drama rules. They are devoted to each other, look great and obey their elders even when this creates problems for them. In contrast, Sam-soon and Jin-heon are a far less attractive couple, are driven more by their physical needs and are perfectly willing to deceive their elders if it means their relationship can continue. By featuring both couples, a binary opposition is set up between the typical type of romance featured in *hallyu* drama and something very different, something more sexy, selfish and more belonging to the real life of the audience than the fantasy world of *hallyu* drama and its impossibly high standards of 'pure love'.

In contrast to the saccharine-sweet romance of much *hallyu* drama and even though sex is absent for the majority of *My Lovely Sam-soon*, it is manifestly ever-present in terms of what the characters want. Both Sam-soon and Jin-heon, at different times in the drama, clearly want to sleep with the other. Indeed, neither of them are oblivious to the possibility of having sex with each other and rather than being for spiritual reasons it is purely for bodily reasons that they do not engage in intercourse. Sam-soon feels overweight and thus her low self-esteem prevents her from getting naked (ep.13). Later on in the series the lack of a condom prevents sex from occurring (ep.16). Physical reasons rather than high minded ideals or childlike innocence stand in the way of sex in this drama, most probably because this is funnier. Although romance is the driving force behind the narrative as in most *hallyu* drama, it is unresolved sexual tension that is this drama's notable difference. Rather than the two main characters having purely romantic yet sexually innocent feelings for each other, Sam-soon and Jin-heon's carnal desires are frequently put to the test when they are put in positions where they can have sex, want to have sex, but are forced to deny their urges.

Arguably then *My Lovely Sam-soon* reframes (at least in part) 'pure love' romance as the guiding principle behind the narrative, visual and auditory construction of much *hallyu* drama. As Dong-Hoo Lee (2004, p. 266) has suggested, *hallyu* trendy drama is 'image oriented' drama, and Soo-yoon Lee (2008, pp. 113–14) has argued that *hallyu* drama in general can be virtually defined through the 'pulling out all the stops' manner in which it presents a visualization of love. For example, a defining image of the drama *Spring Waltz* (KBS, 2006) is the euphoria of love being visually depicted through the hero and heroine joyfully riding on a bicycle together through a sunny field of vibrantly yellow canola flowers, a dazzlingly spectacular external display of their internal exhilaration and elation at being in love. The image of love offered could not be sweeter or more innocent. In contrast to such a depiction of romantic bliss and harmony, we have a scene in *My Lovely Sam-soon* when Sam-soon wakes up in Jin-heon's apartment after getting drunk and, assuming he would not have been a gentleman, questions him as to what he has done to her. He says he has not done anything and enquires as to why he would have wanted to as she has thrown up on her own face and wet herself. Hardly a beautiful, sweet image! When Sam-soon and Jin-heon's moment of romantic realization finally does come, when he openly admits his feelings for her, it is an antithetical image to the transcendental, visually sumptuous expressions of love found in the likes of *Spring Waltz* as their 'moment' occurs in a men's public toilet.[6] Yet although it does not offer an attractive 'visualization of love', rather wonderfully, it is still a moment that is clearly just as sincere and important to them both as the *Spring Waltz* bike ride is to that drama's couple. It also underlines that most of us do not have the opportunity to have a first kiss in the snow by a beautiful frozen lake (*Winter Sonata*) or have a first dance in a field full of flowers (*Spring Waltz*). The Sam-soons watching the show can recognize that 'pure love' is highly unlikely (because just how many of us really marry our childhood sweethearts or resist each other physically for years) whereas real love can find expression in the strangest of places. Despite her obvious failings, as the drama continues we as an audience begin to learn, along with the hero, why

Sam-soon is lovely after all, that love is largely idiosyncratic, that beauty is in the eye of the beholder and that she is as deserving of happiness and love as any of the 'pure' blemish free and rake-like beauties that populate *hallyu* drama.

As aforementioned, Sam-soon is not the hero's childhood sweetheart and nor is he her first love. In fact, these bastions of *hallyu* drama relationship construction are only of concern to other, unsympathetic characters rather than the couple at the centre of the drama. Sam-soon's jealous ex-boyfriend, Hyun-woo, blurts out to Jin-heon that he slept with her first and that he was her first man (ep.7). As Brenda Chan (forthcoming) in her analysis of the trendy drama *Wedding* (KBS, 2005) explains, *hallyu* drama tends to offer highly traditional gender roles. Previous sexual encounters, particularly on the part of women, signify a problem in that the female character is depicted as feeling guilty and ashamed of her indiscretion.[7] Yet in *My Lovely Sam-soon*, rather than this being a shocking revelation for the hero as something that besmirches Sam-soon's reputation or will damage his feelings for her, an argument ensues wherein he actually defends her honour, eventually fighting Hyun-woo for his boorish behavior rather than because he is angry at hers. Rather than admonishing her for being a loose woman afterwards and slipping from the 'pure love' ideal, he instead unlocks his own secrets to her about how he killed his brother and his brother's wife in a car accident that, as he was driving, he feels responsibility for. Thus, his knowledge of her previous physical intimacy is responded to with emotional intimacy on his part rather than jealousy.

One can view the fight as not only about her but more broadly as against the kind of offensively masculine sexual bravado displayed by Sam-soon's ex-boyfriend. As a modern man it is simply of no concern for Jin-heon that she has had a previous lover, although within the conventions of *hallyu* drama it should be a revelation of seismic proportions. As he has no problem with the fact that his relationship with Sam-soon will not be 'pure love', it renders the 'pure love' ideal unideal as it cannot accommodate somebody's past or overcome an ill-chosen romantic liaison. This exposure of 'pure love' as the stuff of fantasy and drama is quite a departure from the generic conventions of much *hallyu* drama and its conservative and patriarchal depiction of the social and cultural sexual norm whereby females abstaining from sex is the primary signifier of their 'goodness' and status as a worthy heroine.

In *My Lovely Sam-soon*, rather than obliviousness to sex, it is abstinence that is the defining feature of the central couple's relationship. So humorous is it that two mature adults should be oblivious to sex that at times the drama pokes fun at the *hallyu* convention by parodying it through the naïve responses of a woman who, as sexually experienced, really should not be so naïve. Episode 13 offers one such case in point as it features an amusing seduction scene in which Sam-soon responds to the sexual overtures of Jin-heon with such mystification and bewilderment that she comes across as comically slow on the uptake rather than 'pure'.

In episode seven it is revealed that when Jin-heon lost his brother and sister-in-law in the car crash he went to the top of Mount Halla (the second highest mountain in Korea) to try to get over the tragedy. In episode 13 and following his example, Sam-soon, on her thirtieth birthday, goes to the top of the same mountain in order to get over something too, her relationship with Jin-heon himself, and thereafter begin the start of a new chapter in her life. On the stormy summit, she shouts into the wind 'I am going to live as Hee-jin. I am no longer Sam-soon', but to her amazement a voice from the wind replies 'You can't do that. I like Sam-soon!' Initially believing the voice to be a result of her tiredness and hunger, she is then taken aback by the sight of Jin-heon standing there in the middle of the beating rain. He immediately begins to take care of the exhausted and starving Sam-soon who, having acted on a whim, had undertaken the grueling climb up the mountain completely unprepared. In the process of feeding her, he reveals that he has also brought seaweed soup, which is traditionally given to Koreans on their birthdays, and she is deeply touched that he remembered and went to the trouble to bring it. Consequently, the scene becomes far more romantic in tone with the couple gazing at each other accompanied by soft, romantic music. Another tonal shift quickly ensues though when, with a cheeky grin, Jin-heon tells her that she will need to eat plenty in order to build up the energy she will need much later on. It is clear from his expression and the manner of his delivery what he is referring to, yet she appears confused by the innuendo and completely unaware of his sexual insinuation. However, the following scene suggests that she finally understood what he was getting at. The camera pans across a hotel room where clothes are scattered everywhere and moaning is coming from where we imagine the bed must be. We also hear her saying 'It hurts. It really hurts' and 'Please, gently' in between her groans. 'Don't exaggerate. Please stay still' we hear him reply. When the panning camera finally reaches the bed, it is revealed that he is only massaging her legs to relieve a muscle pain she developed from climbing the mountain. Comical music then begins which accentuates the sexless nature of what the scene has immediately become, removing the sexual tension that had existed for the few moments it had taken for the camera to reach the bed.

However, after releasing the sexual tension, the possibility of sex immediately reoccurs because, as he insinuated on the mountain, Jin-heon is in the mood for sex. Sam-soon, who after what seems like an eternity realizes what his intentions are, explains that sex is not on the table because she wants to lose weight first, desiring to lose at least 5kg. She informs him that he has to wait until she achieves her target weight and when he asks her how long this will take she estimates two to three months. Jin-heon, in one sense, behaves like a typical *hallyu* hero by being considerate and understanding regarding her feelings about her weight issues. Yet he also behaves untypically by being totally appalled by the length of time he is being asked to wait until he can have sex. The discussion transforms into a quarrel and adult sex takes a back-seat to childish bickering, presented in a comical fashion as the couple regress to behaving like two children by rolling around in the bed fighting, immaturely wrestling rather than maturely sexually writhing. Eventually she kicks him off the bed and he hurts himself which results in him being incapable of having sex anyway. Even though the end result is abstinence, which we have come to expect from *hallyu* drama, Jin-heon's sexual desire is clearly revealed. Sam-soon's is also then established when, after insisting he sleep on the floor, she confesses that if he were with her on the bed all night she would not be able to resist him. Her sexual attraction is expressed in a frank way when she explains that 'she has been starved for a long while' (meaning she has not had sex for a long time) and as a result 'inside she is crying' (meaning that she too is frustrated at having to wait so long to have sex with him).

In the final episode Sam-soon and Jin-heon meet after several months of separation and end up in bed together in Jin-heon's apartment. When they are about to have sex, Sam-soon insists that she wants him to say 'I love you' to her as a condition to their consummation taking place. This leads to another delay. They again fight like children and Sam-soon finally squeezes out 'I love you' from him (literally as she has to strangle him). The condition to respectable sex occurring being met (any sex that now happens is in a loving relationship), we next see them under a moving duvet suggesting that something of a sexual nature is happening, although it is so totally obscured by the duvet that not even a hair, arm or foot is visible. Then Sam-soon's face emerges from the top of the duvet and she asks him 'Do you have it?' He says no and so she orders him to go out and buy some condoms as she does not want to get pregnant. This creates yet another delay to sex. In the next sequence, Jin-heon is seen walking around all-night shops with little success. The pharmacy is closed and some convenience stores that do stock condoms have sold out. In one store the last one is snatched by another customer right in front of him. When Jin-heon finally tracks down the elusive packet of condoms and comes back home, Sam-soon has fallen fast asleep. Then the scene shifts tone to a romantic one as Jin-heon confesses his feelings to the sleeping Sam-soon (and more importantly to the audience as we are the ones listening).

In the morning, in spite of Jin-heon and Sam-soon finally facing up to their feelings for each other, they still have not yet had sex. Further, another obstacle to their union remains – his mother's disapproval. In order to overcome this final hurdle to their being together, Jin-heon lies to his mother that Sam-soon is pregnant. Seeing through the ruse, his mother calls his bluff by stating that they should all go and see the family doctor for a check-up. In something of a panic in the next scene, Jin-heon announces to Sam-soon that 'We need to make a baby right now' and drags her off by the arm to his apartment. Although Sam-soon is reluctant to get pregnant before the wedding, Jin-heon insists that this is the only way to get his mother's approval for their marriage.

The following scene is reminiscent of the earlier scene after the mountaintop with the camera again panning across a room revealing clothes on the floor and moving towards the bed. We eventually see Jin-heon and Sam-soon lying in bed but completely covered up with bedding so that only their heads are poking out. Unlike the earlier scene that suggested sex was occurring but revealed it not to be, this one reveals that sex has indeed occurred. Yet the act of sex which had been built up towards for so long is comically undercut. Both look completely exhausted rather than loved-up and both have tissues pushed up their nostrils because they have both suffered nosebleeds, signi-fying the effort that has been put into trying to make a baby. When Sam-soon points out how long they have been at it by saying 'Honey, it's dawn', Jin-heon can hardly muster his reply of 'yeap!' As the camera continues to move slowly towards the couple, Sam-soon wonders 'Has Sam-sin Hal-mae been here for us?' (Sam-sin Hal-mae is a Korean fairy godmother-like figure who grants couples their wish to have a baby). Jin-heon again hardly manages a reply. Sam-soon then gives voice to her worry: 'What if we do not get pregnant after all this?' The camera by this time has now reached an extreme close-up of the exhausted Jin-heon's face who realizes (with tired horror) that they need to have even more sex. The duvet covers are then pulled up over the couple again.

The following scene features the couple having a well-earned sleep in bed. Sam-soon is woken by the sound of a television and, following the sound, finds her dead father sitting in the living room watching a football game. She says 'What are you doing here?' He says 'What on earth are you doing in someone else's house?' Sam-soon feels awkward that her father knows what has just happened but he then asks her 'Are you happy?' When she responds that she is he says 'As long as you are happy. That is the most important thing'. He approves and obviously that is her dream.

At the end of the drama, sex does take place (albeit sex for reproductive rather than non-procreative, recreational pleasure) and the hero and heroine become a couple. Yet whilst her father approves of their being together, his mother never comes around which leads to an ambiguous conclusion to the series. A family photograph of Sam-soon and Jin-heon with triplets appears on the wall of his apartment. It suggests that the fairytale ending has been achieved and that Sam-soon now has her perfect family, that Sam-sin Hal-mae was there for them and that the sex was reproductively successful. However, then Sam-soon's voiceover explains that this is another dream, an unfulfilled one, as she says that Sam-sin Hal-mae did not grant their wish for a baby that night. Despite the picture-perfect family image being proven to be false and the fact that the sex did not produce a baby, it clearly at least acted as a consummation of love as the last shot is of the couple holding hands and walking together up a long flight of stairs that represents their future journey together through life. They stop half-way up and kiss, ending the drama, their final static pose accompanied by Sam-soon's voiceover that they will live for the moment and that she will love herself more. Still childless, still unmarried, still overweight and still disapproved of, it is an ending for Sam-soon that promises nothing but also has all the possibilities of a real problem-filled relationship open before her. Even though the drama threatens throughout to contain her and make her abide by the conventions of the genre (even to the extent of tempting her with the same name of the more traditional heroine), she resists throughout or at the most, only partly concedes. She remains Sam-soon who to her partner is lovely, and to the audience is recognized as lovely too because of her big heart, even if she never quite fits in to the template of 'lovely' demanded by the genre.

Two articles (Chung, 2007b; Hoon-Soon Kim and Mi-Sun Kim, 2008) that discuss whether *My Lovely Sam-soon* is a feminist text or not rather sit on the fence as to whether the series challenges or bolsters Korean patriarchal attitudes and values. On the one hand it could be argued Sam-soon is taught self-worth by a man, but on the other it could be argued that she recognizes that her own self-worth is not dependent on how others see her (as a result of her name) nor on how she looks (she never loses her weight). However, I think the drama asks even bigger questions than how the battle of the sexes is fought because it is as inward looking as it is outward, recognizing that there is a relationship between the impossible values that are sold to people by the conventions of *hallyu* drama and the ways such values impact upon people's lives. To a certain extent the drama obeys the conventions of its genre as characters avoid having sex and are aware of family responsibility by wishing to please their parents. At the same time, however, the hero and heroine want to have sex, are prepared to deceive their parents in order to make everybody happy and make the audience laugh at the ways in which they rather childishly go about trying to make love (perhaps with as much fumbling ineptitude as the naïvely unworldly *hallyu* heroes and heroines would if they were ever allowed to touch each other with sexual intimacy).

Indeed, so well-drawn was the character of Sam-soon that the show is still referred back to as a yardstick of realism (although its relative sexual explicitness remains overlooked) in more recent discussions of female characters in more contemporary trendy dramas such as *Secret Garden* (Hwas & Dam Pictures, 2010), *Scent of Women* (SBS, 2011–) and *Protect the Boss* (SBS, 2011–) (*Weekly Hankook,* 2011). In the process of telling its tale the drama critiques many of the values of *hallyu* drama by relegating pure love and idealized heroes and heroines to the sidelines, and suggesting that the imperfect relationship at its centre is a more achievable and perhaps ultimately more honest and accepting form of love than the untarnished 'pure' imaginary at the heart of the make-believe world of *hallyu* drama.

Endnotes

1 For a detailed discussion of the origins of the term 'the Korean Wave,' see Jeongmee Kim (2007), 'Why does *hallyu* matter?: the significance of the Korean Wave in South Korea', *Critical Studies in Television*, 2, (2), 47–59. Various Romanized versions of the term *hallyu* exist including *hanryu* and *hanliu.*

2 For detailed discussions of Japanese trendy drama and its cultural context, see Koichi Iwabuchi ed. (2004), *Feeling Asian Modernities: Transnational Consumption of Japanese TV Dramas.* Hong Kong: Hong King University Press and Gabriella Lukács (2010), *Scripted Affects, Branded Selves: Television, Subjectivity, and Capitalism in 1990s Japan.* Durham and London: Duke University Press.

3 Yukie Hirata (2008, p. 149) found that middle-aged Japanese fans enjoyed other old fashioned elements in *hallyu* drama too such as the desirable and nostalgic depictions of family relationships.

4 As this is a literal translation of the Korean title, I have followed the convention of placing the surname before the forename. In this chapter, directors and actors names also follow this word order as this is how they are known within Asia and in on-line communities.

5 Specifically this rating means that 37.7% of households with a television set tuned in to watch the series.

6 Young-Hee Chung (2007a) points out that toilets feature quite a lot in this drama and, as this is a space not typically shown in Korean dramas, that this unusual aspect adds to its reality effect.

7 Chan relates how in the drama the female heroine's premarital sexual experience presents the main obstacle to the couple realizing true love. She asserts that it is ultimately a 'redemption narrative' in which the female protagonist is eventually forgiven by her saintly husband for not being a virgin and is tamed and transformed into a traditional housewife.

PART THREE

TV Sex and Heritage: Sexual Representation and Re-presentation

9

'Why Should I Hide My Regard?': Erotic Austen

Jonathon Shears

1

The following chapter examines the use and reconstruction of the erotic content in television and film adaptations of Jane Austen's novels *Pride and Prejudice* (1813), *Sense and Sensibility* (1811) and *Northanger Abbey* (1818). The chapter will argue that the sexual behaviour of Austen's central male and female figures in the novels is contained by codes of courtship that were designed to uphold social standards in the Regency. In film and TV adaptation, I will argue, these codes are restructured in order to control erotic feelings in different ways, primarily to make them appear consistent throughout the story. For readers unfamiliar with the adaptations, I will primarily focus the argument on several case studies, whilst ranging into other scenes. In Joe Wright's 2005 adaptation of *Pride and Prejudice*, the case studies in question are two Ballroom scenes – the Lucas' Ball in which the main characters are initially introduced, and the Netherfield Ball where Lizzie (Keira Knightley) and Darcy (Matthew Macfadyen) dance for the first time – and Lizzie's encounter with Caroline Bingley (Kelly Reilly) in the study at Netherfield. In the *Sense and Sensibility* adaptation of 1996 by Emma Thompson and Ang Lee, I will be looking at the scenes where Colonel Brandon (Alan Rickman) unsuccessfully attempts to woo Marianne Dashwood (Kate Winslet) early in the adaptation and the conversation between Elinor Dashwood (Emma Thompson) and Lucy Steele (Imogen Stubbs), when Lucy reveals her engagement to Edward Ferrars (Hugh Grant). The chapter will conclude by comparing Maggie Wadey's *Northanger Abbey* adaptation for the BBC in 1986 with Andrew Davies' 2007 adaptation for ITV's Jane Austen season. In both cases I will be focusing primarily on the opening sequences and the use of dream vision to reveal Catherine Morland's sexual desires.

2

Jane Austen became sexy in 1995 when Andrew Davies' screenplay of *Pride and Prejudice* first aired on BBC television. At least, we can date this as the birth of 'the Darcy phenomenon', Lisa Hopkins' (2001, p. 120) memorable term for the media response to Colin Firth's muscular portrayal of the character who has become Austen's keynote male figure. Davies and Firth give the viewer a Darcy who fences to release his sexual frustration, swims to 'cool off' and is happy to drip dry in breeches and a linen shirt after diving into the lake at Pemberley. Hopkins felt that this adaptation was unashamed in appealing to women, and that it appropriated the language of the cinematic gaze for a female audience, inverting as it did so, the association of the camera with the male point of view: 'what the camera picks out [...] is primarily how *men* are seen' (*ibid.*, p. 113).

Davies was by no means parsimonious, however, in spreading around the erotic content and sexual display throughout the cast. He acknowledged that Elizabeth's tomboyish behaviour was presented in the miniseries as 'a coded way of Jane Austen telling us she's got lots of sexual energy' and that 'this is probably what appeals to Darcy' (Birtwistle and Conklin, 1995, p. 4). Jennifer Ehle, playing Elizabeth Bennet, was still primarily associated with her sexually explicit performance as the platinum blond Calypso in Ken Taylor's 1992 adaptation of *The Camomile Lawn*, while Julia Sawalha, at the age of twenty-six, was cast in the role of the fifteen-year-old Lydia Bennet who elopes with Mr Wickham (Adrian Lukis). Sex was also very much part of the milieu of Emma Thompson's 1996 adaptation of *Sense and Sensibility*. This was not only because, as Cheryl L. Nixon (2001, p. 35) has argued, the viewer gets 'extra Edward and Brandon' in the physical display of romantic feeling that makes the two characters more convincing as love interests for Elinor and Marianne, but also due to Hugh Grant's arrest for lewd conduct in a public place during filming.

Jane Austen on screen in the 1990s was, we could argue, only catching up with the Austen that gender theory had been recasting for several years previously. Eve Kosofsky Sedgwick's 'Jane Austen and the Masturbating Girl' (1993, pp. 109–28) most sensationally represented the irritability and abstractedness of Marianne Dashwood and Edward Ferrars as emblematic of autoerotic behaviour. Marianne is a girl who can't sit still, while Edward's 'desponding turn of mind' results from 'an improperly supervised youth' (*ibid.*, p. 122). Here we find that 'energy' also equates with sexual feelings, but the problem for the screenwriter exists in the fact that the erotic life that we recognize most readily in Austen's men and women is primarily a matter of interiority, exclusivity and self-inspection: 'Austen's position in the history of the novel is due, in part, to her mastery of techniques for the representation of the inner life, or interior consciousness' (Wiltshire, 2001, p. 78). Attempts to make Austen heroines speak their mind, or find techniques for representing the erotic inner life that work on screen, have proved a challenge for directors like Joe Wright and Emma Thompson. Thompson was, for example, heavily criticized by Rebecca Dickson (2001, p. 56) for misrepresenting Elinor as a woman who damagingly represses her sexual feelings (presumably without having recourse to the self-instructed pleasure of Sedgwick's Marianne) in a way that ultimately leads her to break down publicly or 'come emotionally unglued'. What offends so deeply here? It is Thompson's apparently uncritical insinuation that the exploration of erotic feelings are healthful and that Elinor's self-control and self-regulation in the novel equates to a lack of depth or miserliness of feeling – something that Tony Tanner (1986, p. 100) and Sue Parrill (2002, pp. 18–19) believe is a misguided representation of the novel – which is to privilege Marianne's, and not Austen's, view that her sister should be more open about her romantic side.

The specific concern that we are facing here is the way that directors have sacrificed the rigorous balance of Austen's courtship heroines in the novels, thus coarsening the lines of socialized Regency sexuality, in favour of either 'the imprint of modern feminism' or other 'substitutive means' that reconstruct interpersonal relationships within the novels into an over-simplified on-screen vocabulary (Wiltshire, 2001, p. 91). Roger Garis (1968, p. 61) represents the received view of the *Sense and Sensibility* novel, maintaining that Austen's Elinor, unlike Emma Thompson's, does not need to change her well-regulated behaviour (even if this makes her a less interesting or sexy character) while Marianne learns that management of her wayward emotions is seemly and socially desirable. The keynote example, for Dickson (2001), of the way that this balanced social-sexual content is altered for the screen comes in a scene in Thompson's adaptation when Elinor breaks down and admits her feelings for Edward to Marianne. This is an addition made by

Thompson to the plot, and it is only after this emotional release of repressed sexual energy that Elinor's relationship with Edward Ferrars becomes a viable proposition. Earlier, at the London Ball, where Willoughby (Greg Wise) snubs Marianne she is forced into an equivalent confessional moment that *is* part of the novel, admitting to Elinor that her romantic connection to Willoughby is actually very slight: 'It was everyday implied but never declared'. Viewers will find that the emphasis has therefore switched: in the novel Elinor is rewarded for her restraint, whereas in Thompson's adaptation she is rewarded because she breaks down under duress and admits she has sexual desires for Edward.

Thompson's Elinor is repressed and needs to alter and publicly repent of her earlier attitude towards sexuality in order to gain her lover, becoming more honest and open like Marianne. The explosive breakdown of Elinor gives the viewer access to an 'inner Elinor' and a satisfaction that she nursed unspoken sexual desires all along that were akin to those that her sister felt for Willoughby. The story of Thompson's Elinor can be seen thereby as a type of therapeutic journey wherein the importance of the intricacies of such Regency issues as courtship, propriety and economic responsibility – the manifest virtues of Austen's Elinor – are relegated behind a desire to humanize the character and to bring sex out into the open. Prompted by these introductory observations, I want to argue in this chapter that television's appropriation and deployment of the sexual content of Austen's novels – we will see that camerawork, costume, body language and various types of visual symbolism all play a part alongside additions to the plot – can mean that directors sometimes neglect the importance of the social mechanisms for erotic regulation and containment that are already part of the Regency society that Austen's novels reflect and construct. As an interesting by-product of this, I believe we will discover that television adaptation of Jane Austen embeds and naturalizes a privileged sexual interiority more deeply within our responses to erotic relationships that actually cuts against the grain of much of the work of modern feminism in which gender acts are construed as performed rather than abiding.[1] It becomes apparent that the ways in which television has adapted Austen in order to regulate the erotic content that is already being socially regulated in her novels, bespeaks a contemporary need for adherence to issues such as romantic consistency, character coherence and conservatism that underlies, I will argue, the more crudely sketched attraction to the masturbatory fantasies of Darcy's body and the sexing up of female characters from Lizzie Bennet in 1995 and Marianne Dashwood in 1996, to Caroline Bingley in 2005 and Catherine Morland (Felicity Jones) in 2007.

3

While overt displays of sexual feeling may not always be punished in Austen's novels, inappropriate or gauchely constructed performances usually are. This is largely a matter of characters misreading their social expectations and responsibilities. Those who have read the exhibited signs of sexuality awry, normally in a social arena such as a ball, music party or formal meal, tend to review their actions with shame and self-rebuke. The privilege of the viewer of Austen adaptations is the access to a visual grammar of sexuality, common to all the adaptations that I consider in this chapter, that frames and attempts to codify what is already socially coded behaviour. The relationship between these codes and what it might tell us about the erotic inner life of Austen characters has yet to be sufficiently accounted for.

The regulation of Eros in Austen adaptations appears normally to be designed, we might agree with Cheryl L. Nixon (2001, p. 25), to underline Austen's socially conservative mode whereby 'the hero proves his masculinity by learning to regulate his emotions in accordance with the constraints dictated by public courtship'. The attempts made by characters to read sexual signs in social settings is paralleled by the choice of the filmmaker to redistribute erotic content on screen in order to facilitate the kind of social and psychological containment that we have seen Thompson's Elinor undergo. This holds true for television and film alike, both of which feature in this chapter, where 'the artful spectacular projection of an elite conservative vision of the national past' is inscribed (Higson, 2003, p. 233). Indeed the vogue for films made for television that has dominated Austen adaptation in recent years suggests little or no deviation in this practice across big and small screen, with the emphasis on the conservative brand of 'heritage' in the latter leading and directing the more polished, big-budget versions in the former.

In Joe Wright's 2005 feature film of *Pride and Prejudice*, for example, inappropriately exaggerated sexuality, particularly from females, becomes an index against which the performance and 'natural' appearance of Keira Knightley as Elizabeth Bennet is gauged. Wright's earthy palette of browns, faded yellow and eggshell blue points throughout to a pastoral English landscape (clearly referencing Constable in several panning shots at Longbourn) and slightly flyblown interiors, that find a correspondence in the muted browns and greys of Knightley's dresses and her unwashed hair. The same applies throughout to the other Bennet sisters who contrast sharply with their energetic but shimmering and ringletted counterparts in the Davies television series. While Davies has Lydia Bennet encounter Mr Collins (David Bamber) in her shift on the stairs of Longbourn (at which he retreats in embarrassment to the sound of girlish giggles off screen), Wright's equivalent bedchamber scene is much less titillating. Lizzie and Jane (Rosamund Pike) prepare their hair for the Netherfield Ball dressed in bodices, but any whisper of sex is averted by the water-colour blue walls, the non-diegetic chamber music and the presence of Mrs Hill (Janet Whiteside), the Bennet's maid-servant, carefully ordering clothes into neat piles at the opening of the scene. Equally, the disorder and impulsiveness that defines the actions of a character like Lydia Bennet is made sexually neutral in Jena Malone's 2005 performance. Wright places emphasis on the wilfulness of youth and the absence of makeup that shows pale skin and an uneven complexion, but he hardly keeps this distinct from the behaviour and presentation of the other sisters. Julia Sawalha's Lydia is altogether more rounded and her recklessness is signposted by overt sexual imagery: the notorious dance with Captain Denny's (David Bark-Jones) sword at the Netherfield Ball and Caroline Noble's decision to give her a 'lopsided' look in contrast to the perfect symmetry of Lizzie and Jane (Susannah Harker) to indicate emotional irregularity.[2]

If Wright's Lydia is sexed down, then Davies' Lydia invokes the wholesome (but alluring) sexuality common to the pastoral poetry of Robert Herrick's *Hesperides* or a character such as Mariette Larkin in the novels of H. E. Bates. Wright's key decision in distributing erotic content does not, however, involve the Bennet sisters at all; rather it is to be found in the associations that accrue around a more sexually aggressive portrayal of Caroline Bingley and the sexing down of Mr Wickham (Rupert Friend). Caroline's first appearance onscreen comes at the Lucas' assembly. Grimy and boisterous country dancing is interrupted by the entry of Darcy, Bingley (Simon Woods) and Caroline; a party slimmed down from chapter two of the novel, which also includes another of Bingley's sisters and her husband, Mr Hurst. The decision to exclude characters emphasizes the singularity of those that remain, as the revellers part to allow the trio to pass down the middle of the hall in silence before taking up awkwardly stylized postures in front of the fireplace. Caroline's costume places emphasis firstly on the icy paleness of her skin in contrast to artfully curled red hair dropping over one shoulder. The perfectly white ball gown with low décolletage stresses the length of her neck, while the ruffs at the shoulders and silk evening gloves correspond to the white linen neckwear of Darcy and Bingley but also to Caroline's contrived sense of poise. As Mrs Bennet (Brenda Blethyn) introduces her daughters to the Netherfield party via Mr Lucas (Sylvester Morand), Caroline's wandering eyes suggest an appropriately haughty contempt, which is later emphasized by her inspired comment to Darcy (not in the novel): 'I can't help thinking that at any point this evening someone is going to produce a piglet and we'll all have to chase it'. Switching from the point-of-view of Mr Lucas and the backdrop of revellery to a portrait shot, Wright frames Caroline with a Gothic composition of candles flickering against dark oak panels and half-empty wine glasses that encourages a view of femininity isolated, objectified and made monstrous by sexuality and sexual signifiers.[3] The dishevelled Bennet sisters could only look natural in comparison.

Reilly's Caroline is very different from her portrayal by Anna Chancellor in 1995, where Davies emphasizes the comic pomposity of the Bingley sisters through their shot silk gowns, lace and 'exotic' head-dresses (Birtwistle and Conklin, 1995, pp. 53–4). There is never a hint in the Davies adaptation that Caroline has a genuine chance of Darcy's hand or that she could arouse his ardour. The overtly sexualized performance of Reilly as Caroline goes to the other extreme and so we might expect more sexual competition, but in reality this serves to highlight her artificial sexual display in contrast to that of Knightley's Lizzie. However, the danger of paraphrasing the sexual content in this way is that it produces a false binary that encourages a misreading of the social construction of sexual interaction.

It is apparent that there exists a mismatch between the coded behaviour of flirtation – deriving from the issues of propriety and decorum I mentioned above – appropriate to the Regency and the symbolic motors that drive romantic screen drama. The key scene of contrast comes in the study at Netherfield, which in the film condenses the material of three chapters from the novel. Lizzie's frustration with Darcy is indicated when she abruptly snaps shut her book as he remarks that an accomplished woman 'must improve her mind by extensive reading': clearly signposting sexual unavailability. Caroline then invites Lizzie to 'take a turn around the room' in a studied display of sexuality which Darcy tries to ignore (by reading a book of his own in the novel, by writing a letter in the film). Caroline's motivation to show herself at best advantage in comparison with Lizzie is emphasized by the disjunction of her red silk dress and the creased grey cotton one worn by Lizzie. Lizzie's wish to be disassociated from Caroline's tactless play is made clear as she responds to her gambit – 'It's refreshing, is it not, after sitting so long in one attitude' – with an addition made by Wright: 'It is a *small* kind of accomplishment I suppose'. The camera also punctures any erotic content on Darcy's side, as it remains fixed to a medium shot rather than moving to his point-of-view.

Wright's composition of careful camera-work with the costume choices and Lizzie's witty put-down paraphrases the equivalent scenes in the novel of *Pride and Prejudice* in a way that isolates and contains Caroline's vulgar display of sexuality. This is unnecessary in the novel where Elizabeth triumphs by wholesale participation in the same coquettish behaviour. Anne Mellor

(1995, p. 412) has argued that in the Regency 'women were encouraged to be fundamentally hypocritical and insincere. Forced to be flirts and sexual teases, they were encouraged to arouse male sexual desire by allowing their suitors to take "innocent freedoms" or "liberties" with their persons'. The key for Austen lies in Lizzie's more sophisticated performance and not her unwillingness to perform. The latter is used by Wright to straightforwardly align Lizzie with Darcy (even though she may not know her 'real' feelings or want to admit to them). Austen actually uses it to distinguish between the two. The abruptly closed book in the film indicates a sexual inner life being frustrated by the unresponsive Darcy. This is an erotic attachment that Lizzie simply does not feel at this point in the novel: 'she liked him too little to care for his approbation' (Austen, 1813; 2001, p. 35). Rather her ability to flirt more successfully than Caroline arises not out of sexual desire but from the exact opposite: a pronounced dislike of Darcy. It does not enter Lizzie's head at this point of the novel that such a wealthy and socially embarrassing person could be a future partner (no matter how much the reader might wish to believe that she is in denial). Georg Simmel (1984, p. 142) describes both sides of the phenomenon: 'Inwardly, the flirtatious woman is completely resolved in one direction or the other. The meaning of the entire situation lies only in the fact that she has to conceal her resolve and that, as regards something that is intrinsically certain, she can place her partner in a state of uncertainty and vacillation which holds true only for *him*'. In the novel Caroline and Lizzie are equally resolved then, but in different directions. In Wright's film they are resolved in the same direction, but Caroline is performing while Lizzie is being 'natural'.

Simmel (1984) goes on to record that in a heterosexual flirtatious exchange like this one, the male is aroused because of uncertainty as to whether the woman will ultimately yield or resist. In Austen's novel Darcy experiences nothing of the male uncertainty in social-sexual display with Caroline, but this is because she is a poor flirt and not because she intimidates him. Wright's camera work captures his mood of disgust at Caroline's behaviour accurately, but he is perhaps less successful than Davies in communicating the sexual friction that arises from Darcy's uncertainty about Lizzie's flirtations. In the Ball scenes at the Lucas' gathering and at Netherfield, for example, Davies continually shoots Firth's Darcy in three-quarter shot framed between two foregrounded female characters, usually Lizzie and one other, emphasising his awkwardness in what is a largely confined female space of soft furnishings and soft lighting. This contrasts strongly with those energetic displays of masculine energy that Davies adds to the story while Darcy is at Pemberley. Hopkins (2001, p. 122) describes this 'fetishizing' and feminizing of Darcy as another form of visual containment, regulating any misconstrued sexuality for the viewer. The visual grammar impacts, however, on our need (and Darcy's too) to read the social signs of Regency sexuality correctly. As Molly Engelhardt (2009, p. 95) notes, the ballroom is probably the most codified area of Regency social life where 'marrying for love and, even more important, for safety and security required skilfulness in reading through the exterior manners of dance participants to penetrate that hidden interior realm where motivations and feelings reside'.[4] The communal acknowledgement of such signs is underlined at two key points in the novel. The first is when Lizzie receives a proposal of marriage from Mr Collins, who mistakenly takes her refusal to mean that she is playing hard to get: 'I know it to be an established custom of your sex to reject a man on first application, and perhaps you have even now said as much to encourage my suit as would be consistent with the true delicacy of the female character' (Austen, 1813; 2001, p. 74).[5] The second comes when Lizzie is scolded by her aunt for flirting with Mr Wickham to which she responds: 'At present I am not in love with Mr Wickham; no, I certainly am not. But he is, beyond all comparison, the most agreeable man I ever saw – and if he becomes really attached to me – I believe it will be better that he should not. I see the imprudence of it' (Austen, 1813; 2001, p. 97). This speech shows the clear distinction Austen has in mind between the behaviour of Lizzie and that of Lydia, but allied with Collins' proposal it also reveals that Lizzie's flirtation with Wickham is undertaken because, not despite, of the certainty that it will not result in union.

The sexual threat of Mr Wickham could only become real to Lizzie were she to start to believe that the coquette's behaviour is sincere.[6] Wright's need to balance the sexual attractiveness of Darcy and Wickham on screen, however, makes him lean once more towards the use of visual indicators of containment rather than towards the social figurations of Austen. When Wickham first appears on the street at Meryton he is suitably dressed in scarlet military uniform but, unlike Caroline's dress, the effect is softened by the fact that his long fair hair is bound neatly in a feminine ribbon. Wickham is symbolically associated with delicate fabric, twice picking up a handkerchief dropped by one of the Bennet sisters. On the first occasion this leads to a short dialogue with Lizzie in a draper's shop where ribbons cascade from the displays. Wickham's admittance that 'I have very poor taste in ribbons' and Lizzie's rejoinder 'Only a man with true confidence in himself could admit to that', function rather weakly as comments on his firmness and is a poor shorthand for flirtation in Austen. Sexual attractiveness is momentarily indicated by Lizzie's brief glance at Wickham's body as he walks across screen and she strokes a ribbon suggestively but the overall effect lacks abrasion.

More substantial sexual contact is suggested in equivalent moments at Pemberley when Lizzie gazes at the sculpture of Darcy – only a portrait in the novel – the camera panning slowly across the torsos of male statuary and the baroque display of flesh on the ceiling of the great hall, mostly shot from Lizzie's point-of-view. The scene is unmistakably a moment of sexual awakening, a well-conceived visual counterpoint to the earlier encounter with Wickham and the ribbons. Frippery is replaced by genuine taste and aesthetic substance that tallies symbolically with Lizzie's first view of Pemberley in the novel: 'It was a large handsome, stone building [...] without any artificial appearance [...] where natural beauty had been so little counteracted by an awkward taste' (Austen, 1813; 2001, p. 159).

And yet the sexing down of Wickham and the sexing up of Caroline Bingley reveal an anxiety about the erotic depths of Austen's characters that needs management beyond that of social codification (no matter how faithfully it may be represented by individual filmmakers). For Wickham or Caroline to represent a genuine romantic alternative would interfere with the primary erotic storyline. This induces Wright to mistakenly depopulate the Netherfield ballroom at the climax of Lizzie and Darcy's dance sequence, leaving them alone in what appears to be a mutually-constructed fantasy (the camera-work offers no clue as to whose erotic inner life this scene should be attributed). I would argue that the scene is a mistake not only because it is overdone but because it runs counter to Austen's careful use of character discrepancy: 'This is not a relationship in which each mirrors the other but of distinct subjec-tivities whose very alterity is the ground of their rapport' (Wiltshire, 2001, p. 122). The desire to prove otherwise is the basis, according to John Wiltshire (2001), of the erotic Darcy who becomes 'a focus of fantasy'.

A seemingly inevitable effect of the visual grammar of a *Pride and Prejudice* adaptation is, then, to align Lizzie's feelings throughout the novel with those that she holds for Darcy at the end in order to make them appear more natural than the substanceless performances of characters like Caroline and Willoughby. The fantasy sequence indicates feelings not experienced by Lizzie until much later in Austen's novel. What Wright's use of the scene at the Netherfield Ball does do is to allow the viewer to enter an erotic inner space that is coherent and consistent with, to quote Wiltshire again, 'settled devel-opments' in character, by which I mean Lizzie is seen as gradually coming to terms with continually and consistently held feelings for Darcy.[7] Using screen imagery to make legible an otherwise concealed erotic history in a character such as Elizabeth Bennet suggests a conservative act of romantic rescripting, an attempt to introduce a private life in which Lizzie was in love with Darcy from the off.

4

In comparison to the BBC *Sense and Sensibility* adaptation of 1981, Emma Thompson is permissive in her use of erotic content. A quick contrast between the equivalent scenes in which Marianne sprains her ankle and is carried home by Willoughby is sufficient to demonstrate the difference. Rodney Bennett in the BBC version directs the sisters on a summer's day and has Elinor (Irene Richards) hastily cover the ankle of Marianne (Tracey Childs) at the approach of Willoughby (Peter Woodward) on foot. The action indicates restraint and the independence of Elinor. Thompson, in contrast, sets the scene during a rainstorm in which Marianne's companion is not Elinor but her younger sister Margaret (Emilie François). Her helplessness thus compounded, the arrival of a storm-drenched Willoughby on a white horse is thoroughly more dramatic and erotic as he proceeds to massage Marianne's ankle while Winslett's bosom heaves responsively in a head and shoulders shot. The overt sexual chemistry between Marianne and Willoughby is then problematized by some more rescripting: in this case it is Thompson's decision not to include Willoughby's return to Cleveland during Marianne's illness at the end of the novel. As Parrill (2002) and Nixon (2001) have observed, it is a decision made to clear up the distribution of the film's sexual signifiers. Early in the action Willoughby drives a curricle with bright yellow wheels (showmanship), throws away a half-eaten apple (impatience), gives Marianne wild flowers (naturalness) and reads to her from a volume of 'pocket sonnets' (intensity). His apparent openness is matched by Marianne – 'Why should I hide my regard?' – and counters the 'repressed' Elinor and Brandon.

The erotic inner space of the latter two characters is drawn, however, from similar symbolic simplification. Nixon's notion of Alan Rickman as a more sympathetic and loveable Brandon than the novel allows may well hold true, but his externalized erotic drives are frequently those of impotence rather than of concealed virility. In the reed-cutting scene (added to the story by Thompson), for example, a red-faced Marianne frustratedly tries to snap a damp reed from the ground to add to her basket. The camera remains focused on Marianne as Colonel Brandon enters from right of shot, his body revealed from his jacket down. He swiftly draws out a pocketknife that he offers to Marianne who takes it and proceeds to cut the reed in two. Her facial expression is particularly hard to read here; annoyance seems to be aimed at both the stubborn reed but also the presumption of Brandon's interference. The scene cuts abruptly to Mr Jennings in conversation with Brandon on the subject of Marianne. Jennings' suggestion of a love match sees Brandon raise his eyes momentarily in contemplation of the idea while he tentatively polishes a shotgun. The phallic symbolism is hard to miss, but it is also hard to sift. Partly we might ascribe this to Brandon's uncertainty about Marianne's affections, but on Marianne's side the visual imagery points wholly to frustration. In the following scene Mrs Jennings (Elizabeth Spriggs) gossips indiscreetly about Brandon, which leads Marianne to run to the house – wrestling with the knot in her bonnet's ribbon that refuses to come undone. It is Elinor, and not Brandon, who undoes Marianne's knot. The visual signs point towards the fact that Marianne wants to wrest herself of the unwanted sexual attention of Brandon.

By translating the inner life into visual equivalents, Thompson perhaps overplays Brandon's inadequacy, which is what results in the need to rescript and leave out key elements of the plot involving Willoughby later on. He is visually referenced when Brandon reprises the earlier heroism in the storm as he carries Marianne back from her wild dash to Combe Magna (Willoughby's lodgings). The difference between the ages of the men is made apparent as Brandon is seen to struggle under the exertion. There were no such problems for Willoughby earlier who swaggered into their cottage at Barton Park with ease. For Elinor, the sexual signposting also indicates feelings that must be contained and cannot be spoken. But her depth of passion is considered on the terms of Marianne rather than the other way around, contrary to Austen's undoubted intentions. The same is true of other characters translated from the novel. Lucy Steele, for instance, at first appears friendly but turns out to be Elinor's rival for the affections of Edward Ferrars. As in the novel, Lucy reveals that she has secretly been engaged to Edward for some time before the plot begins. In this scene of sudden shock for Elinor, she and Lucy Steele walk away from the social group for more private discussion on the matter. The moment of revelation in Thompson's adaptation comes while the camera places Elinor in front of a Gothic picture similar to Fuseli's *Nightmare* in which a woman lies across a bed clearly ravished by an erotic experience. The painting visually recalls Marianne – often shot by Ang Lee in supine posture – particularly as she lies helpless and panting during the storm scene mentioned above. The implication is that Elinor and Marianne share the same erotic content – the difference being that we see Marianne's bodied forth in her physical display while Elinor's needs to be embodied elsewhere in the film through the redistribution of sexuality in visual code.

In adapting Austen for the screen a pattern seems then to recur whereby the desire to reveal, inspect and objectify private sexual feelings, particularly those held by women, leads to a corresponding movement through which they can then be supervised and contained. The social codes of Regency sexual engagement require supplementary codification. This is most obviously the case in the two adaptations of *Northanger Abbey* in which sexuality, particularly of an autoerotic variety, is linked with punishment and retribution. Davies' increasing portfolio of period drama gained the addition of a *Northanger Abbey* for ITV's Jane Austen season in 2007 and it is notable for the use of erotic fantasy sequences that explore Catherine Morland's psychological desire for domination. However, this was also a feature of the 1986 BBC adaptation by Maggie Wadey and in fact the fantasy sequences of the earlier production are more disturbing in their use of recurring imagery of virginal sacrifice, heavily Gothicized makeup and music that recalls 1980s heavy metal. Sue Parrill notes that in Wadey's screenplay Cathy's dreams obsessively return to images of bondage, spilt blood, animals and aggressive medieval settings and costumes. In both adaptations the relationship between dreamscape and reality becomes the abiding visual concern, abstracting their plots into a symbolic Freudian narrative of repressed libidinal drives.

The desire to visualize sex is established early on as a theme in the BBC adaptation's opening sequence where Cathy (Katherine Schlesinger) reads a Gothic novel: Ann Radcliffe's *The Mysteries of Udolpho*. Her copy of the thriller includes line illustrations, one of which the reader sees in which a sinister male figure carries a maiden in a state of semi-conscious ravishment. The picture gradually infiltrates Cathy's fantasies as General Tilney (Robert Hardy) starts to feature in the role of this aggressive seducer. The camera cuts between the picture and Cathy's face with lips parted and eyes glazed over in an approximation of sexual ecstasy. This private moment is then interrupted by the arrival of Cathy's younger brother Edward (Oliver Hembrough) – representing symbolic regression to childhood – and Cathy comments 'Literature and solitude are as necessary to a young woman's development as sunshine is to ripe fruit' before suggestively biting into a plum. Cathy's confident use of innuendo and semi-sexual puns comes back to haunt and punish her in a later dream sequence in which she hears in a mantra the words of John Thorpe (Jonathan Coy), an unwelcome romantic interest, who had taken her against her will in his carriage: 'I thought you and I were going for a ride' he repeats hypnotically.

Davies' opening sequence, along with many of the dream visions, recalls the visual motifs used by Wadey, but in the ITV adaptation even more emphasis is placed on the prurience of the camera-work as it hovers above Cathy whilst she reads in a secluded corner of the garden, gradually closing in on her solitude. This comes immediately after she has been seen becoming heated while playing baseball with her younger siblings – the athletic activity leading directly to the need to withdraw and read alone. In this instance the furtiveness and guilt attached to her behaviour is signalled as she is interrupted by two children and hides the copy of *Udolpho* behind her back. Guilt is indicated later in the film where Cathy admits to Eleanor Tilney (Catherine Walker), who often plays the role of reassuring confidant, 'I don't think I am very pure in heart. I have the most terrible dreams sometimes'.

But just how much erotic content do Cathy's dreams hold and to what purpose do the adaptations put them? The first part of this question is rightly addressed by Parrill (2002, p. 175) concerning Wadey's script: 'It makes very good sense for a modern cinematic adaptation of this novel about a young girl who is looking for love and adventure to show her indulging in erotic fantasies. Although [...] one should notice that the fantasies show only male domination and nothing specifically sexual. Catherine's limited sexual experience allows her to imagine nothing more graphic'. The same holds true for the Davies adaptation, and in both cases it becomes apparent that Henry Tilney, Cathy's preferred suitor, appears in her dreams and fights off the more aggressive and rudimentary sexual advances of John Thorpe. The fantasy sequences act as a release of nocturnal libidinal energy, but are nevertheless heavily policed by the function of the main plot in which Tilney's gentle masculine endearments win out over Thorpe's crudeness. The protective heroism of Davies' Henry within the dream sequences tones down some of Wadey's more extreme fantasies that suggested a 'Ken Russell-style romp' to more than one reviewer: at one point Cathy, dressed in virginal white, is held to her bed by John Thorpe, dressed in the gold and fur regalia of Henry VIII, while low red lighting casts flickering shadows and Thorpe stares malevolently at a white mouse in a glass jar! (Stovel, 1998, p. 236).

It is not always possible to take these sequences as anything more than comic entertainment, and they fulfil this function extremely effectively. Nevertheless, Cathy's dreams in the Davies adaptation are an endorsement of, rather than a threat to, the social and narrative equilibrium and they do not always make full sense in the context of the rest of the film. When, for example, Eleanor tells Cathy about her brother's seduction and abandonment of Isabella Thorpe (Carey Mulligan) – the would-be social climber who Cathy befriends at Bath – the viewer is left in absolutely no doubt by Cathy's reaction that phrases such as 'having his way' and 'easy conquest' mean sexual inter-course. Relative restraint in the dream sequences hardly seems to fit with such open conversation. But then again the sexual sequences are not open: they are unmistakably autoerotic. It is noticeable that in both adaptations the dreams are always related on screen to reading or writing, the camera usually panning across Cathy's sleeping body prior to the dream sequence to a book resting open on her chest. In the Davies adaptation Cathy is also often a viewer rather than a participant in the action of the dreams. She leans against a tree in a state of sexual abandon, for example, as Henry and John Thorpe engage in a sword fight nearby.

We could argue that both adaptations of *Northanger Abbey* further privilege the erotic inner life as opposed to the social figuring of sexual behaviour. Hiding to read or write – Cathy pretends to Henry that she does not keep a journal – equates to autoeroticism in what Kosofsky Sedgwick (1993, p. 110) described as an 'open secret': 'how hard it is to circumscribe the vibrations of the highly relational but, in practical terms, solitary pleasure and adventure of writing itself'. To this we can of course add reading. Cathy Morland writes and performs her own private sexual narrative in the contained unconscious spaces of the cinematic dream vision. This is not surprising as reading is frequently a site of sex in Austen adaptations. In Thompson's *Sense and Sensibility*, first Willoughby and then Brandon court Marianne Dashwood by reading to her. Joe Wright's *Pride and Prejudice* opens with Lizzie walking across a field reading a book upside down, her mind on the Lucas' forthcoming Ball. During their dance at Netherfield Lizzie Bennet tells Darcy 'I cannot talk of books in a ballroom', the implication being that this is too dry a subject for such a glitzy gathering: such material is just not sexy. But books in Austen adaptations represent solipsism and therefore also signify the depths of unsupervised sexual experience. It is exactly these depths that we have seen becoming an anxiety on screen, requiring visual and metaphoric solutions. As Parrill (2002, p. 70) writes, 'One may protest that Jane Austen did not say anything about her characters' sexuality, but she was not blind to the existence of sex'. Austen said nothing explicitly; but her novels indicate more than enough about the erotic inner life. It is an understandable but substantial irony that the paternalistic anxieties Austen satirized in *Northanger Abbey* are being reduplicated in her adaptation for television and film.

Endnotes

1   For the most important argument about gender performativity see Judith Butler (1990), *Gender Trouble: Feminism and the Subversion of Identity*. New York and London: Routledge.

2   Noble recounts that the 'lopsided' look was one of the visual signifiers chosen to indicate Lydia's sexuality (Birtwistle and Conklin, 1995, p. 58).

3   For a discussion of the history of viragos on the screen see Barbara Creed (1993), *The Monstrous Feminine: Film, Feminism, Psychoanalysis*. London: Routledge.

4   Engelhardt precisely delineates the social codification that governed sexual engagement in the Regency Ballroom. There is not space in this chapter to fully explore the function of the camera in these settings but I would say that the general principle follows the main pattern of my argument in which the visual markers of film detract from the importance of social signs and their readers.

5 Simmel (1984, p. 140) confirms that while Collins is wrong about Lizzie he is right about the custom: 'It was not proper for a man to reject a woman, regardless of whether it was improper for her to offer herself to him [...] Rebuffing the zealous suitor is, so to say, a thoroughly appropriate gesture for the woman'.

6 Tamara Wagner (2008, p. 93) has argued that this is actually what saves Lydia: 'she takes their flirtations seriously, misguidedly reading them as part of courtship'.

7 Wiltshire (2001) is writing at this point about Elizabeth Bennet's receipt of Darcy's letter revealing the true nature of Wickham's behaviour. He (*ibid.*, pp. 114–15) properly notes 'I do not think at this point we are meant to feel that Elizabeth is mistaken, nor do I think that Elizabeth is ever – here or earlier – unconsciously, in the normal sense of the words, "in love with" Darcy'.

10

Performance Anxiety and Costume Drama: Lesbian Sex on the BBC

Amber K. Regis

Terry Castle's (1993, pp. 2; 31) famous invocation of the 'apparitional' lesbian exposes the insidious obscurity of 'deviant' female sexual desire in modern culture. The lesbian is forced to occupy 'a recessive, indeterminate, misted-over space'; she is paradoxically 'elusive, vaporous, difficult to spot – even when she is there, in plain view'. But why might this be so? All the better, it seems, to contain her threat. The lesbian's body and desires circulate beyond patriarchy; they circumvent 'the moral, sexual and psychic authority of men', undermining the dominance of normative heterosexuality (*ibid.*, p. 5). The lesbian can only appear, therefore, to the extent that she is 'simultaneously "de-realized"' – apparitional because 'sanitized [...] in the interest of order and public safety' (*ibid.*, pp. 5; 34). Studies of lesbian representation in contemporary popular culture testify to this heavy mediation. Tamsin Wilton (1995, p. 2) speaks of the 'fleeting moments' and 'flickering shape' of the lesbian on screen, invariably immortalized in heterosexual roles or subject to the heterosexual gaze. Similarly, Yvonne Tasker (1994, p. 172; 176) identifies the 'heavily coded and "disguised"' recurrence of lesbian tropes in popular film, but she offers a more optimistic reading: 'hints of perversion' speak to the pervasiveness of lesbian desire. Here Tasker reveals an important consequence of the lesbian's apparitional status: her ability to return, to haunt. For

Castle (1993, p. 7; 18; 46), the lesbian retains a 'peculiar cultural power': she is provocative, inciting containment and sanitation, and despite her cultural invisibility, she is 'legion': 'To be haunted by a woman [...] is ineluctably to see her'.

In our living rooms, on our televisions, the lesbian has certainly enjoyed greater visibility in recent years, returning to haunt us in the form of soap opera kisses and American imports dedicated to *The L-Word* (Showtime/ Viacom, 2004–9). The 1990s appear to have been a watershed moment, with the emergence of what Diane Hamer and Belinda Budge (1994, p. 1) have called 'lesbian chic', a glamorized opening up of mainstream opportunities for lesbian representation. One surprising manifestation on British television has been the appearance and subsequent recurrence of lesbian-themed costume drama, particularly on the BBC. But why so surprising? Classic serials have been a staple of 'Auntie' BBC since the early days of radio broadcasting, forming part of its avuncular (tanticular?) public service ethos to inform, educate and entertain (Giddings and Selby, 2001, p. 1). The roots of contemporary costume drama thus lie in conservative traditions, designed 'not only for our amusement but also for our betterment' (*ibid.*). As such, the genre has long remained a bastion of polite, traditional values, associated with middle-class audiences and constitutive of a culturally hegemonic 'heritage Britishness' (De Groot, 2009, p. 184).

This chapter explores the strategies and rhetorics used to frame and enable representations of lesbian characters and lesbian sex in BBC costume drama. My primary case study is *Portrait of a Marriage* (dir. Stephen Whittaker, 1990), a dramatized account of Vita Sackville-West's tempestuous relationship with Violet Trefusis. As an adaptation of life writing (part-biography, part-autobiography), *Portrait* is relatively unique among costume dramas, but this also raises particular concerns over authenticity: the series' depiction of 'real' lesbian lives and 'real' lesbian sex. How does *Portrait* marry its controversial subject matter with its participation in conservative traditions of quality programming? To what extent does the lesbian remain apparitional, obscured by the series' use of a legitimating, heterosexual framework? Broadcast twelve years later, *Tipping the Velvet* (dir. Geoffrey Sax, 2002) enjoyed less troublesome source material; it was an adaptation of fiction, not life writing. As such, the series exceeded its predecessor in terms of sexual content and explicitness, but a legitimating framework continued to be used – in this case, metatheatrical artifice. *Tipping* was not, therefore, an unqualified triumph for tolerance and increased visibility. Rather, it demonstrates the survival of anxieties that contain and mediate 'authentic' lesbianism.

Adapting Vita's confession

Nigel Nicolson discovered his mother's autobiography after her death in 1962. The document was a confession, an account of Vita's lesbian relationship with Violet Trefusis, and Nigel published it in 1973 as part of a larger work entitled *Portrait of a Marriage*. As this title suggests, the work developed new emphases; it was to be 'a panegyric of marriage', an account of Vita's relationship with Harold Nicolson, Nigel's father, and a description of 'one of the strangest and most successful unions that two gifted people have ever enjoyed' (Nicolson, 1992, p. xiii). *Portrait* was thus a work of composite life writing: Vita's autobiography was reproduced 'verbatim', but set within chapters of biography provided by Nigel, re-telling, questioning and extending her account (*ibid.*, p. xiv). On its first publication, therefore, Vita's autobiography was already adapted. Nigel's embedding of her text within a heterosexual framework was an appropriative act – a transformative mode of adaptation involving a 'decisive journey away from the informing source' (Sanders, 2006, p. 26). In an unpublished memoir of 1985, Nigel reflects on his motives and treatment of the text:

> But I determined that in order to reduce the impact of Vita's confession, I must continue the story of their marriage till its happy end. It would become a sort of joint-biography of two people. I would make it very clear that the crisis of Violet actually deepened their love for each other. It was the love story of V. & H., even more than that of V. & V. But of course I foresaw that the public would ignore the latter part, and make hay with the Violet part (Nicolson, 1985)[1].

Nigel's appropriation was intended to contain the threat of lesbian desire, to reduce the significance of 'V. & V.' and replace their story with the privileged narrative of 'V. & H.'. The confession is seen to require adaptation, and yet Nigel's unpublished memoir makes clear his anxiety that lesbian desire will escape containment – that Vita's story will be *mis*appropriated, with the public 'making hay' with the confession.[2]

Adapting *Portrait*: 'Quality' and 'Authenticity'

Portrait of a Marriage was transformed into a sumptuous four-part drama and broadcast on BBC 2 between 19 September and 10 October 1990. Much of the action occurs in flashback, with a telephone call from Violet disrupting the 'present' of 1940s war-time Britain: childhood memories and scenes from Vita (Janet McTeer) and Harold's (David Haig) courtship are followed by an extended flashback, a sustained re-telling of the events of 1918–1920 and Vita's affair with Violet (Cathryn Harrison). *Portrait* was adapted for the small screen by the novelist and screenwriter Penelope Mortimer, and she chose to focus almost exclusively on Vita's relationship with Violet. The series was thus an adaptation of the confession alone, eliding much of the material added to Vita's story by Nigel's biographical chapters – his concern that the story of 'V. & V.' would escape containment thus proved remarkably prescient.

As a classic serial and costume drama, *Portrait* laid claim to be quality programming. As Jerome de Groot (2009, p. 184) has argued, costume dramas are invested with 'an instant cultural value' – a recognition of prestige derived from their typically canonical source material, high production values and depiction of saleable, 'heritage Britishness'. Prestige is similarly tied to the genre's claim to historicity: an audience must accept 'the validity of the programmes' representations of the past', even if it adheres to a 'popular conceptualisation' rather than holding a mirror to history (Cardwell, 2002, p. 114; De Groot, 2009, p. 187). For de Groot (*ibid.*), the dual recognition of source text and historical setting requires a delicate balancing act: the audience must 'keep two separate concepts in tension – the idea of authenticity and that of fiction'. This model applies specifically to adaptations of novels, a mainstay of costume drama. While the audience concedes the unreality of characters, they expect the narrative to unfold 'within [a] framework of authentic historical representation' (*ibid.*). For example, Elizabeth Bennett (Jennifer Ehle) depends on nothing exterior to *Pride and Prejudice* for her thoughts and experiences, but we expect the clothes she wears and the spaces she inhabits in the famous BBC adaptation (dir. Simon Langton, 1995) to be historically accurate. *Portrait*, however, unsettles and complicates this paradigm. The series does not negotiate competing claims to fiction and history, but rather makes a redoubled claim to authenticity. As composite life writing, the source text participates across genres that claim a truth-value. On screen, therefore, *Portrait* promises an accurate portrayal of 'real' lives in addition to its authentic historical framework.

The series thus blends into the genre of television biopic. Broadly defined, biopic 'depicts the life of a historical person, past or present' and, according to George F. Custen (1992, p. 3; 6), the form is 'embroiled in the same controversies about truth, accuracy, and interpretation' that surround literary biography. As such, we might borrow from theorists of documentary to suggest that biopic, with its claim to truth, is a contractual genre. As viewers, we expect the relationship between documentary and 'the real' to be 'direct, immediate and transparent' (Nichols, 1991, p. 4). In turn, documentaries construct a 'meta-language' to signify and guarantee their authenticity (Kilborn and Izod, 1997, p. 134). For Annette Hill (2007, p. 137), this reciprocal arrangement is a 'contract of trust': programme makers 'agree' to depict reality, while viewers accept this claim to referentiality. As a dramatized reconstruction, biopic does not share in this seemingly unproblematic relation to real life – any 'contract of trust' is undoubtedly more complex. Yet, as audience members, we retain an expectation that what we see is an accurate re-telling of events; according to Custen (1992, p. 2), biopics '[provide] many viewers with the version of the life they [hold] to be the truth'. As a result, the BBC's *Portrait* constructs a comparable meta-language designed to guarantee authenticity. Exterior shots of Sissinghurst and Knole locate the on-screen Vita and Violet within the same spaces occupied by their real life counterparts, while interior shots reveal the careful *re*construction of period detail and living space – scenes that appear to take place in Vita's writing room were, in fact, filmed on set. But *Portrait*'s meta-language is also pervasive and subtle. In episode three, for example, the camera sweeps across an open photograph album. The displayed images depict David Haig and Janet McTeer, in costume and in role, as Harold and Vita respectively. These photographs demonstrate a strikingly literal pose of authenticity, recreating a number of iconic images: McTeer holding a baby, imitating a 1914 photograph of Vita with her son Ben; McTeer with upturned stare, imitating a photograph of Vita taken in the early 1920s; Haig and McTeer standing together, hands in pockets, imitating a 1932 photograph of Harold and Vita at Sissinghurst. Paradoxically, the adaptation *performs* referentiality, dramatizing its relation to real, historical persons.

Portrait on screen was thus subject to two distinct legitimating discourses: quality programming and authentic representation. At first glance, the latter appears to reinforce the former. As television biopic and adaptation of life writing, the accurate portrayal of 'character' and events seems part of the series' high production values. And yet, a potential conflict is thrown into relief by the lesbian content of the source material. How might lesbian sex in *Portrait* impact on the conservative, 'heritage Britishness' of costume drama? Would this 'product' be devalued as a result? Could authenticity undermine perceptions of quality? *Portrait* negotiates these competing claims, shaping its representation of lesbian sex accordingly.

Screening 'Quality' Sex in *Portrait*

Portrait was broadcast two years after the implementation of Section 28 of the Local Government Act – an amendment prohibiting the 'promotion' of homosexuality in public institutions. This nebulous yet far-reaching legislation served to silence debate and inquiry; it was aimed, in particular, at schools and schoolchildren, where the teaching of homosexuality 'as a pretended family relationship' was explicitly censured (HM Government, 1988). It should thus come as little surprise that a costume drama whose *raison d'être* was a lesbian relationship courted controversy. But as Mandy Merck has argued, *Portrait* was broadcast in a pervasive context of repression. The series coincided with the Conservative Party Conference bemoaning the rise of divorce and single-parent families, the publication of a government 'white paper' providing 'for greater powers to extract maintenance payments from absent fathers' and the drawing up of new proposals 'to retard divorce' on the part of the Law Commission (Merck, 1993, p. 114). *Portrait* thus appeared at a time when the nuclear family seemed under threat. Responding to this climate, Elizabeth Wilson (1990, p. 31) argued that the series had more to say about heterosexuality than it did about homosexuality:

> Brideshead for dykes (aka *Portrait of a Marriage*) is over. But, if everyone hates lesbians, why screen it at all? [...] But, could it be that gay love is the lens through which heterosexual society is desperately peering at its own problematic practices? [...] Although the message is usually that hetero-sexuality, or just men, wins out over love between women in the end, these narratives also hint that not all is well in the world of heterosexuals.

Wilson exposes concerns over the visibility of lesbian sex – was *Portrait* a further manifestation of declining morality and defunct values? But her notion of a 'lens' through which heterosexuality is scrutinized suggests an underlying conservatism – homosexuality may act as 'a strange, illicit, subliminal utopia [...] by contrast with the clapped-out world of heterosexuality', but it does so at the cost of finite, mediated expression. Order is restored and normative heterosexuality 'wins out' (*ibid.*). But how does this work in *Portrait*? What strategies enable the depiction of lesbian sex, and how is order restored?

Portrait was more explicit than *Oranges Are Not the Only Fruit*, the first BBC drama to depict lesbian sex (broadcast nine months earlier). In *Oranges*, nudity and the suggestion of sex was limited to a single sequence in the second of three episodes: Jess (Charlotte Coleman) and Melanie (Cathryn Bradshaw) kiss and lie naked together, cue the use of de-realizing slow-motion and dystopic, non-diegetic organ music (techniques that recall the drama's fantasy sequences). In *Portrait*, by contrast, each of the series' four episodes contained scenes of nudity and sex (or, at least, their suggestion). There was not, however, a comparable leap forward in explicit content – no more human flesh was on display, with both series restricted to the acceptable terrain of breast and buttock. Indeed Jennifer Harding (1998, p. 134) bemoans the reticence of *Portrait*, with sex scenes comprised (in the majority) of 'lingering passionate kisses and (non-genital) stroking in the afterglow'. One marked difference, however, was the series' strategic contextualization of lesbian sex.

Hilary Hinds (1995, p. 63) has explored the 'romantic idealism' that characterized popular and critical reactions to *Oranges*. Sex was perceived in terms of youthful naivety – Steve Clark, writing in *The Sunday Times* (21 January 1990), described the relationship between Jess and Melanie as 'almost Disneyesque in its innocent wonderment' – while delicate sensibilities were more concerned by the series' depiction of repressive religion (cited in Hinds, 1995, p. 63). If innocence had helped to contain the threat of lesbianism in *Oranges*, then the careful (re-)setting of desire in terms of heterosexuality served the same purpose in *Portrait*. I would not be the first critic – or the first audience member – to notice this marked heterosexualization. Penny Florence (1995, p. 124) describes *Portrait* as 'masculinist and heterosexist', noting in particular the absence of self-identified lesbians among the cast and crew. But what is the evidence in terms of the series' aesthetic? Most notably, Vita is often seen in masculine dress, whether in full drag or trousers (the 'breeches and gaiters [...] like the women-on-the-land' she describes herself wearing in her confession), or the masculine fashions of 1920s Britain (Nicolson, 1992, p. 99). Vita's costumes appear in stark contrast to the delicate lace, flowing dresses, shawls and pastel shades of the indisputably feminine Violet. As Jennifer Harding has observed, *Portrait*'s sex scenes are predicated on Vita's performance of masculinity, on her 'theatrical "crossing over"' (Harding, 1998, p. 131). Vita is shown to identify as a man in her relationship with Violet and, as a result, she is invested with sexual agency. For example, in episode two, we see Vita in full drag, dressed as a wounded soldier and later as a tango-dancing lover in the bars and cafes of the Parisian *demimonde*. Two sex scenes result from this 'crossing over'. In the first, Violet sucks and kisses Vita's toes. Having entered the room as the 'wife' of a male-identified Vita, in the guise of a soldier, this scene can be read as a displaced act of fellatio – Vita is thus in possession of the phallus and the authority it confers. This is manifest in the episode's second sex scene: Vita, again in the guise of a soldier, stalks Violet in their darkened hotel suite, grabbing her and silencing her playful scream, kissing her and forcing her to the ground. Here Vita is physically and sexually dominant; her desire is active and tinged with violence, finding its counterpart in Violet's demure vulnerability.

But how does this heterosexualized performance contain the threat of lesbian desire? For Jennifer Harding, *Portrait*'s repeated use of drag and butch/femme serves to regulate non-normative sexuality. Costumed and performed, lesbian sex becomes a temporary aberration – a finite imitation of the 'norm'. Lesbianism is thus ultimately 'brought to heel', bending to the responsibilities of marriage (Harding, 1998, p. 129). *Portrait*'s reticence also serves to obfuscate lesbian sex. Again, Harding (*ibid.*, p. 132) argues that the tendency to fade out sexual encounters produces 'a space usually filled by images of heterosexual copulation. Viewers were directed towards thinking of heterosexual penetration or drawing a blank'. *Portrait* does little, therefore, to challenge the dominance of normative heterosexuality – deviant desires are highly mediated and, to return to Elizabeth Wilson, heterosexuality 'wins out'. Gender might be performative, but sexuality remains tied: Vita's masculinity desires Violet's femininity. Thus lesbianism in *Portrait* is 'visible *only* though these particular enactments of butch/femme stereotypes' (*ibid.*, p. 131; my emphasis).

In his study of biopic, George F. Custen (1992, p. 221; 226) suggests the intimacy of the small screen has encouraged an increasing concern with 'the lives of typical people' – television biopics 'enshrine normalcy'. But it would be difficult to confuse *Portrait* with kitchen-sink drama, while the class privilege of Nicolson, Sackville-West and Keppel/Trefusis families elevates the series above the 'typical'. Despite this, the maintenance of norms is certainly key to *Portrait*'s treatment of lesbian sex. For Custen (*ibid.*, p. 226), 'villains' in television biopic embody factors that threaten family life, and he includes homosexuality among these ranks. Despite the series' containment of this 'villain' within a heterosexual framework, *Portrait* failed to 'enshrine normalcy' to the required standard of its American audience. The broadcaster PBS cut 34 minutes from the series, claiming the decision was based on efficiency: 'mostly for pacing and to move the story along'. But a second, 'softer' version was also made 'in accordance with the public's "concerns and sensibilities"', and local stations were able to choose which version to broadcast (Macintyre, 1992, p. 12).[3] The Gay and Lesbian Alliance Against Defamation protested the decision. In an article for *The Nation*, one of their members, Charlotte Innes, claimed the cuts enacted a thorough curtailment of the women's relationship. Excised material included: 'a childhood scene suggesting that Vita and Violet's lesbianism was inherent and their love for one another mutual; a wonderful tender moment in which Violet sings to Vita; and several shots in which the two women are seen having fun together' (Innes, 1992, p. 338). In other words, they removed 'the pleasurable, enduring aspect of the relationship' (*ibid.*). These cuts reveal the protectionist aspect of television biopic identified by Custen, but the requirement to 'enshrine normalcy' was also integral to *Portrait*'s status as quality programming. The series' careful screening of sex was intended to appease traditional audiences of costume drama, burying lesbianism within a heterosexual framework to protect the series' appeal to middle-class respectability. The result was a strange denial of lesbianism in the face of its presence. In the *Radio Times*, for example, the series' producer Colin Tucker was able to assert that 'lesbianism was irrelevant', universalizing (and reducing) the story to 'a *human* triangle' (Brompton, 1990, p. 4; my emphasis).

But one aspect of *Portrait* and its screening of sex remains problematic. I have argued that Vita is invested with sexual agency and this marks a clear break between source text and adaptation. The heterosexual framework adopted by the series follows the clear precedent set by Nigel's treatment of the confession: his reduction and containment of 'V. & V.'. Thus far, book and costume drama appear to agree. But Vita's confession mediates sexual agency – the relationship is predicated on Violet's precocious sexuality and Vita claims to be seduced: 'She was infinitely clever [...] it was all conscious on her part, but on mine it was simply the drunkenness of liberation' (Nicolson, 1992, p. 100). Vita's 'drunkenness' suggests the loss of rational self-control and, by implication, her lack of responsibility. Violet, however, is sexually aware, with her passive femininity being actively performed: 'She let herself go entirely limp and passive in my arms. (I shudder to think of the experience that lay behind her abandonment)' (*ibid.*, p. 101). Nigel extends this trope in his biographical chapters. In his account of Vita's relationship with Virginia Woolf, for example, he uses evidence from letters to insist their relationship was 'a mental thing; a spiritual thing [...] an intellectual thing' (*ibid.*, p. 188). All this, however, is in stark contrast to the television series' depiction of rape.

In episode three, after Violet's marriage to Denys Trefusis (Peter Birch), Vita intercepts the newlyweds on their honeymoon. She abducts Violet and takes her to a darkened room somewhere else in Paris. She shouts at her – 'Bitch!' and 'Whore!' – then kisses her passionately, forcing her onto the bed. When Violet attempts to rise, she slaps her across the face. Forcing herself on top of Violet, she kisses her and tears her dress, forcing her hand up Violet's skirts and penetrating her: 'Is this what he feels like? Is it?'. Violet cries and struggles throughout, screaming at the moment of penetration. This is the series' most explicit scene in terms of sex and violence, yet it remains on the periphery of the heterosexual framework. While the scene is a perverse imitation of heterosexual practice, it is not contextualized through a clear performance of butch/femme. The act of penetration is male-identified, but the scene is not made safe by a theatrical performance of masculinity – Vita does not 'cross over'. She wears layered skirts and a long, flowing beige coat; in style and colour palette, the women appear remarkably similar. As such, this is the closest the series gets to sex between two feminine-identified women. And yet, it is also *Portrait*'s most negative portrayal of lesbianism. The demands of television biopic and quality costume drama require this to be so: lesbianism that escapes the series' heterosexual framework must be rendered abject – it is allied to rape, an extreme, non-normative and 'deviant' sexual practice.

Disputing Authenticity

Portrait's most outspoken critic was Nigel Nicolson. At first, he acknowledged the strange experience of seeing his mother's story re-told, confessing to the *Radio Times* that he found it 'all a bit spooky' and was 'particularly unnerved' by the sight of Janet McTeer in Vita's clothes (Brompton, 1990, p. 4). The series' performed reality, it seems, was uncannily accurate. But Nigel would later revise this assessment and he begins here, in his first post-broadcast interview, to distance himself from the production. In particular, he is dismayed by the portrayal of his parents' marriage and he confesses to feeling 'embarrassed' by the 'intimate "very sexy" love scenes': 'I was conscious of looking away from some of the more erotic scenes, feeling I was a voyeur' (*ibid.*). Here Nigel averts his gaze from the screening of lesbian sex and, in subsequent statements to the press, he would attempt to avert the gaze of the public.

In an article for *The Times* entitled 'Portrait of a love betrayed?', Nigel (1990) repeated his objections, returning again to the series' too-explicit depiction of lesbian sex. He suggests the adaptation contravened a 'gentle-man's agreement' between himself and the series' producers. As evidence, he (Nicolson, 1990, p. 16) quotes from a letter written during a previous adaptation project, a copy of which was sent to the BBC:

> The story must be told with delicacy and with no overtly sexual scenes. By that I mean that Vita and Violet should not be shown making love. There must be no pawing or mutual undressing or passionate embraces [...] Their elopement was a crazy escapade, from which Vita just recovered in time, largely owing to Harold's extraordinary gentleness and understanding. At the end it might be suggested (I don't know how) that this crisis in their marriage made it all the more successful and secure. In other words, the drama might show the triumph of love over infatuation.

Nigel concedes there was no contractual agreement and, placing the ethics of this issue aside, what this letter reveals is an assumption that he would retain control of his mother's text – that any adaptation would replicate his focus on 'V. & H.'. His letter attempts to censor the depiction of lesbianism; there should be *no* sex scenes, nor any physical expression of desire. Nigel thus sought to render the lesbian body invisible: 'Penelope Mortimer [...] had little patience with my suggestion that the love between the two women should be expressed by look and gesture more than touch' (ibid.). Despite the clear heterosexualization of lesbian sex in the BBC's Portrait, Nigel feared its stark visibility would inevitably undermine the dominance of his parents' marriage.

In order to wrestle back control, Nigel disputes the series' authenticity, setting the script in contradistinction to his book. Penelope Mortimer was 'determined to tell the story her way, not mine', and thus an uncomfortable stalemate is produced: '"But it's my script," she said. "It's my book," I replied' (ibid., pp. 16; 17). Reasserting the authority of his source text, Nigel engages in 'fidelity criticism' (in which 'fidelity to the adapted text' is 'the criterion of judgment'), with the starkest example occurring in Nigel's memoir, Long Life (1997) (Hutcheon, 2006, p. 6). Material from The Times article is reproduced near-verbatim, but the issue of authenticity is more prominent. Significantly, Nigel questions the series' historical framework. He recounts the filming of a dining room scene – in which Vita sits far apart from her mother, discussing personal matters in front of three male servants – and recalls his response: 'It would never have happened like that, I said. I was reminded that this was not fact, but drama. The scene suggested the period as most would imagine it to have been' (Nicolson, 1998, p. 27). As such, the adaptation is exposed as imagined history; performativity is emphasized, with the 'fact' of Vita's life contrasted to the fiction of television. The lead actors' performances are similarly exposed, despite tentative praise. Nigel is positive in his Times article: Cathryn Harrison's Violet is 'astonishingly true' and he is 'moved and startled by [Janet McTeer's] resemblance to my mother'. But praise is mediated by disclaimer and reservation, with Nigel emphasising the inevitable difference between adaptation (i.e. an actor's performance) and original: 'No actress or actor can portray with any exactness a person they have never met' (Nicolson, 1990, p. 17). Returning to this argument in Long Life, Nigel insists that authentic performance is impossible: 'the personality of an actor necessarily dominates the personality of the person whom he or she is trying to represent' (Nicolson, 1998, p. 27).

As a result of Nigel's 'fidelity criticism', disbelief is no longer suspended: McTeer remains McTeer, while the 'original' of Vita can only be glimpsed through his source text. But how does this rhetoric revise the series' depiction of lesbian sex? With its authenticity undermined, sex and nudity are returned to the body of the actress: 'When I saw the rough cuts, I gasped inwardly at the sight of Janet and Cathryn in the nude (how they must have hated it!)' (ibid.). Here we are reminded that the bodies on screen, and the actions they perform, are part of the series' artifice. No longer averted, Nigel's gaze is fixed on the bodies of McTeer and Harrison; he figures *their* response, and not the 'characters' they play. In doing so, he extends the series' de-realization of lesbian sex, further containing (his own) anxieties surrounding the public exposure of private lives and 'real' sex.

Tipping the Velvet: An Alternative Framework?

It would be tempting to read the BBC's adaptation of *Tipping the Velvet*, broadcast twelve years after *Portrait*, as a product of increasing tolerance and greater visibility. *Tipping* was certainly more explicit: sex scenes did not fade out and the series' stars were shown to engage in a range of practices, from under-the-sheets cunnilingus to female-female penetration with a strap-on leather dildo. Sex also formed part of the series' promotional blurb; it was marketed as 'the most sexually explicit period drama ever shown on British TV' and screenwriter Andrew Davies described it as 'absolutely filthy' (Cozens, 2002). Progress appears to have been made with lesbianism emphasized, rather than denied, in public soundbites (compare this to Colin Tucker's 'lesbianism is irrelevant').

As an adaptation of Sarah Waters' neo-Victorian novel, *Tipping* was freed from *Portrait*'s ties to 'real' life and its redoubled claim to authenticity. Speaking in *The Telegraph* shortly before the first episode was broadcast, Waters revealed her source text was 'as much "historical fantasy" as research', and in the *Radio Times* she described her urge to 'queer' the period: to impose 'startling lesbian action' onto a 'familiar Victorian backdrop' (Cohu, 2002; Dickson, 2002, p. 24). *Tipping* thus unsettles paradigms of costume drama, undermining 'popular conceptualisation[s] of the past' (compare this to *Portrait*'s faithful adherence to the period 'as most would imagine it to have been') (De Groot, 2009, p. 187). For Jerome de Groot (*ibid.*, p. 193), this necessitated the 'queering of [...] genre'. *Tipping* disrupts realist traditions in order to render non-normative sexuality visible, while artifice is signalled through a range of metafictive and metatheatrical devices. For example, a shot of Sarah Waters in the opening sequence of episode one provides an intertextual nod to the series' status as fiction; slow motion and fast motion disrupt representations of time and action – including a comically-frantic, speeded-up sex scene – while fades between scenes often take the form of a spotlight. This stylized production reinforced the series' pervasive concern with performativity, from the 'queer electric spaces' of the theatre – including stage, dressing room and players' lodgings – and the tableaux performed for Mrs Lethaby (Anna Chancellor), to the social construction (and manipulation) of gendered, sexual roles, such as male renter or 'angel in the house' (both performed by Nan (Rachael Stirling)) (Waters, 2006, p. 38). Performativity enables a profusion of sexual identities and behaviours to be represented. As such, lesbian sex in *Tipping* was not dependent on butch/femme imitations, but rather sought to confuse this heterosexual logic. In episode one, for example, a montage sequence depicts Nan as she learns her new role as a music hall 'masher', intercutting footage of rehearsal and on-stage performance. The kiss shared by Nan and Kitty (Keeley Hawes) on stage, while both are costumed in male suits, is a subversive moment of butch/butch desire contained by their acknowledged performance. But the kiss shared by Nan and Kitty in rehearsal is less easily quantified. As they rehearse, Nan and Kitty wear a combination of male and female dress, donning skirts and bowler hats, and thus their desires do not fit neatly into strict binaries of gender.

Tipping breaks the heterosexual frame employed by *Portrait*, but does this mean it was more successful as a representation of lesbian lives and sex? If explicitness is to be the measure, then the answer must be yes. But lesbianism in *Tipping* was contained by unreality. Where *Portrait* had raised anxieties due to its paradoxical performance of 'real' lives and sex, *Tipping* was made safe by its 'innate inauthenticity' (De Groot, 2009, p. 193). It was this that enabled Andrew Davies to 'sell' the series' depiction of lesbianism – insisting 'We are not pornography, we are drama' – and which prompted much of the popular and critical response (Cohu, 2002). In an interview for *The Telegraph*, Rachael Stirling described the resulting atmosphere of titillation: 'you get all these male journalists asking you what it's like to kiss a girl. I just think, you're a bloody man, you tell me!' (Donaldson, 2002). *Tipping* had thus become a spectacle adapted for, and consumed by, the heterosexual male gaze – its playful representation of lesbian sex providing a *frisson* of excitement. In fact, it was widely reported that audiences clamoured for more. The *Daily Mail* asked 'Where was the blue Velvet?', claiming viewers had complained, 'aggrieved that the sex scenes were too tame' (Bonnici, 2002). Such a response suggests the series was not perceived as a threat to normative sexuality or traditional values, but any residual fears could be easily contained via a denigration of the series' quality. According to Jerome de Groot (2009, p. 193), those who considered *Tipping* offensive 'were mourning a particular type of conservative, culturally one-dimensional "classic" series'. In *The Independent*, for example, the series' stylized production came in for criticism: 'This isn't a subtle or decorous adaptation at all – it's the equivalent of a Victorian playbill, all period typefaces and arresting changes of scale' (Thomas Sutcliffe cited in *The Guardian*, 2002). Whereas *The Telegraph* drew an explicit connection between the series' screening of sex and poor quality: '*Tipping The Velvet* apparently hoped that the lesbian angle would be sufficient to disguise the thinness of last night's material' (James Walton cited in *The Guardian*, 2002). For de Groot (2009, p. 193), this denigration forms part of a broader attempt to 'remarginalise [...] lesbian identities' – to reinstate traditional (i.e. heteronormative) depictions of history and historical persons. Thus, *Tipping* can be safely exiled from the canon of costume drama – a poor quality, sexually-explicit 'blip' in an otherwise consistent realm of quality BBC programming.

Tamsin Wilton (1995, p. 4) suggests it is important for lesbians to 'break into' conventional cultural forms and thus 'destroy [their] monolithic heterosexism'. From this perspective, all depictions of lesbianism in costume drama are potentially subversive. But while the heterosexism of costume drama may have been unsettled, it has nonetheless remained intact. Depictions of 'real' lesbian lives – in dramas claiming redoubled authenticity – have been tentative and sexually tame. Reliant on butch/femme pairings, they have heterosexualized lesbian sex. We are thus returned to the apparitional: in *Portrait*, lesbianism is contained, or 'ghosted', by the pre-eminence of marriage (Castle, 1993, p. 4). In terms of visibility, *Tipping* has been the most successful lesbian costume drama, achieving a level of explicitness still to be repeated or bettered.[4] But sex in *Tipping* was fully de-realized by the playful, metatheatrical production, while the series itself was subject to (potentially phobic) criticism. To return to Terry Castle (1993, p. 7), the recurrence of the lesbian figure in costume drama testifies to her 'peculiar cultural power'. But we are yet to see her fully, unambiguous and unapologetic.

Endnotes

1 I am grateful to Adam Nicolson for his permission to quote from this source.
2 For a detailed account of the publication and containment of lesbian desire in *Portrait of a Marriage*, see my article: Amber K. Regis (2011), 'Competing life narratives: *Portrait*s of Vita Sackville-West', *Life Writing*, 8, (3), 287–300.
3 Prairie Public Television in North Dakota chose not to broadcast the series at all, claiming it '[violated] community standards beyond saving'. See *The New York Times* (1992), 'PBS mini-series rejected in N. Dakota', *The New York Times*, [online] 20 July. Available at: <http://www.nytimes.com/1992/07/20/arts/pbs-mini-series-rejected-in-n-dakota.html>
4 In 2005 the BBC broadcast an adaptation of Sarah Waters' *Fingersmith* (dir. Aisling Walsh). This series was not as explicit as *Tipping*, nor was its lesbianism as central to the plot. In 2010 the BBC broadcast *The Secret Diaries of Miss Anne Lister* (dir. James Kent). This series marked a return to the legitimating framework and heterosexualized lesbianism of *Portrait*, employing an intensified rhetoric of cultural legitimacy to insist on Lister's universal relevance: 'It's not about being gay or lesbian – the story is about anybody who wants to be who they want to be' (Osborn, 2010).

11

The Conquests of Henry VIII: Masculinity, Sex and the National Past in *The Tudors*

Basil Glynn

Peter Kramer has made the argument that certain American television shows are now superior to cinema films (cited in Jancovich and Lyons, 2003, p. 1). While the question as to whether one form is superior to the other is debatable, it is certainly becoming increasingly difficult to separate one from the other given the cross-fertilization that occurs today between the two mediums in terms of stars, financing, production and creative talent. It is also becoming more and more difficult to discuss the two as national products, as American or British for example, given the number of films and series being produced by studios in international partnerships and with these studios themselves often being owned by global conglomerations.

The Tudors (2007–10) is a television series that is a prime example of such contested national status. In its interpretation of the story of Henry VIII, it can be placed within a larger meta-text as it draws on previous versions and renditions of the king's life that go back at least as far as Shakespeare. It draws on generally known historical facts, previous cinematic and television portrayals of Henry himself and owes a great debt to British costume dramas and historical films. In addition, it also owes its existence to non-British influences such as American and Canadian production companies. It features an international all-star cast and was filmed in Ireland with an Irish actor as the English king. Given the series' intercontinental production credentials and wide-ranging historical credentials and influences, this chapter discusses *The Tudors* as an international product, explores how the series portrays British history and considers what this particular portrayal of the king reveals about on-screen Englishness and British masculinity on the international stage (and television screen).

Since the early days of cinema, Henry VIII has been a figure who has fascinated British filmmakers and, at times, the tellings of his story have been instrumental in shaping the British film industry. In 1911 William George Barker, who in 1910 had built the first Ealing studio, brought a stage production of Shakespeare's *Henry VIII* to the screen with the selling point that all prints of the film would be burnt within six weeks (and as there are no surviving prints, there is nothing to suggest that he was anything other than true to his word).[1] Running at over half an hour at a time when most British films were less than ten minutes long (Street, 1997, p. 36), it was in the film historian Rachael Low's (1949, p. 209) post-war appraisal, Britain's 'first really important feature film'. Roy Armes (1978, p. 30) argues that 'the intense interest which its production aroused' helped break 'the stagnation of the British cinema' whilst James Spark (1990, p. 44) suggests that the fact that it brought Shakespeare's gravitas to the cinema 'was welcomed by exhibitors, who felt that stage adaptations would enable them to attract a better class of customer'. In Spark's (*ibid.*) opinion, however, rather than saving the British film industry this film was only important for damaging it by sounding a death knell for innovative films that offered 'excitement' in favour of 'London stage actors running through potted silent versions of Shakespeare'.

Similarly, Alexander Korda's *The Private Lives of Henry VIII* (1933) has been viewed as both helping and hindering the British film industry. Greg Walker (2003, p. ix) proclaims that it was 'probably the most important film produced in Britain before the Second World War' because with this one film Korda effectively 'put British pictures on the world map'. Negatively, however, because it broke box office records in America, Sarah Street (2000, p. 55) argues that it 'encouraged other British producers to aim at world markets ... [and] ... many blamed the example set by Korda for promoting profligacy and overextension, contributing to the famous "crash" of many British film companies in 1937'. Despite such cinematic ups and downs, however, the focus on the personal lives of Tudor monarchs continued on in England with Gainsborough's *Tudor Rose* (1936, dir. Robert Stevenson, 1936) and in Hollywood with Warner Bros' *The Private Lives of Elizabeth and Essex* (1939, dir. Michael Curtiz, 1939), MGM's *Young Bess* (1953, dir. George Sidney, 1953) and Twentieth Century Fox's *The Virgin Queen* (1955, dir. Henry Koster, 1955).

When not starring, Elizabeth and Henry became established supporting players in British and American films, Elizabeth in London Film Productions' *Fire over England* (dir. William K. Howard, 1937), Warner Bros' *The Sea Hawk* (dir. Michael Curtiz, 1940) and Universal Pictures' *Mary Queen of Scots* (dir. Charles Jarrott, 1971), and Henry in Warner Bros' *The Prince and the Pauper* (dir. William Keighley, 1937), Disney's *The Sword and the Rose* (dir. Ken Annakin, 1953), Highland Films' *A Man for All Seasons* (dir. Fred Zinnemann, 1966), Hal Wallis Productions' *Anne of the Thousand Days* (dir. Charles Jarrott, 1969), Rank's *Carry on Henry* (dir. Gerald Thomas, 1971), International Film Productions' *The Prince and the Pauper* (dir. Richard Fleischer, 1977) and BBC Films and Focus Features' *The Other Boleyn Girl* (dir. Justin Chadwick, 2008).

A number of these later films were neither distinctly British nor American but were instead 'international' in nature. Robert Murphy, in *Sixties British Cinema* (1992, p. 6), went so far as to exclude detailed discussion of films like *A Man for All Seasons*, *Anne of the Thousand Days* and *Mary, Queen of Scots* because they were either directed or funded by Americans and thus belonged 'to an international Hollywood-dominated cinema'. If one were to look for more bona fidely British representations of the Tudor dynasty at the time, then it would have been on television, particularly in BBC costume dramas such as *The Six Wives of Henry VIII* (1970), *Elizabeth R* (1971) and *The Shadow of the Tower* (1972), which respectively depicted the lives of Henry and his wives,[2] Elizabeth I and Henry's father Henry VII.

Television interest in the Tudors would not reach early 1970s levels again until the early noughties when several dramatic works appeared, prompted in no small part by the success of the film *Elizabeth* (dir. Shekhar Kapur, 1998) in the cinema. *Henry VIII* (Granada, 2003) starred Ray Winstone as the eponymous king and *The Other Boleyn Girl* (BBC, 2003) featured Jared Harris as Henry. Elizabeth I reappeared in 2005 in the BBC's *The Virgin Queen* with Anne-Marie Duff as Elizabeth and Channel 4's *Elizabeth I* with Helen Mirren (who had a busy time playing royal Elizabeths, starring as Elizabeth II the following year in *The Queen* (dir. Stephen Frears, 2006)).

In terms of being authentic British products, however, things had begun to change in the noughties. Just as in the 1960s when the British monarch film became 'international', foreign production companies also began to take an interest in the 'high end'[3] monarch television series, *Elizabeth I* receiving production investment from America's HBO. *The Tudors* falls into this same category, with its co-production status even more convo-luted with involvement from the British Working Title Films, Irish Octagon Films, Canadian Peace Arch Entertainment and American based Reveille Productions and Showtime (a subsidiary of CBS). Although the series was exclusively shown on the BBC (which is understandable given its reputation for quality costume drama), it had nothing to do with its production.

While there are financial advantages in multi-national co-productions, such as gaining easier access to the partner's markets and shooting locations as well as foreign government incentives and subsidies,[4] an important side-effect is that aesthetically and subtextually internationally created texts such as *The Tudors* have become increasingly unbounded by specific national context and this has ramifications for the critical study of such texts. In the 1980s a British heritage film like *Chariots of Fire* (dir. Hugh Hudson, 1981) could, relatively unproblematically, be 'construed as the embodiment of Thatcherite patriotic rhetoric' (Hall, 2001, p. 191) and the heritage genre itself be seen to be 'fuelled by resurgent Thatcherist nationalism' (Allrath and Gymnich, 2005, p. 212) because the texts under discussion were seen as British films that said things about and to Britain. Just like BBC costume dramas that were 'a touch-stone of national culture – "passion plays" broadcast to millions of homes' (Pidduck 2001, p. 131), such films were understood as a loosely defined body connected, as Sheldon Hall (2001, p. 191) argues, by their 'common invocation of British history, literature and/or an "approved" cultural tradition'.

When there are complicated co-production deals, however, this notion of 'Britishness' becomes harder to assert. *Elizabeth* (1998), for example, which was written by the British writer Michael Hirst (who also executive produced and wrote all four seasons of *The Tudors*), was co-produced by the British Working Title Films, Channel Four Films and also the American Polygram Filmed Entertainment. In addition, it was directed by Shekhar Kapur, a veteran of Bollywood films, which further complicated its British creden-tials.[5] International in both creation and intended target audience, there was something very 'un-British' about this particular rendition of the iconic queen's early life. Julianne Pidduck (2001, p. 134–5), for example, argues that its 'sex, intrigue, raw physicality and violence' distinguished it 'from a largely demure British tradition'. 'In an affront to costume drama's tender sensibilities', she continues, 'the costumes come off' (*ibid.*, p. 135).

The sexual and violent explicitness of *Elizabeth* is actually only surprising if one examines the film in relation to an exclusively British tradition of historical films or within the context of British costume drama. If one were instead to consider it in relation to the far less demure contemporary cinema of the era then it would be easy to comment that the costumes still remain on more than usual and the violence is rather tame. What perhaps an international film like *Elizabeth* more tellingly reveals, as Robert Murphy (1992) found with earlier monarch films, is that its production credentials make it extremely difficult to discuss such texts in relation to exclusively British traditions.[6]

On television, similar internationalization is occurring in the form of multi-company, multi-national historical television series like *Rome* (BBC/HBO, 2005–7), *Camelot*[7] (CBS/Ecosse/Octagon/Starz/Take 5, 2011–), *The Borgias* (Mid Atlantic Films/Octagon/Take 5, 2011–), *Spartacus: Blood and Sand* (Starz, 2010–) and *Spartacus: Gods of the Arena* (Starz, 2011).[8] All of these series suggest that the historical specificity of national pasts are becoming secondary to a transnational televisual rendition of sex, violence and bad language set in period but performed and visually rendered in a very modern manner for an international audience. These series are alike not only in their departures from historical factuality but also in the conformity of male behaviour depicted. Rather than the cultural and historic uniqueness of Rome, Capua or Dark Age England being explored, these dramas offer instead picturesque eras and places populated by dehistoricized male characters who have magnificent bodies, engage in energetic sex and commit brutal and spectacular violence. They present the erotic spectacle of female bodies being sexually abused and the violent spectacle of male bodies being physically abused.

Unlike traditional British costume and historical dramas, these series do not present to audiences the grand heritage of a national past through the location shooting of splendid manor houses, cathedrals and castles. Instead, the worlds the characters in these series inhabit are largely CGI conjured and, just as in more contemporary historical films like *300* (dir. Zack Snyder, 2006), suggest less the past (the CGI period depicted) than now (the CGI technology used to depict it). In contrast to L. P. Hartley's suggestion in his novel *The Go-Between* (1953) that 'the past is a foreign country: they do things differently there', contemporary historical transnational television co-productions propose that the past is not that foreign at all. Period sensibility has given way to modern receptivity in that internationally produced historical drama does not strive to meet audience expectation of the past. Instead, part of its appeal is to offer a modernization of history that runs counter to audience expectation of what the past was like. History in these dramas has become populated with people who are clean, buff and toned and who have sex at the drop of a period hat. Modern hair gels, breast implants and teeth whitening agents anachronistically exist and bloodshed is viewed in slow-mo, close-up and multi-angles. Rather than concealing this revamping of the past, the overhauling of history and its largely 'demure' depiction has become an essential part of their draw.[9]

In 1933, at the beginning of *The Private Life of Henry VIII* (dir. Alexander Korda) and after keeping the audience waiting for seven minutes of the running time, Charles Laughton appeared as the king in a doorway looking as if he had just stepped out of Hans Holbein's famous portrait. So powerful had this painting been in creating the image of Henry that Greg Walker (2003, p. 20) suggested 'any actor taking on the role of the King must [...] come to terms with the impact and legacy of Holbein's portrait'. Laughton 'grew his beard to precisely the length indicated by Holbein', and 'combed his hair meticulously' and 'tried to turn the image from a two-dimensional portrait into a living character' (ibid., p. 22). Similar interpretations faithful to the portrait have been attempted by the likes of Richard Burton, Montague Love, Keith Mitchell, Robert Shaw, Charlton Heston and even Sid James. In contrast, however, The Tudors flaunts the fact that it does not offer the expected depiction of Henry. When Holbein's portrait of the old, overweight king appears in the credits, it is immediately followed by the young, thin and handsome Jonathan Rhys Meyers smirking and widening his eyes directly into the camera as if to say 'Yes, that's right! I look nothing like him'. From the very beginning the central conceit of the drama is made clear; this is the past as you do not know it. The voiceover intones at the beginning of each episode, 'You think you know a story but you only know how it ends. To get to the heart of a story you have to go back to the beginning'.

As a brief trawl through the internet will reveal, The Tudors is rife with historical solecisms such as Henry having red hair rather than brown, two sisters rather than one and so on. The series, not particularly interested in authentically telling how 'the story' of the historical Henry started or ended, tells as the voiceover informs us, 'a story'. As Michael Hirst admitted, 'Showtime commissioned me to write an entertainment, a soap opera, and not history. And we wanted people to watch it'.[10] The result, rather than largely 'being educational' (Gerry Scott cited in BBC Education, 1994, p. 30) as the BBC classic dramas were encouraged to be viewed, is instead as Allesandra Stanley of The New York Times (2007, p. E1) described The Tudors, 'renaissance romping with Henry and his rat pack'.

By discarding Holbein's portrait (and with it many of the popular associations the image of the aged king conjured up) the past became a largely blank canvas allowing The Tudors to bring it in closer proximity with the present. One very noticeable way in which it achieved this was through occupying period verisimilitude with jarring modern vernacular. For example, the Duke of Norfolk (Henry Czerny), upon observing Henry's anger at Cardinal Wolsey (Sam Neill), turns to Thomas More (Jeremy Northam) and says 'indignatio principis mors est', which More translates for us as 'the anger of the prince means death'. This 'period' scene is immediately and jarringly followed by a temporal non sequitur with the king ranting to a servant about the Pope's refusal to grant him a divorce in very modern idiom: 'I want you to force his fucking holiness into submission, if necessary by telling him that if he does not grant me my fucking annulment then England will withdraw its submission to Rome' (1.8). On another occasion the elevated period language of Sir Thomas Wyatt's beautiful poem, 'They Flee from Me That Sometime Did Me Seek' (1.6), about the pain of being jilted that features in one episode, is brought right up to date in another when Wyatt (Jamie Thomas King), considering the same woman, less poetically exclaims 'for what it's worth, I did fuck her'(1.10). Hirst clearly intended his Tudor past to contain 'an idea [...] of modernity' populated by 'characters who were not distanced in time but right in your face and you could talk to'.[11] Throughout, the series continually makes use of modern frames of reference to negate the strangeness of the past with the characters indeed 'right in your face' with 'cock' and 'cunt' just as commonplace as the occasional heightened language of the age.

The casting of the handsome and athletic Meyers as Henry certainly sexed up the character away from the popularly held image of the overfed king and the drama focuses upon him as an attractive young man rather than a bloated monster. Although unexpected, this was initially a not altogether historically inaccurate approach because, as Camille Naish (1991, p. 41) explains, at the age of twenty-three Henry had been described as '"the best-looking royal person in Christendom". He was also the most learned, the most liberal, and probably the most athletic. He excelled at tennis and dancing [...] he played the lute, organ and other keyboard instruments, and could have made a living as a professional musician, had he not been King [...] a friend to humanists and scholars, he was surrounded with the best minds of his time; he was, in short, the ideal Renaissance prince'. As Natalie Dormer (the actress who plays Anne Boleyn in *The Tudors*) describes him, he was in his prime 'the charismatic alpha male of Europe'.[12] Hirst had already been attracted to the youth of Henry's daughter in *Elizabeth*, stating that he 'wanted to show her as a young woman – the young woman arrested for treason and afraid for her life; the young woman passionately in love with Robert Dudley – and not the white-faced, pearl-encrusted icon of her later years, and of historical memory' (Pidduck, 2001, p. 134). In *The Tudors* he repeats the same trick of taking a famous Tudor historical figure with something of an image problem and giving them a modern makeover. However, season four of *The Tudors* in particular reveals, in terms of maintaining a semblance of historical factuality, the problem in overly relying upon sexing up historical figures to make the past more appealing because this season depicts the life of the aged king. In this season at least one would expect him to become obese, to become like Holbein's portrait, but he never does. Meyers just gains a few wrinkles, speaks in a husky voice and wears thicker clothes.

The fact that Henry never really loses his sex appeal, even in season four, is understandable if one considers the way the dramatic world of the series is constructed around male power, male beauty and male heterosexual desire. In *The Tudors'* body politic the king is the head of state and all of the arms of government are controlled by men put in positions of power by the king himself. Within the drama, the king's power is absolute and as a result his sexual affairs directly impact upon the affairs of state. In the first two seasons proceedings are dominated by the love triangle between Henry, his wife Catherine of Aragon (Maria Doyle Kennedy) and Anne Boleyn, the woman he loves and wants to marry. England's great schism with Rome and the English Reformation are both presented as a direct result of his lust for Anne Boleyn. The king's sexual desires drive the transformations of the nation and many of its great and powerful men are ultimately brought low because they cannot accommodate these desires: Cardinal Wolsey for not managing to obtain a divorce for the king, Sir Thomas More for refusing to approve it and Thomas Cromwell (James Frain) for failing to find a suitable wife.

Throughout the series, Henry is led as much by the 'member' in his codpiece as he is by the members of his cabinet. For example, during negotiations between England and France, Henry meets Anne Boleyn's sister, Mary (Perdita Weeks), and asks what 'French graces' she has learnt at the French court. She answers by giving him oral sex, a scene immediately followed by the king signing the 'Treaty of Universal and Perpetual Peace', suggesting that any anger he may have felt towards the French has now been well and truly assuaged (1.2). In the next episode, during a play performed in honour of the king, Henry falls for Anne Boleyn while she is playing the role of 'Perseverance', one of the Graces, but this time in a very different rendition of a 'grace' to the one performed by her sister. In response to her perseverance and ambition to be queen, the series depicts how he showers her with gift after gift, bestows her with a title, the Duchess of Pembrokeshire, and even presents her with the jewels of the queen of England. Once the couple consummate their love, however, the king's ardour quickly cools and turns to murderous intent, particularly when she fails to provide him with a son.

Historically, as Camille Naish (1991, p. 5) observes, 'in western societies of every type in almost every era numbers of women have mounted the scaffold in ultimate obeissance to laws they have sometimes violated but seldom, until the present time, have had the possibility to make'. *The Tudors* does a fine job of conveying this political powerlessness as again and again women like Anne Boleyn are forced to face courts consisting entirely of men. On each occasion we know they are facing a lie, and on each occasion we know that the lie will win. From the very first episode it is also made evident that even in the domestic space women have little power. When we see Henry's wife, Catherine, being prepared to receive him by two ladies-in-waiting it is apparent that both of these women have slept with the king. One is even pregnant with his child. It is a world, as Henry says, in which women 'must shut' their 'eyes and endure' (2.6). The only power women have is sexual. As the Duke of Norfolk explains, only when a woman 'opens her legs', can she 'open her mouth' and have some influence (1.3). In Henry's wives cases, this influence depends upon continuing to satisfy his sexual appetites and meeting the reproductive demands he places upon their bodies. Any female power attained is ultimately ephemeral as it always succumbs to the king's when allure fades, usually when his eye falls upon another and always if she fails to produce a son. It is a particularly masculinized view of history that *The Tudors* offers, in part because women were oppressed in the period depicted but also because the depiction suited the period in which the series was made.

James Chapman (2005, p. 322) suggests that historical films often gain their contemporary resonance as a result of coincidental contemporary events that have a 'major bearing on the ways' they are 'understood'. For example, Hirst's *Elizabeth* was seen in some quarters to 'bond heritage to a more modern sensitivity' and 'embody Tony Blair's "Cool Britannia'"' (Vincendeau 2001, p. xxi) while in others the young queen spoke in a more Conservative voice, Renée Pigeon (2001, p. 19) suggesting she had the 'vulnerability of a Diana and the ruthlessness of a Thatcher'. The resonance with audiences of Hirst's *The Tudors* can similarly be attributed to the bonding of 'heritage to a more modern sensitivity', but in this case it dealt with international rather than purely British preoccupations and did so in a way that would prove quite different from a 'typically' British approach.

In 2003, Granada Television produced a quaintly old-fashioned British version of *Henry VIII* starring quintessentially British actors such as Ray Winstone, Charles Dance, David Suchet, Helene Bonham Carter and Joss Ackland. In the course of detailing Henry's relationships with his six wives, the king's passion was depicted as, variously, hand wringing, sweaty staring, face wiping, letter writing and soft-focus skinny dipping. In contrast, only four minutes into the first episode of *The Tudors* and Henry is shown graphically making love to a married woman. Fifteen minutes later, finding his wife otherwise occupied, he instead makes love to her servant. Twenty-three minutes in, and we are watching his best friend, Charles Brandon (Henry Cavill), vigorously having sex with the daughter of their mutual enemy, the Duke of Buckingham (Steven Waddington). Only half-way through the episode and it is already abundantly clear that this is 'high end' costume drama with more flesh on display in the first sex scene than in the entire running length of Granada's version, more bodice ripping than *Carry On Henry* and as much simulated sex as *The Undercover Scandals of Henry VIII* (Charlton de Serge's 1970 pornographic Henrician romp).

The explicit portrayals of passionate sex presented in *The Tudors* are less part of the tradition of British costume drama than they are of American cable television drama. As a result of *The Tudors* international origins and ambitions, the depiction of period sex along with British masculinity has been 'internationalized' with Tudor men comparable in their sexual behaviour to the non-British characters that populate other international television historical dramas such as *Rome* and *Spartacus: Blood and Sand*. In contrast to the types of readings previously mentioned of *Elizabeth* in specifically British terms as responses to, for example, New Labour's 'Cool Britannia', when considering the depiction of characters like Henry and Charles in *The Tudors* it is perhaps more revealing to consider them in relation to 'mass-cool-inity', a term (and admittedly painful pun) I introduce to describe the series non-nationally-specific, nominally British imaginary of cool, enviable and heterosexual manhood aimed at a mass international audience.

Judith Butler (1990) and Mary Anne Doane (1982) suggest that 'woman-liness' and 'manliness' are masquerades, dramaturgical performances and *The Tudors* reveals that some performances are considered more attractive than others when dramas are produced for and by multiple countries. John Beynon's (2002, p. 16) distinction between 'hegemonic masculinity' (that reinforces dominant gender ideology) and 'subordinate variants' (that oppose and challenge it) is evident in the series with the latter subordinated in the extreme. Heterosexual men look and behave in ways that are approved of by dominant culture and that broad audiences can relate to and admire. In contrast, gay men in *The Tudors*, rather than critiquing such behaviour, serve what Adrienne Rich (1980, p. 632) terms 'the bias of compulsory hetero-sexuality' by being revealed as mistaken in their sexual choices or harmful to heterosexual society. To borrow Yvonne Tasker's (1993, p. 95) categories, there are clearly defined '"good" and "bad" masculinities' on display in the series.

Despite the presence of several gay characters, homosexual sex is never shown in *The Tudors*.[13] Same-sex relationships belong either to a higher, spiritual plane (as with the romance between William Compton (Kris Holden-Ried) and the composer Thomas Tallis (Joe Van Moyland)) or become sublimated into violence against women (as in the case of George Boleyn (Padraic Delaney) expressing his desire for the musician Mark Smeaton (David Alpay) by assaulting his own wife). In the first gay relationship depicted in the series, the love between the physically frail Tallis and charming Compton is expressed through a single, brief candlelit kiss (1.5). Other than this momentary expression of affection, Compton acts solely as Tallis' muse for his compositions. Tallis' own devotion is expressed by his turning down the opportunity to have sex with two beautiful women at the same time, who happen to be also twins (1.4), but his resistance to 'good masculinity' only lasts whilst Compton is alive. When he dies, he sleeps with one of them and marries the other.

In contrast to the lack of physical detail shown in relation to contact between the lovers, Compton's death is depicted in graphic detail. He gets 'the sweating sickness' and has blood drained from his back. He dies surrounded by and soaked in his diseased blood and his wife is warned to burn his bedding and clothing and that he should be put in the ground first thing. However, his disease infects and causes the death of his wife. As he is the first character to contract this mysterious plague, it is seen to radiate from this one gay man and infect much of the country. Thomas More observes that it is a punishment from god. If left in any doubt as to what the disease actually represents, Henry gives Charles an ointment to protect his 'cock' (1.7).

In the relationship between George Boleyn, Anne's brother, and the dashing Mark Smeaton, Anne's musician friend, there is not even a kiss. Both, as gay men, serve the narrative function of offering Anne sensitive, non-threatening male support (kindness that she does not receive from her father or uncle). Even though George is gay, he too has slept with the same twins as Tallis (who seem to act as a form of litmus test for how gay a character actually is) and he too gets married. With a character unable to fully abandon his homosexuality as Tallis did, in a drama unwilling to show gay sex, George acts out his desire for Smeaton through brutally anally raping his wife, a deeply unpleasant, but at least heterosexual act, shown at some length.

In contrast to the sorry confusion of the gay men in the drama, the athletic and heterosexual Henry and his rugged best friend Charles act out their heterosexual fantasy lives with ungay abandon. Their 'good' masculinity is accentuated as they play tennis, joust and wrestle in front of adoring female audiences. They make love to an array of young, willing and beautiful women (perhaps 'firm-ininity' is another term we could coin here in reference to the toned nature of the women who are serially seduced and displayed in these dramas). In an arm-wrestling competition between Henry and Charles, the king's straining bicep almost fills the screen accentuating his 'musculinity'[14] (1.6). In order to have sex with a woman, all the king has to ask is 'do you consent' and, of course, she always does. These are not the males of British television costume drama or much British cinema. There is no insecurity or charming inability to express feelings. Henry is not a Mr D'Arcy or a prevaricating Hugh Grant figure (from *Four Weddings and a Funeral* (dir. Mike Newell, 1994) or *Notting Hill* (dir. Roger Michell, 1999)) who endlessly considers and reconsiders the merits of entering into a relationship. There is no bumbling awkwardness, no stiff upper lips, no unspoken desire. Instead, as Henry Cavill said of his character Charles, the type of man on display here 'really can't keep his dick in his pants'.[15] Henry and Charles seduce, cast aside or send women running back to their husbands. They are heterosexual supermen.[16]

In terms of period depiction, the king pays lip service to the rituals of courtly love and enacts the chivalric code by wearing his wife's colours when jousting, but he is clearly no chivalrous king or English gentleman. If looking for British influences and antecedents one is better looking not to BBC television costume drama with their reserved English gentlemen, but rather the romps of Gainsborough and Woodfall with their dangerous, beautifully costumed, irresistibly handsome and seductive leading men. However, in contrast to these depictions of British masculinity that were considered transgressive in their day, there is little that is interrogative about the images of heterosexual masculinity on display in *The Tudors* in relation to national characteristics. One suspects that they are not challenging any particular notions of Englishness at all but are instead just spectacles of manhood, fine physical specimens that are cool and emulous and as empty of national context as Spartacus is in terms of his Thracian-ness in *Spartacus: Blood and Sand*.[17] Unlike the love lives of James Mason's Captain Jerry Jackson in Gainsborough's *The Wicked Lady* (dir. Leslie Arliss, 1945) or Albert Finney's *Tom Jones* (dir. Tony Richardson, 1963) which caused controversy upon their release, there is little shocking or even particularly surprising to our modern sensibilities about Henry or Charles' far more explicit sexual behaviour in *The Tudors*. In today's international historical dramas, whether it be Tudor Brits or ancient Romans, they all make love with the same athletic energy and multi-positioned variety we have long become accustomed to from American shows like *Sex and the City* (HBO, 1998–2004) and even appear cosier in doing so by presenting their sex acts as occurring in the distant past.

This is not to say that the Britishness of the subject matter plays no part in the popularity of *The Tudors*. In spite of its international production background, like *Elizabeth* (which starred Richard Attenborough and John Gielgud), *The Tudors* does recognize the value in the symbolic 'Englishness' of its subject and its genre. It has a veneer of British quality television costume drama by featuring recognizable British actors such as Peter O'Toole, Simon Ward and Jeremy Northam.[18] However, given the number of years English national identity has been exported by the British film and television industries, then been reconstructed and revised by Hollywood and 'internationalized' by the likes of the 'monarch' films Murphy excised from his history of 1960s British cinema, the on-screen depiction of Englishness perhaps no longer 'subliminally' suggests, as British costume pictures used to, 'the superiority of British culture and its role in world affairs' (Walker, 2003,

p. 33). Instead, in today's international television historical dramas, the Britain on offer has less to do with national superiority than with accommodating an international consensus notion of Western WASP ascendency.

Just as in various cinematic renditions of Robin Hood as performed by the Tasmanian Errol Flynn,[19] Scottish Sean Connery,[20] American Kevin Costner[21] and Australian Russell Crowe,[22] the Englishness of Henry is of secondary importance to his white, Western heroic qualities (and so it is of little consequence that he is portrayed by the Irish actor Jonathan Rhys Meyers). *The Tudors* presents the king of a Christian country standing firmly against the military aggression of Catholic Spain and the religious intolerance of the Pope in Rome, a position of defiance against a menacing external religion and threatening foreign powers that broad Western audiences familiar with 'the war on terror' can easily identify with. The Spanish have agents who blend in and plot to overthrow the British government and the status quo. In response, Henry founds the Church of England and becomes, quite literally, the first and most powerful symbol of WASP resistance and power.

As a result of the contemporary resonance of foreign religious threat to WASP security, one of the great 'heroes' of British costume drama becomes significantly transformed in *The Tudors*. Sir Thomas More, canonized as a man of great conscience and religious principle in *A Man for All Seasons*, is recast as a religious fanatic. The religiously moderate and worldly Cardinal Wolsey, who is content to work within the existing order, sees More's obsession with the next world rather than this one as misguided, and bemoans how 'evil men pray louder, seek penance and think themselves closer to heaven' than people like him (1.10). Capable of terrible brutality to enforce his position of intolerance, More follows a leader in the Pope who speaks glibly of the glories of martyrdom, conspires with foreign powers to enforce archaic religious practices and believes those who sacrifice their lives in the name of their religion will 'receive all of heaven's graces' (2.5).

By presenting a monoethnic society in which WASP values triumph, *The Tudors* offers a masculinist rescue of white Western heritage from its threatened present in which Western countries have been drawn into questionable military expeditions abroad and heightened security at home. Under threat from foreign powers overseas and threatening religious ideas domestically, *The Tudors* resonates with the present in its depiction of a country struggling for strength and security. England's dynamic nature is presented as bound up with the king's forceful virility and militaristic aggression as he propels his country towards a better future, a reclamation of Western masculinity under threat by weakness on the international stage following events such as the London bombings of 7 July 2005 that directly preceded *The Tudors*.[23]

In 1960s Britain, following the Suez debacle and Britain's subsequent international humiliation, writers such as John Osborne, Alan Sillitoe, Stan Barstow and David Storey all deliberated the effects that a crisis of national confidence has on men facing a future in a country perceived as weaker than in the past. John Hill (1983, p. 307) argued that such 'failed confidence in colonial certainties' went 'hand in hand with a failed confidence on the terrain of sexuality' whilst Stephen D. Arata (2000, p. 162) referred to such crises as symptomatic of an erosion in 'confidence in the inevitability of British progress and hegemony'. It is telling therefore that in the post-Suez British New Wave cinema (which spoke to domestic audiences but did not export well) the response of the angry young men to their moment of national crisis was largely a performative reclamation of their masculinity through bedding as many women as they could.[24] However, in The Tudors, although Henry too beds a significant number of women, his sexual activities serve more than 'keeping the British end up' at a time of national distress. Because he occupies an iconic position in a period of perceived imperial greatness, he also reasserts WASP masculinity for a wide variety of Western audiences whose countries share the same national distress as each other. Unlike the Suez crisis when an Islamic nation threatened the national confidence of just Britain and France, a more widespread and internationally shared crisis of confidence has existed post 9/11.

As well as speaking to an international audience because it addresses international concerns, The Tudors also appeals because it balances popular international styles of television. In the process of telling the story of Henry's political and sexual life, The Tudors displays American influences, notably a reproduction of Showtime and HBO's graphic depictions of sex and violence as seen in shows like Dexter (2006–) and The Sopranos (1999–2007). Yet it is so effective because it is also a costume drama set in Britain which as a genre has long been synonymous with quality British national cinema and television. Thus, in addition to presenting British heritage in an American style, the drama also draws upon a broad British heritage of sexual depiction in television and film, including Gainsborough and Woodfall's historical romances. It is because of this hybridity that the drama essentially 'gets away with' its graphic depictions of explicit sex and violence. Vivian Sobchack (1994, p. 320) argues that 'the containment provided by literary tradition, generic convention, and period costume allows ... [certain texts] ... to exploit eroticism and sadism beyond' that which is 'generally acceptable in more realistic genres'. Drawing upon British heritage provides 'high-end' status whilst generic hybridity and its Anglo-American-Irish-Canadian co-production status deflect potential criticism of the series' 'inauthentic' depiction of Britain's historical past. Through referencing British historical events, it enables the drama to be placed nearer to the respectable end of television culture. By emphasising period atmosphere and costuming, manor houses and manners, *The Tudors* has many of the accoutrements of a traditional heritage product. Ultimately it is the combination of the historically distant and traditional with the visceral and the new that makes *The Tudors* so effective. Rather than the past as depicted after the war[25] and in the 1980s where 'there is endless cricket, fair play with bent rules, fumbled sex, village teas and punting through long green summers'(Woollen, 1991, p. 182), *The Tudors* depicts the past as beneath the surface violent and sex-ridden. Rather than presenting it with the weightiness of historical costume drama or theatrical adaptation, however, it is wantonly popular television. For this it owes its more explicit aspects, or semantic components, to borrow Rick Altman's (1996, p. 283) term, to its American influences.

The Tudors is now over, but its explicitly sexual and violent approach towards the past has clearly become an established global alternative to BBC television costume drama. As the British *Radio Times* (Graham, 2011) television guide said after its demise: 'Has life never been quite the same since *The Tudors* ended for good? Do you feel the need of a tawdry historical drama full of toned bare bottoms and parting bimbos? Well, hello and welcome to *The Borgias*'.

Endnotes

1 Henry VIII also featured in other silent films such as the British *Henry VIII and Catherine Howard* (1911, Urban Trading Company) and the French *Jane Seymour and Henry VIII of England* (1912, Pathé Frères).

2 Each of the six episodes was devoted to one wife in turn.

3 I borrow here Robin Nelson's (2007, p. 2) definition of the term 'to indicate big budgets and the high production values associated with them, along with a "primetime" position in the schedule of a major channel'.

4 For a discussion of the economic advantages of co-production deals in television see: Colin Hoskins, Stuart McFadyen and Adam Finn (1997), *Global Television and Film: An Introduction to the Economics of the Business*. Oxford: Clarendon Press.

5 As, incidentally, did the crucial role played by the Indian producer Ismail Merchant in heritage cinema.

6 This has not stopped numerous critics from doing so. The critical and popular readings of *Elizabeth* and how the queen's portrayal related to British cinema at the time and Britain itself were debated by Andrew Higson (2003) and James Chapman (2005) in their respective books on British costume dramas and historical films.

7 This was co-created and executive produced by David Hirst.

8 Whilst the two *Spartacus* series were made by an American production company, they were made in New Zealand with much local personnel involvement.

9 It is important to note that British costume and historical films have not always had 'tender sensibilities'. The director Ken Russell, for example, is an important figure in British costume drama whose depictions of the past were far from 'demure'.

10 Interview with David Hirst in '*The Tudors*: The Complete First Season' DVD boxset (2007).

11 Interview with David Hirst in '*The Tudors*: The Complete First Season' DVD boxset (2007).

12 Interview with Natalie Dormer in '*The Tudors*: The Complete First Season' DVD boxset (2007).

13 Gay sex does feature in *Spartacus: Blood and Sand* and *Spartacus: Gods of the Arena*. It is notable, however, that the gay gladiators are weaker fighters, tend to be swarthy and Middle-Eastern and that the main heroes of both series are staunchly heterosexual.

14 A term used by Yvonne Tasker (1993, p. 2) to describe physical aspects of masculine representation in the cinema. 'Musculinity' is not exclusive to men but is also utilized to portray women behaving outside of their ascribed cinematic gender roles and behaving like men, as in the case of Sarah Connor (portrayed by Linda Hamilton) in *Terminator 2: Judgement Day* (1991, dir, James Cameron, 1991).

15 Interview with Henry Cavill in '*The Tudors*: The Complete First Season' DVD boxset (2007).

16 Cavill has actually been cast in the role of Superman in the forthcoming *Man of Steel* (dir. Zack Snyder, 2013).

17 For a discussion of mainstream masculinity as a 'collective norm' see: Richard Dyer (1979), *Stars*. London: BFI, pp. 53–68.

18 Even non-British-set dramas like *The Borgias* (with Jeremy Irons), *Spartacus: Blood and Sand* (with John Hannah) and *Camelot* (with Joseph Fiennes) star established British actors in important roles. For a long time, as Robin Nelson (1997, p. 150) explains, the funding for much flagship BBC costume drama had been 'made possible by the world sales potential of a prestigious British period drama with established actors'. Masterpiece Theatre and PBS, for example, distributed *Elizabeth R* in America. International costume dramas are perhaps simply following suit by hiring British stars to add a veneer of British costume drama.

19 *The Adventures of Robin Hood* (dir. Michael Curtiz, US, 1938).

20 *Robin and Marian* (dir. Richard Lester, US, 1976).

21 *Robin Hood: Prince of Thieves* (dir. Kevin Reynolds, US, 1991).

22 *Robin Hood* (dir. Ridley Scott, US, 2010).

23 Other significant incidents of the time include the Madrid bombings of 11 March 2004 and the foiled plot to blow up American commercial aircraft on 10 August 2005.

24 Reassertion of masculinity on screen can take many forms. For example, Susan Jeffords (1994) suggests fragile masculinity in the Reagan era was bolstered by the muscular hard bodies of the action heroes of American cinema of the 1980s. See also: Yvonne Tasker (1993), *Spectacular Bodies: Gender, Genre and the Action Cinema*. London: Routledge.

25 Sue Harper (1998, p. 109) points out how heritage was actively used in the war effort during World War II, explaining that 'the Ministry of Information was enthusiastic about the efficacy of history for propaganda purposes, and it promulgated films that used Britain's heritage in an exhortatory manner'.

Notes on Contributors

Dr James Aston is Director of Studies for the Film Studies Degree at the University of Hull, United Kingdom and teaches extensively on the programme including American Alternative Cinema, East Asian Cinema and Global Nightmares: Horror From Around the World. His principal research interests lie in the field of cinematic representations of the past especially in Hollywood during the 1960s and 1970s and post-9/11. He is active in other research areas that focus on pre-and-post millennium apocalyptic cinema and the films of Michael Haneke. Also, at present, he is co-editing a volume entitled *Small Screen Revelations: Apocalypse and Prophecy in Contemporary Television* (Phoenix Press, 2013).

Dr Emily Brick is Senior Lecturer in Film and Media Studies at Manchester Metropolitan University, United Kingdom. Her current research is on screen representations of female serial killers. She has co-edited *European Cinema: Horror Cinema in Europe Since 1945* (Wallflower Press, 2012).

Dr Rebecca Feasey is Senior Lecturer in Film and Media Communications at Bath Spa University, United Kingdom. She has previously published work on the celebrity gossip sector, contemporary Hollywood stardom and the representation of gender in popular media culture in journals such as *Continuum: Journal of Media & Cultural Studies*, *Journal of Gender Studies*, *Journal of Popular Film and Television*, *European Journal of Cultural Studies* and *The Quarterly Review of Film and Video*. She is also the author of the recent volume *Masculinity and Popular Television* (Edinburgh University Press, 2008) and is currently writing a book on motherhood and the maternal role on the small screen.

Dr Basil Glynn has lectured in film and television studies with the Open University and other universities in the United Kingdom and Europe. His research interests include post-colonialism and representations of the body in film and television and his recent publications include 'Corpses, Spectacle, Illusion: The Body as Abject and Object in *CSI*' in *The CSI Effect: Television, Crime, and Governance* (Lexington, 2009) and 'Approximating Cultural Proximity and Accentuating Cultural Difference: Cross Border Transformations in Asian Television Drama' in *Reading Asian Television Drama* (I. B. Tauris, 2012).

Dr Ruth Y. Y. Hung is Assistant Professor of Comparative Literature at Hong Kong Baptist University and Assistant Editor for *boundary 2* published by Duke University Press. She has published on the Chinese critical intellectual Hu Feng and on the genre of Chinese memoir writing in English since the Cultural Revolution. She is author of the article 'The State and the Market: Chinese TV Serials and the Case of *Woju* (Dwelling Narrowness)', *boundary 2* 38.2 (summer 2011): 155–88.

Dr Beth Johnson is a lecturer in Television, Film and English Studies at Keele University, United Kingdom. Her present research focuses on expressions of filmic extremism and televisual chaos. Beth is currently completing a monograph on the television auteur Paul Abbott (forthcoming, 2012, Manchester University Press) and is the author of various extant and forthcoming publications including: 'Sex, Psychoanalysis and Sublimation in *Dexter*' in *Investigating Dexter: Cutting Edge Television* (I. B. Tauris, 2010) and 'Realism, Real Sex and the Experimental Film: Mediating New Erotics in Georges Bataille's Story of the Eye' in *Realism and the Audiovisual Media* (Palgrave Press, 2009).

Dr Jeongmee Kim is Senior Lecturer in Film and Television Studies at Manchester Metropolitan University, United Kingdom. She has published in such academic journals as *Critical Studies in Television* and *Media, Culture & Society* and is the editor of the book *Reading Asian Television Drama: Breaking Boundaries and Crossing Borders* (I. B.Tauris, 2012). She is currently working on a number of projects looking at Asian cinema and contemporary Korean television drama.

Dr Amber K. Regis completed her PhD at Keele University and is a Visiting Lecturer in English Literature at the University of Chester, United Kingdom. Her research interests include nineteenth and twentieth-century life writing and the representation of lives across different genres and media. She has published work on Virginia Woolf, Vita Sackville-West and John Addington Symonds, and she is currently working on a book-length study of Victorian experiments in auto/biography.

Dr Jonathon Shears is a lecturer at Keele University, United Kingdom. His main research interests lie in nineteenth-century literature, literary theory and the nature of poetic influence. He is currently working on a monograph on Byron titled *From Change to Change We Run* and editing a volume of essays titled *Literary Bric-à-Brac: Victorian Oddities and Commodities*. Longer term ventures include a monograph on 'voice' in Romantic poetry that he has been exploring first in relation to Coleridge's ballads and an interdisciplinary project on excess in the long nineteenth-century provisionally titled *Sermons and Soda Water: A Cultural History of the Hangover*.

Madeleine Smith is a post-graduate Film Studies student at the University of Hull, United Kingdom. She is currently researching vigilantism and revenge narratives in American film and television and is writing a chapter for a forth-coming book on a popular film franchise. As an avid *Buffy* fan, Madeleine is very excited that this is her first publication.

Melanie Waters is Senior Lecturer in Modern and Contemporary Literature at Northumbria University. She has published essays on feminist theory, popular culture, and twentieth-century women's poetry, and is the editor of *Women on Screen: Feminism and Feminity in Visual Culture* (Palgrave, 2011). She is the co-author of *Feminism and Popular Culture* (I. B. Tauris, 2012) and has co-edited special issues of *Life Writing* (2009) and the *Journal of International Women's Studies* (2007, 2008, 2009).

Bibliography

Abbott, S. (2010), 'TV loves fangs: Sookie Stackhouse reconceived through the excesses of TV horror', *Vegetarians, VILFs and Fang-Bangers: Modern Vampire Romance in Print and on Screen Conference*. De Montfort University, Leicester, 24 November.

Akass, K. and McCabe, J. ed. (2003), *Reading 'Sex and the City'*. London: I. B. Tauris.

Allrath, G. and Gymnich, M. ed. (2005), *Narrative Strategies in Television Series*. Houndmills: Palgrave MacMillan.

Altman, R. (1996), 'Cinema and genre', in G. Nowell-Smith ed., *The Oxford History of World Cinema*. Oxford: Oxford University Press, pp. 276–85.

Arata, S. D. (2000), 'The occidental tourist: *Dracula* and the anxiety of reverse colonisation', in K. Gelder ed., *The Horror Reader*. London: Routledge, pp. 161–71.

Armes, R. (1978), *A Critical History of the British Cinema*. London: Secker & Warburg.

Arnold, M. (1994), 'Preface', in S. Lipman ed., *Culture and Anarchy*. New Haven: Yale University Press, pp. 3–27.

Arthurs, J. (2004), *Television and Sexuality: Regulations and the Politics of Taste*. Maidenhead: Open University Press.

Ashby, J. and Higson, A. (2000), *British Cinema, Past and Present*. London: Routledge.

Attwood, F. (2009), *Mainstreaming Sex: The Sexualisation of Western Culture*. London: I. B. Tauris.

—(2010), '"Younger, paler, decidedly less straight": the new porn professionals', in F. Attwood ed., *Porn.com: Making Sense of Online Pornography*. New York: Peter Lang, pp. 88–106.

Austen, J. (1813; 2001), *Pride and Prejudice*. Repr. London and New York: Norton.

Baker, S. (2009), '*Shameless* and the question of England', *Journal of British Cinema and Television*, 6, 452–67.

Barthes, R. (1986), 'The reality effect,' in R. Howard (trans), *The Rustle of Language*. Oxford: Blackwell, pp. 141–8.

BBC Education (1994), *Middlemarch: A Viewer's Guide*. London: BBC Education.

BBC News (2008), 'Rise in arrests of women drunks', *BBC News*, [online] 2 May. Available at: <http://news.bbc.co.uk/1/hi/uk/7379333.stm>

Beynon, J. (2002), *Masculinities and Culture*. Buckingham: Open University Press.

Bignell, J. (2004), 'Gender representations: *Sex and the City*', in J. Bignell ed.,

Television Studies: An Introduction. London and New York: Routledge, pp. 216–19.

Birtwistle, S. and Conklin, S. (1995), *The Making of Pride and Prejudice*. Harmondsworth: Penguin and BBC Books.

Bloch, E. (1988), *The Utopian Function of Art and Literature: Selected Essays*. Cambridge, Massachusetts: The MIT Press.

Bonnici, T. (2002), 'Where was the blue Velvet?', *Daily Mail*, [online] 11 October. Available at: <http://www.dailymail.co.uk/tvshowbiz/article-142244/Where-blue-Velvet.html>

Booth, P. (2010), *Digital Fandom: New Media Studies*. New York: Peter Lang.

Borland, S. (2010), 'The legacy of ladette: women's binge drinking is linked to alarming rise in teenage promiscuity and abortions', *The Daily Mail*, [online] 21 August. Available at: <http://www.dailymail.co.uk/news/article-1304833/The-Legacy-ladette-binge-drinking-women-linked-rise-casual-sex-abortions-prescriptions-morning-pill.html>

Botting, F. (1995), *The New Critical Idiom: Gothic*. London: Routledge.

Bradberry, G. (2002), 'Swearing, sex and brilliance', *The Observer*, [online] 20 October. Available at: <http://www.guardian.co.uk/theobserver/2002/oct/20/features.review97.>

Bragg, S. and Buckingham, D. (2009), 'Too much too young?: young people, sexual media and learning', in F. Attwood ed., *Mainstreaming Sex: The Sexualisation of Western Culture*. London: I. B.Tauris, pp. 129–46.

Brompton, S. (1990), 'Vita, violet and me', *Radio Times*, 15–21 September, 4.

Brown, C. (2009), 'Feminism and the vampire novel', *The F Word: Contemporary UK Feminism*, [online] 8 September. Available at: <http://www.thefword.org.uk/features/2009/09/feminism_and_th>

Brownworth, V. A. ed. (1996), *Night Bites: Vampire Stories by Women*. Seattle, Washington: Seal Press.

Bruzzi, S. and Church Gibson, P. (2004), '"Fashion is the fifth character": fashion, costume and character in *Sex and the City*', in K. Akass and J. McCabe (eds), *Reading Sex and the City*. London and New York: I. B.Tauris, pp. 115–29.

Buchanan, G. (2010), 'Adapt or die!', in L. Wilson ed., *A Taste of True Blood: The Fangbanger's Guide*. Dallas: Benbella Books Inc, pp. 211–22.

Burton, J. (2001), 'Artistic achievements bring a culture of rich success', *The Financial Times*, 24 October, 4.

Butler, J. (1990), *Gender Trouble: Feminism and the Subversion of Identity*. New York and London: Routledge.

Cardwell, S. (2002), *Adaptation Revisited: Television and the Classic Novel*. Manchester: Manchester University Press.

Castle, T. (1993), *The Apparitional Lesbian: Female Homosexuality and Modern Culture*. New York: Columbia University Press.

Chan, B. (forthcoming), '"Like a Virgin": sex, marriage and gender relations in the Korean television drama *The Wedding*', in J. Kim ed., *Reading Asian Television Drama: Breaking Boundaries and Crossing Borders*, London: I. B. Tauris.

Chapman, J. (2005), *Past and Present: National Identity and the British Historical Film*. London and New York: I. B. Tauris.

Cherry, B. (1999), 'Refusing to refuse to look: female viewers of the horror film', in R. Maltby and M. Stokes (eds), *Identifying Hollywood's Audiences*. London: BFI, pp.187–203.

—(2010), 'Stalking the web: celebration, chat and horror film marketing on the internet', in I. Conrich ed., *Horror Zone: The Cultural Experience of Contemporary Horror Cinema*. London: I. B. Taurus, pp. 67–86.

Chung, Y.-H. (2007a), 'A study on the audience's realistic sympathy and pleasure in the television drama <My Name is Kim Sam-Soon>', *Korean Journal of Journalism and Communication*, 51, (4), 32–57. (in Korean).

—(2007b), 'Cohabitation of patriarchal order with feminist demands in a successful television drama series <My Name is Kim Sam-soon>', *Media, Gender & Culture*, 8, 41–70. (in Korean).

Cohu, W. (2002), 'The BBC make it sound quite filthy', *The Telegraph*, [online] 8 October. Available at: <http://www.telegraph.co.uk/culture/4728952/The-BBC-make-it-sound-quite-filthy.html>

Cooke, L. (2003), *British Television Drama: A History*. London: BFI.

Cozens, C. (2002), 'Davies boasts of "filthy" lesbian drama', *The Guardian*, [online] 19 September. Available at: <http://www.guardian.co.uk/media/2002/sep/19/bbc.broadcasting1>

Creeber, G. (2004), *Serial Television: Big Drama on the Small Screen*. London: BFI.

Creed, B. (1993), *The Monstrous Feminine: Film, Feminism, Psychoanalysis*. London: Routledge.

—(2005), *Phallic Panic: Film, Horror and the Primal Uncanny*. Carlton: Melbourne University Publishing Group.

Custen, G. F. (1992), *Bio/Pics: How Hollywood Constructed Public History*. New Brunswick: Rutgers University Press.

Daily Express, The (2008), 'Surge in violent females –police', *The Daily Express*, [online] 8 August. Available at: <http://www.express.co.uk/posts/view/56128/Surge-in-violent-females-police>

De Groot, J. (2009), *Consuming History: Historians and Heritage in Contemporary Popular Culture*. London: Routledge.

Derrida, J. and Stiegler, B. (2002), *Echographies of Television*. Trans. by J. Bajorek. Cambridge: Polity Press.

Dickson, E. J. (2002), 'Velvet underground', *Radio Times*, 5–11 October, 24–8.

Dickson, R. (2001), 'Misrepresenting Jane Austen's ladies: revising texts (and history) to sell films', in L. Troost and S. Greenfield (eds), *Jane Austen in Hollywood*. Lexington: The University Press of Kentucky, pp. 44–57.

Dirlik, A. and Zhang, X. (1997), 'Introduction: postmodernism and China', special issue of *boundary 2: An International Journal of Literature and Culture*, 24, (3), 1–20.

Doane, M. A. (1982), 'Film and the masquerade–theorising the female spectator', *Screen*, 23, (3–4), 74–87.

Donaldson, S. (2002), 'It's not just two birds snogging', *The Telegraph*, [online] 8 October. Available at: <http://www.telegraph.co.uk/culture/tvandradio/3583845/Its-not-just-two-birds-snogging.html>

Douglas, M. (1982), *Natural Symbols: Explorations in Cosmology*. New York: Pantheon.

Drake, P. (2003), 'Mortgaged to music: new retro movies in 1990s Hollywood cinemas', in P. Grange ed., *Memory and Popular Film*. Manchester: Manchester University Press, pp.183–201.

Durex (2010), 'Durex condoms' [online] Available at: <http://www.durex.com/en-gb/products/condoms/pages/CondomHomepage.aspx>

Dyer, R. (1979), *Stars*. London: BFI.

Eden, J. (2008), '*Pushing Daisies*: taste of success', *TV Zone*, [online] no 228, May. Available at: <http://www.visimag.com/tvzone/t228_feat01.htm>

Elliott, M. (2007), 'The Chinese century', *Times Weekly*, [online] 11 January. Available at: <http://www.time.com/time/printout/0,8816,1576831,00.html>

Ellis, H. (1910), *Studies in the Psychology of Sex, vol. VI, Sex in Relation to Society*. Philadelphia: E. A. Davis.

Engelhardt, M. (2009), *Dancing out of Line: Ballrooms, Ballets and Mobility in Victorian Fiction*. Athens: Ohio University Press.

Faludi, S. (2007), *The Terror Dream: Fear and Fantasy in Post–9/11 America*. New York: Metropolitan Books.

Florence, P. (1995), 'Portrait of a production', in T. Wilton ed., *Immortal, Invisible: Lesbians and the Moving Image*. London: Routledge, pp.115–30.

Foucault, M. (1990), *The History of Sexuality. Volume 1: An Introduction*. London: Penguin Books.

Freud, S. (1908), 'Character and anal erotism', *The Standard Edition of the Complete Psychological Works of Sigmund Freud, Volume IX: Jensen's 'Gradiva' and Other Works*. Vol. IX. Ed. and trans. by J. Strachey and others. 1953–74. London: Hogarth Press, pp. 167–76.

—(1919), *The Uncanny*. Trans. by D. McLintock. London: Penguin.

Garis, R. (1968), 'Learning experience and change', in E. B. C. Southam ed., *Critical Essays on Jane Austen*. New York: Routledge, pp. 60–82.

Gauntlett, D. (2008), *Media, Gender and Identity: An Introduction*. 2nd Ed. Oxon: Routledge.

Giddings, R. and Selby, K. (2001), *The Classic Serial on Television and Radio*. Houndmills: Palgrave.

Gill, R. (2007), *Gender and the Media*. Cambridge: Polity Press.

Gillis, S. and Waters, M. (date) '"Mother, home and heaven": nostalgia, confession and motherhood in *Desperate Housewives*', in K. Akass and J. McCabe (eds), *Beyond the Picket Fence: Reading Desperate Housewives*. London: I. B. Tauris, pp. 190–205.

Girard, R. (1972), *Violence and the Sacred*. Trans. by P. Gregory. Baltimore, Maryland: The Johns Hopkins University Press.

Global Times (2011), 'National museum, Louis Vuitton reject criticisms of design exhibition', *Global Times*, [online] 9 June. Available at: <http://china.globaltimes.cn/society/2011-06/660772.html>

Graham, A. (2011), *Radio Times*. 14 August.

Grainge, P. (2003), 'Colouring the past: *Pleasantville* and the textuality of media memory', in P. Grainge ed., *Memory and Popular Film*. Manchester: Manchester University Press, pp. 202–19.

Griffin, S. (1981), *Pornography and Silence: Culture's Revenge Against Nature*. New York: Harper & Row.

Grunt, A. (2008), '*Pushing Daisies*, "frescorts": big gumshoe', *What's Alan*

Watching, [online] 24 October. Available at: <http://sepinwall.blogspot. com/2008/10/pushing-daisies-frescorts-big-gumshoe.html>

Guangzhou Daily Post (2010), 'Survey on life of the post-eighties.' *Guangzhou Daily Post*, [online] 24 February. Available at: <http://wenku.baidu.com/view/ a96be21414791711cc79177e.html> (in Chinese).

Guardian, The (2002), 'Tipping the Velvet', *The Guardian*, [online] 10 October. Available at: <http://www.guardian.co.uk/media/2002/oct/10/firstnight. broadcasting>

Gunter, B. (2002), *Media Sex: What Are the Issues?* New Jersey: Lawrence Erlbaum Associates.

Hainan News (2009), 'The media recovers *Woju*'s historical reference: first male protagonist alludes to Qin Yu, personal secretary to Chen Liangyu', *Hainan News*, 4 December. Available at: <http://www.hinews.cn/news/ system/2009/12/04/010625878.shtml>

Halberstam, J. (1995), *Skin Shows: Gothic Horror and the Technology of Monsters*. London: Duke University Press.

Hall, S. (2001), 'The wrong sort of cinema: refashioning the heritage film debate', in: R. Murphy ed., *The British Cinema Book*. 2nd Ed. London: BFI, pp. 191–9.

Hamer, D. and Budge, B. (1994), 'Introduction', in D. Hamer and B. Budge (eds), *The Good, The Bad and The Gorgeous: Popular Culture's Romance with Lesbianism*. London: Pandora, pp. 1–14.

Hankook-ilbo (2005), *Hankook-ilbo* [online], 16 June. Available at: <http://news. hankooki.com/lpage/life/200506/h2005061709065623280.htm> (in Korean).

Harding, J. (1998), *Sex Acts: Practices or Femininity and Masculinity*. London: Sage.

Harper, S. (1998), 'The scent of distant blood: Hammer films and history', in T. Barta ed., *Screening the Past: Film and the Representation of History*. Westport, CT: Praeger, pp. 109–26.

Harris, C. (2001), *Dead Until Dark*. London: Orion Publishing Group.

—(2002), *Living Dead in Dallas*. London: Orion Publishing Group.

—(2003), *Club Dead*. London: Orion Publishing Group.

Herald Business (2011), *Herald Business*, [online] 4 July. Available at: <http://biz. heraldm.com/common/Detail.jsp?newsMLId=20110704000007> (in Korean).

Higson, A. (2003), *English Heritage, English Cinema: Costume Drama Since 1980*. Oxford: Oxford University Press.

Hill, A. (2007), *Restyling Factual TV: Audiences and News, Documentary and Reality Genres*. London: Routledge.

Hill, J. (1983), 'Working class realism and sexual reaction: some theses on the British "New Wave"', in J. Curran and V. Porter (eds), *British Cinema History*. London: Weidenfeld & Nicolson, pp. 303–11.

Hinckley, D. (2007), 'Daisies pushing envelope with no sex', *Daily News*, [online] 22 October. Available at: <http://www.nydailynews.com/entertainment/ tv/2007/10/22/2007–10–22_daisies_pushing_envelope_with_no_sex.html>

Hinds, H. (1995), '*Oranges Are Not the Only Fruit*: reaching audiences other lesbian texts cannot reach', in T. Wilton ed., *Immortal, Invisible: Lesbians and the Moving Image*. London: Routledge, pp. 52–69.

Hirata, Y. (2005), *Japan Consuming Korea: The Korean Wave, Women, Drama*. Seoul: Chaeksesang. (in Korean).

—(2008), 'Touring "dramatic Korea": Japanese women as viewers of *hanryu* dramas and tourists on *hanryu* tours', in K. Iwabuchi and Chua B. H. (eds), *East Asian Popular Culture: Analysing the Korean Wave*. Hong Kong: Hong Kong University Press, pp. 143–56.

H. M. Government (1988), 'Local Government Act 1988: Section 28', *H.M. Government and the National Archives*, [online] Available at: <http://www.legislation.gov.uk/ukpga/1988/9/section/28>

Hollows, J. (2003), 'The masculinity of cult', in M. Jancovich, A. L. Reboll, J. Stringer and A. Willis (eds), *Defining Cult Movies: The Cultural Politics of Oppositional Taste*. Manchester: Manchester University Press, pp. 35–53.

Hopkins, L. (2001), 'Mr. Darcy's body: privileging the female gaze', in L. Troost and S. Greenfield (eds), *Jane Austen in Hollywood*. Lexington: The University Press of Kentucky, pp. 111–21.

Hoskins, C., McFadyen, S., and Finn, A. (1997), *Global Television and Film: An Introduction to the Economics of the Business*. Oxford: Clarendon Press.

Hung, R. Y. Y. (2011), 'The state and the market: Chinese TV serials and the case of *Woju* (Dwelling Narrowness)', *boundary 2: An International Journal of Literature and Culture*, 38, (2), 155–88.

Hutcheon, L. (2006), *A Theory of Adaptation*. London: Routledge.

iCasualties: Iraq Coalition Casualty Count. [online] Available at: <http://icasualties.org/>

Innes, C. (1992), 'Bloomsburied', *The Nation*, 28 September, 337–40.

Iwabuchi, K. ed. (2004), *Feeling Asian Modernities: Transnational Consumption of Japanese TV Dramas*. Hong Kong: Hong Kong University Press.

Jackson, R. (1981), *Fantasy: A Literature of Subversion*. London: Routledge.

Jacobs, J. (2006), 'Television aesthetics: an infantile disorder', *Journal of British Cinema and Television*, 3, (1), 19–33.

Jancovich, M. (2008), 'Cult fictions: cult movies, subcultural capital and the production of cultural distinctions', in E. Mathijs and X. Mendik (eds), *The Cult Film Reader*. Maidenhead: Open University Press, pp.149–62.

Jancovich, M. and Lyons, J. (2003), 'Introduction', in M. Jancovich and J. Lyons (eds), *Quality Popular Television: Cult TV, the Industry and Fans*. London: BFI, pp.1–8.

Jeffords, S. (1994), *Hard Bodies: Hollywood Masculinity in the Reagan Era*. New Brunswick: Rutgers University.

Jenkins, H. (1992), *Textual Poachers: Television Fans and Participatory Culture*. London: Routledge.

Ji, M. (2010), 'An interview with Lian Si: the present condition of youths – from *Woju* to Ant Clans', *book.douban.com*, [online] 29 January. Available at: http://book.douban.com/review/2962892/ (in Chinese).

Jones, E. (1991), 'On the Vampire', in C. Frayling ed., *Vampyres*. London: Faber & Faber, pp. 398–417.

Jowett, L. (2005), *Sex and the Slayer: A Gender Studies Primer for the Buffy Fan*. Connecticut: Wesleyan University Press.

Joy News 24 (2005), *Joy News 24*, [online] 1 June. Available at: <http://news.naver.com/main/read.nhn?mode=LSD&mid=sec&sid1=106&oid=111&aid=0000011394> (in Korean)

Kane, T. (2006), *The Changing Vampire of Film and Television: A Critical Study of the Growth of a Genre.* Jefferson, CA: McFarland and Co.

Keveney, B. (2007), 'Lee Pace and Anna Friel on Ned and Chuck', *The PieMaker*, [online] 21 November. Available at: <http://www.thepiemaker.com/lee-pace-anna-friel-on-ned-chuck/>

Kilborn, R. and Izod, J. (1997), *An Introduction to Television Documentary: Confronting Reality.* Manchester: Manchester University Press.

Kim, H.-S. and Kim, M.-S. (2008), 'Television drama and women['s] discourse: a study on the 30s single women's work and love', *Korean Journal of Journalism and Communication*, 52, (1), 244–70 (in Korean).

Kim, J. (2007), 'Why does *hallyu* matter?: the significance of the Korean Wave in South Korea', *Critical Studies in Television*, 2, (2), 47–59.

Kinsey, A., Pomeroy, W. B. and Martin, C. E. (1948), *Sexual Behaviour in the Human Male.* Philadelphia: W. B. Saunders.

Klaus, A. and Krüger, S. (2011), 'Vampires without fangs: the amalgamation of genre in Stephenie Meyer's *Twilight* saga', *The Looking Glass: New Perspectives on Children's Literature*, [online] 15,(1).Available at: <http://www.lib.latrobe.edu.au/ojs/index.php/tlg/article/view/260/257>

Klein, N. (2007), *The Shock Doctrine: The Rise of Disaster Capitalism.* London: Penguin.

Kristeva, J. (1982), *Powers of Horror: An Essay on Abjection.* New York: Columbia University Press.

Kwon, D. -H. (2006), 'Is it too early to talk about "hallyu" in the Philippines? Koreanovela and its reception among [the] Filipino audience,' Cultural Space and Public Sphere: an International Conference. Seoul, Republic of Korea 15–16 March. Available at: <http://asiafuture.org/csps2006/01program.html>

Kyunghyang-shinmun, The (2005), *The Kyunghyang-shinmun* [online], 13 June. Available at: <http://news.khan.co.kr/kh_news/khan_art_view.html?artid=2005 06131602271&code=900307> (in Korean).

Larbalestier, J. (2004), 'The only thing better than killing a Slayer: heterosexuality and sex in *Buffy the Vampire Slayer*', in R. Kaveney ed., *Reading the Vampire Slayer: The New, Updated Unofficial Guide to Buffy and Angel.* 2nd Ed. London: Tauris Parke Paperbacks, pp.195–219.

Lee, D.-H. (2004), 'Cultural contact with Japanese TV dramas: mode of reception and narrative transparency', in K. Iwabuchi ed., *Feeling Asian Modernities: Transnational Consumption of Japanese TV Dramas.* Hong Kong: Hong Kong University Press, pp. 251–74.

Lee, S.-Y. (2008), *Hallyu Drama and Asian Women's Desire.* Seoul: Communication Books (in Korean).

Leverette, M. (2008), 'Cocksucker, motherfucker, tits', in M. Leverette, B. L. Ott and C. L. Buckley (eds), *It's Not TV: Watching HBO in the Post-Television Era.* New York and Oxon: Routledge, pp. 123–51.

Levy, A. (2006), *Female Chauvinist Pigs: Women and the Rise of Raunch Culture.* London: Pocket Books.

Lichtenstein, O. (2009), '*True Blood* vampires and the explicit TV sucking the innocence out of our children', *Daily Mail*, [online] 5 November. Available at: <http://www.dailymail.co.uk/femail/article-1225388/True-Blood-vampires-explicitTV-sucking-innocence-children.html.>

Lin, A. and Tong, A. (2008), 'Re-imagining a cosmopolitan "Asian us": Korean
media flows and imaginaries of Asian modern femininities', in K. Iwabuchi
and Chua, B. H (eds), *East Asian Popular Culture: Analysing the Korean Wave.*
Hong Kong: Hong Kong University Press, pp. 91–126.

Lin, Y. (2009), 'Final episode of *Woju* earned 7 percent audience rating last night',
Shanghai Youth Post, [online] 10 August. Available at: <http://www.why.com.
cn/epublish/node4/node25435/node25443/userobject7ai188965.html> (in
Chinese).

Longino, H. (1980), 'Pornography, oppression and freedom: a closer look', in L.
Lederer ed., *Take Back the Night: Women on Pornography.* New York: William
Morrow, pp. 40–54.

Low, R. (1949), *The History of British Film (1906–1914).* London: Allen and Unwin.

Lukács, G. (2010), *Scripted Affects, Branded Selves: Television, Subjectivity, and
Capitalism in 1990s Japan.* Durham and London: Duke University Press.

Lyotard, J.-F. (1984), 'Answering the Question: What is Postmodernism?', in
R. Durand (trans), *The Postmodern Condition: A Report on Knowledge.*
Minneapolis: University of Minnesota Press, pp. 71–84.

Macintyre, B. (1992), 'Lesbians angered as TV tones down tale of Vita's love
affairs', *The Times,* 15 June, 12.

Mackie, D. (2009), 'Naming conventions in *Pushing Daisies*', *Back of a Cereal
Box,* [online] 8 September. Available at: <http://kidicarus222.blogspot.
com/2009/09/naming-conventions-in-pushing-daisies.html>

Mamatas, N. (2010), 'Working class heroes', in L. Wilson ed., *A Taste of True
Blood: The Fangbanger's Guide.* Dallas: Bendella Books, pp. 61–74.

Marx, K. (1867), *Capital: Critique of Political Economy.* Vol. 1. Trans. by B.
Fowkes. 2004. London: Penguin.

Mathijs, E. and Mendik, X. ed. (2008), *The Cult Film Reader.* Maidenhead: Open
University Press.

McClintock, A. (1999), 'Female-friendly porn', in R.A. Nye ed., *Sexuality.* Oxford:
Oxford University Press, pp. 389–91.

McCracken, A. (2007), 'At stake: Angel's body, fantasy masculinity, and queer
desire in teen television', in E. Levine and L. Parks (eds), *Undead TV: Essays
on Buffy the Vampire Slayer.* Durham: Duke University Press, pp. 116–44.

McNair, B. (1996), *Mediated Sex: Pornography and Postmodern Culture.* London:
Arnold.

—(2002), *Striptease Culture: Sex, Media and the Democratisation of Desire.*
London and New York: Routledge.

Mead, M. (1948), *Sex and Temperament in Three Primitive Societies.* London:
Routledge and Kegan Paul.

Mellor, A. K. (1995), 'A revolution in female manners', in D. Wu ed., *Romanticism:
A Critical Reader.* Oxford: Blackwell, pp. 408–16.

Merck, M. (1993), *Perversions: Deviant Readings.* London: Virago.

Moyes, J. and Robins, J. (2000), 'The astute businessman who gave us Kirsty
and Cheggers', *The Independent,* [online] 28 October. Available at: <http://
www.independent.co.uk/news/media/the-astute-businessman-who-gave-us-
kirsty-and-cheggers–634822.html>

Mulvey, L. (1981), 'Afterthoughts on visual pleasure and narrative cinema
inspired by *Duel in the Sun*', *Framework,* 15–17, 12–15.

Murphy, R. (1992), *Sixties British Cinema*. London: BFI.

Naish, C. (1991), *Death Comes to the Maiden: Sex and Execution, 1431–1933*. London: Routledge.

Nanfang Weekly (2010), 'Shatter all dreams: an interview with Liu Liu', *Nanfang Weekly*, [online] 12 April. Available at: <http://www.infzm.com/content/43699> (in Chinese).

Negra, D. (2009), *What a Girl Wants? Fantasizing the Reclamation of the Self in Postfeminism*. London: Routledge.

Nelson, R. (1997), *TV Drama in Transition: Forms, Values and Cultural Change*. Houndmills: MacMillan Press Ltd.

—(2007), *State of Play: Contemporary 'High End' TV Drama*. Manchester: Manchester University Press.

NetEase (2009), 'Torrents of thunderbolts, the most obscene TV drama dialogues in history: *Woju*', *NetEase,* [online] 17 November. Available at: <http://bbs.ent.163.com/bbs/tv/156933073.html> (in Chinese).

New York Times, The (1992), 'PBS mini-series rejected in N. Dakota', *The New York Times*, [online] 20 July. Available at: <http://www.nytimes.com/1992/07/20/arts/pbs-mini-series-rejected-in-n-dakota.html>

Nichols, B. (1991), *Representing Reality: Issues and Concepts in Documentary*. Bloomington: Indiana University Press.

Nicolson, N. (1985), 'Unpublished Memoir TS'.

—(1990), 'Portrait of a love betrayed?', *The Times*, 22 September, 16–17.

—(1992), *Portrait of a Marriage*. London: Phoenix.

—(1998), *Long Life*. London: Phoenix.

Nixon, C. L. (2001), 'Balancing the courtship hero: masculine emotional display in film adaptations of Jane Austen's novels', in L. Troost and S. Greenfield (eds), *Jane Austen in Hollywood*. Lexington: The University Press of Kentucky, pp. 22–43.

Onishi, N. (2004), 'What's Korean for "real man"?: ask Japanese women.' *The New York Times*, 23 December, 13.

—(2005), 'Roll over, Godzilla: Korea rules,' *The New York Times*, 28 June, A3.

Onscenity Network (2011), 'ONSCENITY: sex, commerce, media and technology in contemporary society', [online] Available at: <http://www.onscenity.org/>

Osborn, M. (2010), 'Drama gives "first" lesbian fresh life', *BBC News Website*, [online] 31 May. Available at: <http://news.bbc.co.uk/1/hi/entertainment/8710965.stm>

Park, J. (1990), *British Cinema: The Lights that Failed*. London: B. T. Batsford.

Parrill, S. (2002), *Jane Austen on Film and Television: A Critical Study of the Adaptations*. Jefferson, NC and London: McFarland.

Passonen, S., Nikunen, K. and Saarenmaa, L. ed. (2007), *Pornification: Sex and Sexuality in Media Culture*. London: Berg.

People.com.cn (2009), [online] 4 December. Available at: <*http://pic.people.com. cn/BIG5/162952/162956/10511266.html*> (in Chinese).

People's Daily (2009), '"Poor 2nd generation": hot term in China', *People's Daily Online*, [online] 3 September. Available at: <http://english.peopledaily.com.cn/90001/90776/90882/6747456.html>

Piddcuk, J. (2001), '*Elizabeth* and *Shakespeare in Love*: Screening the Elizabethans', in G. Vincendeau ed., *Film/Literature/Heritage: A Sight and Sound Reader*. London: BFI, pp. 130–5.

Pigeon, R. (2001), '"No man's Elizabeth:" the Virgin Queen in recent films', in D. Cartmell, I. Q. Hunter and I. Whelehan (eds), *Retrovisions: Reinventing the Past in Film and Fiction*. London: Pluto, pp. 8–24.

Postman, N. (1993), *Technopoly: The Surrender of Culture to Technology*. New York: Vintage Books.

Radway, J. (1984), *Reading the Romance: Women, Patriarchy and Popular Literature*. Chapel Hill, NC and London: University of North Carolina Press.

Regis, A. K. (2011), 'Competing life narratives: *Portrait*s of Vita Sackville-West', *Life Writing*, 8, (3), 287–300.

Rich, A. (1980), 'Compulsory heterosexuality and lesbian existence', *Signs*, 5, (4), 631–60.

Rogers, P. (2010), 'To live and die in Dixie' in L. Wilson ed., *A Taste of True Blood: The Fangbanger's Guide*. Dallas: Bendella Books, pp. 45–60.

Rolling Stone (2010), 'The joy of vampire sex: "True Blood" on *Rolling Stone* latest cover', *Rolling Stone*, [online] 17 August. Available at: <http://www.rollingstone.com/culture/news/the-joy-of-vampire-sex-true-blood-on-rolling-stones-latest-cover–20100817>

Sanders, J. (2006), *Adaptation and Appropriation*. London: Routledge.

Sarris, A. (1998), *You Ain't Heard Nothin' Yet: The American Talking Film, History & Memory, 1927–1949*. New York: Oxford University Press.

Scannel, P. (2001), 'Public service broadcasting: the history of a concept', in E. Buscombe ed., *British Television: A Reader*. Oxford: Oxford University Press, pp. 45–62.

Sedgwick, E. K. (1993), *Tendencies*. Durham: Duke University Press.

Sepinwall, A. (2008), '*Pushing Daisies*, "frescorts": big gumshoe', *What's Alan Watching*, [online] 23 October. Available at: <http://sepinwall.blogspot.com/2008/10/pushing-daisies-frescorts-big-gumshoe.html>

Shim, D. (2006), 'Hybridity and the rise of Korean popular culture in Asia', *Media, Culture & Society*, 28, (1), 25–44.

Shoji, K. (2004), 'Japan gripped by obsession with pure love', *The Japan Times*, [online] 30 December. Available at: <http://search.japantimes.co.jp/cgi-bin/ek20041230ks.html.>

Simmel, G. (1984), *Georg Simmel: On Women, Sexuality, and Love*. Trans. by G. Oakes. New Haven and London: Yale University Press.

Sina Entertainment (2009), '*Woju* broke records of audience rating and provoked discussions among white-Collar workers', *Sina.com*, [online] 10 August <http://ent.sina.com.cn/v/m/2009–08–10/13342646466.shtml > (in Chinese).

Sisa Press (2005), *Sisa Press*, [online] No. 817. Available at: <http://www.sisapress.com/news/articleView.html?idxno=24692#> (in Korean).

Skeggs, B. (2004), *Class, Self, Culture*. London: Routledge.

Slayden, D. (2010), 'Debbie does Dallas again and again: pornography, technology, and market innovation', in F. Attwood ed., *Porn.com: Making Sense of Online Pornography*. New York: Peter Lang, pp.54–68.

Smith, C. (2007a), 'Designed for pleasure: style, indulgence and accessorized sex', *European Journal of Cultural Studies*, 10, (2), 167–84.

—(2007b), *One For the Girls!: The Pleasures and Practices of Reading Women's Porn*. Bristol: Intellect.

Sobchack, V. (1994), 'The fantastic', in G. Nowell-Smith ed., *The Oxford History of World Cinema.* Oxford: Oxford University Press, pp. 312–21.

Stacey, J. (1994), *Stargazing: Hollywood Cinema and Female Spectatorship.* London: Routledge.

Stanley, A. (2007), 'Renaissance romping with Henry and his rat pack', *The New York Times,* 30 March, E1.

Storr, M. (2003), *Latex and Lingerie.* Oxford: Berg.

Stovel, B. (1998), '*Northanger Abbey* at the movies', *Persuasions*, 29, 236–47.

Street, S. (1997), *British National Cinema.* London: Routledge.

—(2000), 'Stepping westward: the distribution of British feature films in America, and the case of *The Private Life of Henry VIII*', in J. Ashby and A. Higson (eds), *British Cinema, Past and Present.* London: Routledge, pp. 51–62.

Tamsin Wilton, T. (1995), 'On invisibility and immortality', in T. Wilton ed., *Immortal, Invisible: Lesbian and the Moving Image.* London: Routledge, pp. 1–19.

Tanner, T. (1986), *Jane Austen.* Cambridge: Harvard University Press.

Tasker, Y. (1993), *Spectacular Bodies: Gender, Genre and the Action Cinema.* London: Routledge.

—(1994), 'Pussy Galore: lesbian images and lesbian desire in the popular cinema', in D. Hamer and B. Budge (eds), *The Good, The Bad and The Gorgeous: Popular Culture's Romance with Lesbianism.* London: Pandora, pp. 172–83.

Taylor, M.C. (1987) *Altarity.* Chicago: University of Chicago Press.

Telegraph, The (2009), 'The gout on the rise as Britons overindulge', *The Telegraph*, [online] 4 March. Available at: <http://www.telegraph.co.uk/health/healthnews/4936215/Gout-on-the-rise-as-Britons-overindulge.html>

Topping, A. (2008), '*Pushing Daisies* wilts on debut ratings race', *The Guardian*, [online] 14 April. Available at: <http://www.guardian.co.uk/media/2008/apr/14/television.itv1>

Vincendeau, G. (2001), 'Introduction', in G. Vincendeau ed., *Film/Literature/Heritage: A Sight and Sound Reader.* London: BFI, pp. xi-xxv.

Wagner, T. (2008), 'The decaying coquette: refashioning highlife in early nineteenth-century women's writing, 1801–1831', in S. King and Y. Schlick (eds), *Refiguring the Coquette: Essays on Culture and Coquetry.* Lewisburg: Bucknell University Press, pp. 83–102.

Walker, G. (2003). *The Private Life of Henry VIII.* The British Film Guide 8. London: I. B. Tauris, 2003.

Wall Street Journal, The (2011), 'Throwing out the Marxist baggage: veneration of Louis Vuitton is the default ideology of China'. *The Wall Street Journal*, [online] 9 June. Available at: <http://online.wsj.com/article/SB10001424052702304259304576373233534354252.html>

Waters, M. (2011), 'The horrors of home: feminism and femininity in the suburban gothic', in M. Waters ed., *Women on Screen: Feminism and Femininity in Visual Culture.* Basingstoke: Palgrave, pp. 58–74.

Waters, S. (2006), *Tipping The Velvet.* London: Virago.

Weekly Hankook (2011), *Weekly Hankook*, [online] Available at: <http://weekly.hankooki.com/entertain/201108/wk20110802041729105250.htm.> (in Korean).

Weeks, J. (1985), *Sexuality and Its Discontents: Meanings, Myths & Modern Sexualities*. London: Routledge & Kegan Paul.

Whang, I.-S. (1999), 'A theoretical study of structural characteristics of "trendy drama" narrative and its textual pleasure', *Korean Journal of Journalism and Communication*, 43, (5), 221–48 (in Korean).

Wilcox, R. (2005), *Why Buffy Matters: The Art of Buffy the Vampire Slayer*. London: I. B. Tauris.

Williams, L. (1989), *Hardcore: Power, Pleasure and the 'Frenzy of the Visible'*. Berkeley: University of California Press.

—(2009), *Screening Sex*. Durham: Duke University Press.

Williamson, M. (2005), *The Lure of the Vampire: Gender, Fiction and Fandom from Bram Stoker to Buffy*. London: Wallflower.

Wilson, E. (1990), 'Borderlines', *New Statesman and Society*, 2 November, 31.

Wilson, E.O. (1978), *On Human Nature*. Cambridge: Harvard University Press.

Wiltshire, J. (2001), *Recreating Jane Austen*. Cambridge: Cambridge University Press.

Wollen, T. (1991), 'Over our shoulders: nostalgic screen fictions for the 1980s', in J. Corner and S. Harvey (eds), *Enterprise and Heritage: Crosscurrents of National Culture*. London: Routledge, pp. 178–93.

Xin, A. L. (2009), '*Narrow Dwellings*: a TV series that slipped through SARFT's guidelines', *Danwai.org*, [online] 11 December. Available at: <http://www. danwei.org/tv/narrow_dwellings.php>

Zhu, S. (2009), 'Who should be woken up by *Woju*?', Trans. by Ren Zhongxi. *China.org.cn*, [online] November 25. Available at: <http://www.china.org.cn/ opinion/2009–11/25/content_18953464.htm>

Index

Williamson, Millie 57, 58, 60
Wilson, Elizabeth 148, 150
Wilton, Tamsin 143, 156
Wiltshire, John 129, 136, 142n. 7
Winter Sonata 112, 113, 118
Woju xvi, xvii, 93, 94, 109nn. 1–4
  and realism and representation of
    sex 103-8
  and sexuality and consumption
    99–103
  and the *Xiaosan* 95–7

Wright Joe 129
  and *Pride and Prejudice* 127, 131–6,
    141

Xiaosan xvi, xvii, 95
  as commodity 107-8
  and the 'new sexual economy' 99-100
  and *Woju* 95-8, 100, 101-3,,106
Xin, Alice 104, 105

Yahoo! 55, 56, 58, 62